Dance Education and Training in Britain

Published by the Calouste Gulbenkian Foundation
UK and Commonwealth Branch, London
1980

D0542346

© 1980 Calouste Gulbenkian Foundation
ISBN 0-903319-18-7
Printed by Oyez Press Ltd., London
Cover design by Michael Carney Associates

Further copies can be obtained from:-
Calouste Gulbenkian Foundation
98 Portland Place
London W1N 4ET
Telephone 01-636-5313/7
Telex 28331 Assist London

Trade distribution by Dance Books Ltd
9 Cecil Court London WC2N 4EZ Telephone 01-838-2314

Contents

Part I: The Setting

1 Origins of the report 2 Council for Dance Education and Training 3 Scottish Council for Dance 4 Dance Council for Wales 5 Our terms of reference 6 Need for further research 7 Two parts of our task 8 The place of arts in education 9 The arts still peripheral to education 10 Traditional views challenged by our experience 11 Preparing for a different future 12 Roots in the maintained sector 13 Dance a test case 14 A critical situation

15 Purpose of the chapter 16 Historical background 17 Early educational dance companies 18 Expansion of educational work 19 The student connection 20 Initiation of residencies 21 Appointment of education officers 22 Link with community dance 23 Role of Regional Arts Associations 24 Contribution of television 25 Where we stand now 26 Where we might go 27 Dance Umbrella 28 Three pilot projects in schools 29 Provision for mime 30 Provision for archives 31 Need for partnership

32 Purpose of the chapter 33 Music in relation to dance 34 Mutual need for music and dance education 35 The classroom musician — what is needed 36 The dance teacher/student dancer — what is needed 37 The student dancer 38 Student dance teacher 39 Cultural education 40 Need for in-service courses 41 Dance education of musicians 42 Areas of creative contact 43 Action needed 44 Dance and other arts 45 Value of studying related arts

46 Purpose of the chapter 47 Locations of power 48 Central policy-making 49 The educational civil service 50 Other national administrative resources 51 Dance and local government 52 Dance and statutory bodies 53 Dance and voluntary organisations 54 The media 55 Using resources

56 Purpose of the chapter 57 International consultations 58 Formation of national and international organisations 59 Dance and the Child International 60 Urgency of international co-operation 61 Australia 62 Canada 63 France 64 Holland 65 A Swedish Inquiry 66 The United States of America 67 Vocational links with higher education — USA 68 Dancers in schools — USA

Introduction

by the Chairman of the Inquiry

It is unusual for the chairman of a national inquiry to be writer of its report as well as an officer of the Foundation which commissioned it. The situation derives in part from my independent position in British dance education and partly from the position the Gulbenkian Foundation has acquired in recent years as catalyst and contributor across the whole field of education and the arts in the United Kingdom.

During 1972 the Foundation's educational advisers to its Branch in UK, and subsequently its Board in Lisbon, endorsed a recommendation that the arts in education and training for the arts should become a priority of the Branch's education programme. Many practical activities flowed from this decision, all listed in subsequent annual reports of the Branch. One early project, however, was of a different kind. It developed from a joint approach to the Foundation by British Actors' Equity, the Council of Regional Theatres and the Conference of Drama Schools. These three bodies requested an independent inquiry into, the vocational training of actors. Their letter was on my desk when I arrived at the Foundation in January 1972. It was inspired by the example of the Foundation's report, *Making Musicians*, published in 1965.

This actors' initiative subsequently became a Foundation report, *Going on the Stage*,[1] published in 1975. The study which informed it was chaired first by Huw (now Sir Huw) Wheldon and then by Professor (now Lord) Vaizey. The experience of this study made clear to the Foundation the need for more expert information about the arts in education generally and vocational training for the performing arts in particular. Therefore the Foundation commissioned two further studies to be undertaken concurrently. The first, into the training of professional musicians, took place under the chairmanship of Lord Vaizey and reported at the end of 1977 as *Training Musicians*.[2] The second is the present study.

The Foundation considered commissioning a similar study into training for painting and sculpture. But training for these arts had been studied, and the training re-organised to an important extent, only a few years previously. Instead, the Foundation commissioned a study of the economic situation of the visual artist as a contribution to understanding the financial position of all artists in late twentieth century Britain. This major undertaking is being directed by Richard Hoggart and is expected to report during 1980 or early 1981.

A consideration of arts education and vocational training, of course, leads inevitably to the larger problems of arts on the one hand and education on the other. Hence the Foundation has extended its commitment through three further studies undertaken, as always, in consultation with appropriate professional authorities. Two of these have been published: *Support for the Arts in England and Wales*[13] by Lord Redcliffe-Maud and *The Arts Britain Ignores*[12] (a report on ethnic arts) by Naseem Khan. The third is a study of the arts and the curriculum due to be published later in 1980.

In all this work, begun seven years ago and now nearing completion, the dance study has been unique in two respects. First, it did not have, as other areas of study had, the benefit of previous inquiry or some existing collection of facts or statistics. We had nothing from which to start beyond the dance structures of the maintained and non-maintained sectors, created mostly in the last half century. Second, the nature of dance, our belief in its importance to society generally, and the need to start vocational training around the age of 16 or earlier, compelled us to survey what dance is taking place in ordinary schools in the maintained sector as well as to examine the needs of vocational training, almost all of which takes place in the non-maintained sector. We completed the study by reference to appropriate overseas experience, especially in Australia and Canada whose dance situation is comparable to that in Britain and from whom we have learned a great deal. We hope that dancers, students and teachers in those countries may find something useful in this report so that our debt can be repaid, at least in part.

We began, as we always begin, by assuring ourselves of professional support and of the genuine need for study. The actors' inquiry was an actors' initiative supported by representatives of the entire acting profession. The musicians' inquiry was a follow-up to the Gulbenkian study a decade earlier and arose from many approaches by the musical profession. The dance education profession, however, was much less organised and much more divided by its separate interests than the other professions. The Foundation therefore convened in March 1974 an Action-Conference on Dance Education. Details of the membership and programme of this conference are given at Appendix A and its significance is summarised in chapter 1, paragraph 1. It was the first time most of the interests of the dance education profession had assembled under one roof, joined by visitors from Australia, Canada and the USA. It demonstrated that the Foundation had the confidence of these interests. Because of this confidence the Foundation itself agreed to conduct the subsequent dance study rather than invite an outside chairman with supporting staff.

As well as providing the impetus for this study, the Action Conference inspired the beginnings of several very important institutions which complemented or helped develop a number of initiatives, then just beginning. In March 1974 there were no choreographic departments at the London School of Contemporary Dance and Royal Ballet School although the former had taught choreography from 1968; there was no annual international dance course for choreographers and composers at Surrey University, providing a potential centre for advanced choreographic study at the highest level; there were no degree courses at tertiary level in which dance was a major option; above all, there were no national organisations, to provide a 'voice' for dance education and training in the three countries of our concern and no national study assembling the facts and opinions of the dance education profession across the maintained and non-maintained sectors as a basis for further development. All this now exists mostly created in parallel with the dance study and with the help of the Foundation.

As our dance study has evolved other changes have occurred. School rolls have begun to fall; the non-university sector of higher education has been re-organised; dance has become recognised increasingly as a subject for study at tertiary level; the education debate came and went without much reference to the arts; and arts funding throughout the country has had to take greater account of the practice of the arts in the ordinary spaces and places of daily life. Now, under a new Government, the steady expansion of 15 years has come to an end. Significant changes are taking place in the general economic and political fields within which the results of our study will need to be considered. As part of these changes, not only funding but the role, institutions and structure of the arts in Britain are under scrutiny. Our report may be the better for having moved slowly to absorb and consider these changes.

We began the study with open minds and the knowledge that we had to consider two separate but related problems: dance as part of general education, and vocational training for gifted potential professional dancers. Our response has been to treat these problems separately, at the same time emphasising the essential unity of all dance education and the climate of co-operation between its component interests which has developed so noticeably in recent years. It is appropriate now to present something of our hopes at the end of a study which has modified many of our views.

What would we most like to see arising from our report? By far the most urgent need is that all children, male and female, should have the benefit of good dance experience as a central element of upbringing and education. The case for this is set out, I believe, in the body of our report but its realisation carries a number of implications: that dance is important in its own right alongside other arts; that a dance experience, therefore, should be available in every school with its fair share of spaces, time, resources and finance; that the grant system is re-organised to allow children gifted in dance from any section of society and any local education authority to benefit from vocational training; that vocational dance training receives more public support; that linked with this, urgent action be taken to avert the threat to vocational dance training implicit in the application of the present grant system; and that dance teachers in both sectors have career prospects commensurate with their training and responsibilities.

All this is possible now. The teaching skills exist. The training institutions exist. Many successful examples in individual schools exist. There is supporting evidence from the behavioural, medical, psychological and social sciences, some of which is indicated in our report. Most of all it is possible because adequate support for dance in education and vocational training for dance depend on changing attitudes, on persuasion. Implicit in this persuasion, it seems to me, is a re-consideration of the nature of knowledge and, therefore, of the nature of teaching and learning. The need for re-consideration came clear from our encounter with a fascinating difficulty during our discussions. Traditional education in Britain is based on words. It assumes the transmission of knowledge through words. To argue a proper place for dance in education, and more support for vocational training, challenges this tradition. It asserts the reality of a language of movement and the validity of knowledge acquired through movement, of experiential knowledge. Our problem of persuasion includes the problem of helping parents, teachers, principals and educational administrators to grasp that there can be a non-verbal language of communication which, incidentally, is not one dimensional, like words, but three dimensional, like the human body.

This change is achievable because it is, in fact, happening already. The new thinking is demonstrated in the acceptance of dance for honours degree study by the Council for National Academic Awards (CNAA), as we show in chapter 9. But dance is not only the transmission or acquisition of experiential knowledge, nor even a means of artistic communication. To give it more presence in the life of a nation, as our report suggests, is to pose two other arguments. Both have to do with the imagination, dance being what it is. One is to ask schools and teachers to give more time in the curriculum, especially at secondary level, for young people to think through their own inner world through creative activity. Such activity — whether it be writing, dancing, painting, music or anything else — provides an important opportunity to clarify self-development and make it of value to others. This is the more important if one considers the second argument, that Britain's richest resource is neither oil nor coal but the imagination of her people. This imagination is most stirred and developed through education in the arts. The arts not only communicate ideas — they create ideas — they are a way of having ideas, of training the imagination. Arguably, therefore, they should lie at the core of the curriculum.

VIII

The Committee, nevertheless, has made no attempt anywhere to establish any pre-eminence for dance: the study simply postulates that dance, at the various levels at which it is practised, should have at least equal treatment with other subjects on the school curriculum, with other theatre arts in the professional theatre, and with other non-vocational activities in the general provision for tertiary and continuing education. This, we think, constitutes our most powerful case to realise our recommendations. But faith in the arts and in human beings is not our only reason for hope that our recommendations will be implemented. We have tried to balance ideals with realism, and to establish priori-ties. We are anxious not to propose action which is unrealistic in the present economic situation, or in terms of the present Government's policies. As the study progressed it be-came evident that many of our proposals are so inter-related as to constitute, in fact, a comprehensive structure for dance education in Britain which our Committee would like to see established over the next five to ten years. We hope that all those organisations and authorities to whom the recommendations chiefly apply will select their priorities from the plan we offer and will move in their own way towards the common goal of improved dance education and vocational training which we believe can be realised during the 1980s.

The structure of the report reflects this practical approach. Exceptionally busy readers will find our principal recommendations drawn together at the end. Those who wish to concentrate on particular sectors can do this by turning to Parts II or III. We have emphasised above, however, the inter-relationships in the whole field. Dance does not take place in a vacuum: it arises from society expressing personal and social needs and is set in a real world of power, money, state structures, international influences and profes-sional relationships. All these affect the present structures of dance education and train-ing in Britain and, especially, the possibilities of change. This is why we present these factors in Part I as background to the detailed study which follows. It is the reason we urge that our work be read as a whole.

In this introduction I have attempted to set the scene. It would be incomplete without acknowledging the many people whom we consulted, interviewed, invited to conferences, seminars and other gatherings, contacted by letter or watched perform or teach in Britain or abroad. Without them this report could not exist, let alone possess any credibility. The Committee held 26 formal meetings as well as conferences in Cardiff, Edinburgh and Winchester and special seminars in London. The largest of these are listed in Appendix A. It met informally on many other occasions and visited, in groups or as individuals, many institutions and people as well as important conferences in Australia and Canada. Indeed this report has been much influenced by experience in the Common-wealth. Parts of it have been drafted at desks as far apart as Canada, Australia and Hong Kong. We are deeply grateful for the welcome we received from the dance and education professions in Britain and abroad, and the help which so many people extended to us by writing, telephoning, answering our questions and discussing many matters with us. Especially important to us in this dialogue was the continual consultation it stimulated with working teachers in both sectors of education.

Throughout the five years of the study we have received unwavering and generous help from the Board of the Foundation, and we thank them. In particular, I should like to thank my colleagues on the Committee, not only for the high priority they have given to our task, the expertise they have contributed to discussions and the quality of individual responses to the many drafts of this report, but for their confidence and patience in facing many difficulties and delays not all directly connected with our study.

I must thank also Lord Vaizey and Michael Barnes, Chairman and Secretary respectively of the two previous Gulbenkian reports, *Going on the Stage* and *Training Musicians*, for helpful advice and the invaluable example of their work and standards which guided much of what we did. The Committee, and myself in particular as the one who did the writing, owes a great debt to Joan Maxwell-Hudson, our organising secretary, for her tireless efforts and dedication to the work, to Claire Seignior, her successor during the last year of the study who also compiled the Index, and to Millicent Bowerman, the Foundation's literary editor in the UK. They, our other secretaries, research staff and consultants have been unfailing in their response to our demands on them and, what is even better, unfailingly cheerful. Our task has been formidable. We believe it has been worthwhile because it marks a new beginning. Final judgement rests with those who will fashion from our work a new period of development ahead.

Peter Brinson   July 1980

Members of the Committee of Inquiry

Peter Brinson *Chairman*

John Allen *Vice-Chairman*; Chairman, Accreditation Panels, National Council of Drama Training and Council for Dance Education and Training; member of Dance and Drama Boards, Council for National Academic Awards; formerly, HM Inspector with national responsibility for drama; formerly Principal Central School of Speech and Drama; author of many books on drama.

Audrey Bambra Chairman of Governors, London College of Dance and Drama; executive member of International Association of Physical Education and Sport for Women and Girls; council member of the Imperial Society of Teachers of Dancing; executive member of Keep Fit Association; member of exploratory group of the Assessment of Performance Unit, Department of Education and Science; formerly, Principal, Chelsea College of Physical Education; author.

Pauline Clayden ILEA Training Officer for the Youth and Play Centre Service; founder and Director, Islington Dance Factory for Young People; formerly, ILEA Youth Officer for Camden and ballet and gymnastics teacher in youth centres and adult institutes.

Robert Cohan (alternate **Robin Howard**) Artistic Director and Principal Choreographer, London Contemporary Dance Theatre; formerly, Principal of the Martha Graham Company and partner to Graham, creating many roles in her ballets.

Margaret Dunn Member of the Arts Council Advisory Committee, and of the Creative and Performing Arts and Dance Boards, Council for National Academic Awards; formerly, Vice-Principal, Bretton Hall College and teacher and adviser in dance and drama.

Grace Eldridge Headmistress, New Parks Girls School, Leicester; formerly teacher in secondary schools and lecturer in education at colleges in the South West and Midlands.

Andrew Fairbairn (alternates **Maurice Gilmour, Peter Kyle**) Director of Education, Leicestershire; member of the Business Education Council and of the Council of the Association of Art Institutions; formerly, Deputy-Director of Education, Leicestershire; Educational Administrator and teacher; chairman of a committee of the Youth Service Development Council for the Report *Youth and Community Work in the 70s.*

Julia Farron (alternate **James Monahan**) Member of the Ballet Staff, Royal Ballet School; member of the Executive Committee and the Professional Advisory Panel, Royal Academy of Dancing; formerly, principal dancer, the Royal Ballet, now guest artist.

John Field Director, London Festival Ballet; formerly, Director Royal Academy of Dancing; principal dancer, Sadler's Wells Ballet; assistant director, the Royal Ballet, in charge of touring section; Director of the Ballet and Ballet School, La Scala, Milan.

XI

Jane Nicholas (on behalf of the Arts Council of Great Britain) Director, Dance, Arts Council of Great Britain, formerly, assistant director, Dance; drama officer, the British Council; freelance dancer, singer, actress; member, the Sadler's Wells Ballet and Sadler's Wells Theatre Ballet.

Jane Pollard (on behalf of the Department of Education and Science) HMI. (Retired August 1978)

Athalie Knowles (appointed September 1978 on behalf of the Department of Education and Science) HMI; Formerly lecturer in dance at Whitelands College, Putney; Dartford College of Education; the Laban Art of Movement Studio; Chairman, DES Dance Working Party.

The following members withdrew with effect from the dates stated:—

David Blair died April 1976
Margaret Dale July 1976
Norman Morrice March 1977
Alan Storey April 1978
Mary Clarke October 1978

Secretariat

Joan Maxwell-Hudson, Organising Secretary; Shirley Dennison, Claire Seignior.

Research

1 Maintained Sector: National Foundation for Educational Research; Janet Adshead; Joan White.

2 Non-maintained Sector: Gale Law with Sandy Stallen.

NOTE: Almost all of us are connected in one way or another with institutions which may benefit from some of our recommendations. Such connections are inevitable by nature of our experience or appointments. We have been careful to bear in mind at all times these connections, where they occur, and to safeguard against them. It is proper, nevertheless, here to declare our interest.

Terms of Reference

1   Elucidate the facts and make a study of the present provision in Britain of general dance education in primary, secondary and higher education, including its relation to professional training, with an assessment of how far potential talent to perform or teach remains undiscovered for lack of opportunity.

2   Elucidate the facts and make a study of the present provision for vocational education in dance with particular reference to the training available for those who wish to become performing artists on stage and screen, including their early training as children, choreographic and music training, and their needs at the end of a dance career.

3   Investigate the methods and standards of training dance teachers, related to the needs of companies, the requirements of the educational system and the growth of the amateur dance movement.

4   Measure present financial provision for vocational training against actual and potential needs and sources.

5   Investigate the discretionary grant system as regards professional training for dance and the problems caused within this system by the necessity for training to start at an early age.

6   Investigate any disparity between the number of those trained and employment opportunities, including estimated present and future needs of theatre companies and mechanical media of all kinds.

7   Assess the contribution of current dance examinations to the teaching of the amateur and professional student and the relationship to needs of professional companies and teacher training courses.

8   Consider ways of safeguarding and advancing dance education at national and local level in the current economic climate.

9   Make recommendations.

PART I
The Setting

1 The Importance of Dance

1 Origins of the report

Dance is part of the history of human movement, part of the history of human culture and part of the history of human communication. These three elements are brought together and realised through dance activity. Therefore, dance activity is an important factor in human social development. Some societies have accorded it this role. Not, however, British society today, beyond acknowledging that dance has educational as well as artistic value. This national ignorance of the significance of dance has complicated all our work. The starting point of the study was the situation at which dance education had arrived in Britain by the mid 1970s. The need for a study was expressed at an action-conference on dance education called by the Gulbenkian Foundation in March 1974 and described in Appendix A. The conference became an event of major significance for dance education and training in Britain. It brought together many different, often rival, methods at just the right moment. It stimulated new thinking and reinforced the mood of questioning and exploration which was evident already at every level. It identified as equally important the two 'sectors' of dance education and training in Britain — the maintained or public sector, and the non-maintained or private sector. In dance education and training it has led directly to the establishment in England of a Council for Dance Education and Training and, indirectly, to a Scottish Council for Dance and a Welsh Dance Association. It even played a small part in influencing the formation of an Australian Association for Dance Education in August, 1977. This is the first time in each country there has been a single body representing all the major dance interests and methods of teaching. Since we shall refer to these bodies many times and make suggestions for their work, it is appropriate to define them clearly here.

2 Council for Dance Education and Training

The Council for Dance Education and Training in England arose out of discussions between the leading bodies of the private sector brought together by the action-conference in 1974. The Council is now a charitable body with objects described in Appendix F. It aims principally to raise standards; to provide an accreditation system of dance schools for local education authorities and parents; to be a centre of advice and policy study for the dance profession; to speak as a 'voice' on behalf of dance education and training to official organisations at national and local level. It is funded entirely privately and at the moment speaks only for the private and vocational sector. Its Council is composed of representatives appointed by the major bodies involved with representation from the broader educational world.

3 Scottish Council for Dance

The Scottish Council for Dance arose out of a national consultation held on 29/30 April, 1977 at Dunfermline College of Physical Education, near Edinburgh, as part of the information-gathering process of the

1

present study. The consultation drew together the public and private sectors of dance education in discussions which were sufficiently fruitful to justify continued discussion and collaboration. As a result the Scottish Council came into being as a registered charity at the end of 1979. It differs from the English Council in that it embraces both sectors of dance education and training in Scotland, and the members of its Council and Executive are elected, not appointed. Details of its constitution are given at Appendix F. Like the English Council, however, it seeks to promote all forms of dance; to provide a 'voice' through which dance can speak with greater authority to government; to advise and help local authorities, parents, students and the public; and to raise standards. It does not, as yet, provide an accreditation service for schools.

4 Dance Council for Wales A Dance Council for Wales is being formed from the Welsh Dance Association, the oldest of the three national organisations. The first step towards its formation was a consultation for our dance study organised by the Welsh Arts Council at the Sherman Theatre, Cardiff in 1976. This brought together many dance interests in Wales. Two years later the Welsh Dance Association was established at a conference at the Sherman Theatre in May 1978. Like its English and Scottish counterparts, it is privately funded and seeks to raise standards; to advance the cause of dance in Wales; and to bring together all those interested in dance. Further details are given in Appendix F.

5 Our terms of reference The other major result of the action-conference was our dance study. The Conference pointed out how few facts and statistics are available about dance education and training in Britain;* how little dance teachers know about their profession outside their own experience; how much under-estimated by the larger world of education are the achievements of dance education and training during the last 30 years; and how profoundly unstudied is the contribution of dance education at every level. From this derives our terms of reference. In fulfilling these terms our method has been to gather as much factual information as possible supported by illustrative example and opinion from a wide variety of people. We have tried to discuss and present the results in ways which lead to unprejudiced deductions leading to a series of recommendations. To accomplish this objective we needed to supplement the facts we gathered by some original research, although the research we could commission was limited by time and resources.

---

* Including, for example, considerable differences between the Scottish education system and the system in England and Wales, due to historical circumstance and national approach. These differences influence the development of dance education and vocational training north and south of the border and are emphasised by the existence of two departments of state — a Department of Education and Science for England and Wales (DES), and a Scottish Education Department (SED).

6 Need for *further* *research*	In commissioning research we had to differ from the approach of the Gulbenkian Foundation reports on training for drama[1] and music[2] because we had at our beginnings neither an equivalent of the Conference of Drama Schools* to help us, nor any previous report like *Making Musicians.*[3] The Arts Council of Great Britain's report on opera and ballet[4] studied the present and future needs of these arts in the professional theatre leaving education and training outside the terms of reference. We had before us, therefore, virgin territory; our only guide a long but little known history which we ourselves had to begin by studying so as to draw on the experience it offered. There is a need for further research across the whole field. We reflect this need in our recommendations.
7 Two parts *of our task*	Launched, then, as the result of an action-conference which had asserted the unity of the dance world, and believing in this unity ourselves, we have sought to emphasise unity at every opportunity. We think it self-evident that the interests of general dance education and vocational dance training are inseparable. We show, for example, that some gifted potential dancers may be educated within the general dance education provided by county schools, so that for them what county schools offer could be directly vocational. Nevertheless, dance education for the generality of children and vocational training for the gifted potential dancer clearly represent two different parts of the whole. This is why we treat them separately in our report. We draw them together only in this part of our report to show the common context, the efforts now being made, the further efforts needed, and to advance the common cause of winning greater recognition for both.
8 The place of *arts in education*	The case for the arts in education has been supported by every major report on British education since Hadow[5] in 1926 and by a wealth of other evidence, official and unofficial, British and foreign. 'The arts', said the Crowther Report in 1959 'are not the flowers but the roots of education.'[6] The same view has been expressed across the Atlantic. 'Painting, sculpture, music, dance, crafts — these are not frills to be indulged in if time is left over from the real business of education; they *are* the business of education as much as reading, writing, maths or science. For the arts are the language of a whole range of human experience; to neglect them is to neglect ourselves and to deny children the full development that education should provide.'[7] The case is developed further in current Education Surveys of the Department of Education and Science (DES), nos. 2, 11, 12 and 22 covering drama, art and museums in schools, and comparable studies from the Scottish Education Department (SED);[8] in documents from UNESCO, Conseil International de la Danse (CIDD) and Dance and the Child International (DACI) and all the countries discussed in chapter 5; in reports from the Labour Party,[9] the Conservative Party[10] and Trades Union Congress

---

* A grouping of 14 leading drama schools which first requested the drama study in association with British Actors' Equity and the Council of Regional Theatres, then supplied invaluable information.

(TUC);[11] in the Gulbenkian reports on drama,[1] music[2] and ethnic arts[12] as well as Lord Redcliffe-Maud's synoptic *Support for the Arts*;[13] in the Schools Council's *Arts and the Adolescent*;[14] and in the forthcoming Gulbenkian study on arts and the curriculum.[15] All maintain the essential role of the arts at every level of the education of young people, in practice as well as in appreciation. The arts, moreover, help the school as well as the student. Peter Newsam, now chief education officer of the Inner London Education Authority (ILEA) welcomed his Authority's booklet on *The Creative Arts in the Secondary School*[16] 'as a reaffirmation of confidence; it reaffirms the place of creative teachers at the heart of children's learning.'

9 The arts still peripheral to education

How then can it happen that in British secondary schools, 'for all practical purposes, arts education remains a matter of only peripheral concern. Neither the arts subjects nor the teachers have ever been taken seriously. Such has been the reluctant conclusion of every major education report published in the last 50 years, and such is ours'[14]? Why, against so much evidence have the arts remained 'peripheral' to British secondary education and, indeed, British life? The continuing debate about the future of British education suggests an answer. The debate has reflected two conceptions of education, which are not, of course, mutually exclusive. One seeks to provide every child with opportunities for self-realisation and the acquisition of appropriate knowledge to develop potential in interesting and rewarding leisure as well as work. The other, by concentrating mostly on the three Rs, seeks to adapt tomorrow's work force more closely to the needs of modern industry without the 'frills' of wider knowledge and artistic opportunity. This second conception permeated the then Prime Minister's policy speech when he launched the education debate at Oxford in 1976, and appears to guide also the definition of 'training' applied by the Manpower Services Commission (MSC). It reflects especially clearly the strength of the dominant view in our society, that the arts have no significant place in an education concerned primarily with preparation for work.

10 Traditional views challenged by our experience

The traditional view that education should concern itself primarily with education for work is based generally on a concept of knowledge limited to the 'written word' and 'the academic'. It denies the value of experiential knowledge except in the narrowest, functional sense. This narrow approach overlooks the fact that knowledge acquired in one field may have some unpredictable relevance to problems and concerns in apparently unrelated fields. Experiential knowledge appears to us no less valuable than that gained through books. The evidence lies in creative experimental work conducted over many years in the sciences as well as in the arts. Dance *is* experiential knowledge. This is one of its particular values in education illustrated many times in the pages which follow. Traditional attitudes promote the view that the arts are a great civilising force in society but not an important power-house from which society draws its strength. In fact, while better teaching of science and technical subjects will help to solve some of our present economic problems, in the long term we need young people with imagination and commitment to drive events to fruitful conclusions. We believe that these qualities are developed just as effectively by the arts as by science.

11 Preparing for a different future
We have had to bear in mind in our task the changing nature of life and work which lies before young people. We do not accept that a narrowly functional education is appropriate to this future. We have entered an electronic age in which developing automation and division of labour in industry increasingly eliminate the need for unskilled workers. For the mass of the workforce of young school-leavers the prospect is dead-end jobs or the dole queue. Paradoxically, this process creates, at the same time, conditions for increased creative leisure in a shorter working week in which work and non-work are balanced more rationally.* Hence there is a need to educate human beings as much for leisure as for work. The complexities of the age in which we live require, more than ever, human beings who are questioning contributors to a lively democracy rather than unquestioning machine operators, managers and television viewers.

12 Roots in the maintained sector
In view of this future we may seem to give more attention to dance in the maintained sector than to the non-maintained private and vocational, sector on which the Gulbenkian Foundation drama and music reports have concentrated. This is not so. We are bound by our terms of reference to give equal weight to both sectors and to fail in this would be to make nonsense of the study. The maintained sector has to be the beginning of everything else because of the young age at which dancing needs to start for those aiming at a dancing career. 'It really is not possible,' remarked Christopher Price, MP, in a House of Commons debate about the Gulbenkian Foundation Report on *Training Musicians*, 'to develop a system of further education in music in the country as a whole if it is not underpinned by something at secondary school level.'[17] What is true of music is truer still of dance if we really wish to offer opportunity to young people in the widest possible way, and so make sure that our professional dance institutions are nourished by all the resources of potential talent in the United Kingdom. We are glad, therefore, to note the current explosion of dance interest 'in the country as a whole' with a blurring of the distinctions between professional and amateur dancers, and between dance teachers in the maintained and non-maintained sectors.

13 Dance a test case
In all these fields dance is a special case for a special reason. If, as our study suggests, failure to comprehend the nature of the arts is a major reason for underestimating their educational value, then the minority

---

* 'We pay great attention to mitigating inequality in wealth and income but very little to mitigating inequality of employment. If we did, it is estimated each person would be unemployed once every six years.' David Metcalf, Professor of Economics, University of Kent. *The Guardian* 30.7.79.

place of dance makes it a test case for the arts as a whole. Particularly is this true of education, where to argue the case for dance almost always stirs controversy. This realisation has given our work a particular spur and lends a special emphasis to this part of our study which places British dance education and training within the four contexts which influence what it is and what it can become. They are: international relations and cultural exchange; the structure of state and voluntary organisations within Britain at national and local level; relations with the British dance profession; relations with other arts. These four provide also valuable links and liaisons between the public and private sectors of our study, emphasising their common background.

14 A critical situation

Lastly, we draw attention to a triple threat which has arisen particularly during the last year of our study and which overshadows all our report. First, the arts generally in the maintained sector, and dance in particular, are threatened by an additional emphasis on a curriculum of the three Rs which excludes the arts.[18] Second, the application of cuts by many authorities (though not by all) is falling disproportionately upon the arts as expendable 'frills'. Third, in the non-maintained sector the whole of the British vocational training system for the performing arts is threatened by cuts in the discretionary grants system and by the anomalies in treatment by different local education authorities. We return to these dangers in subsequent chapters, but *it is no exaggeration to say that much of what has been achieved in arts education and vocational training during the last 35 years is now seriously at risk. We have to sound the alarm.*

2 The Dance and Education Professions

15 Purpose of the chapter

Among the important conclusions to emerge from our study is the need for a new relationship between the dance profession and the education profession, each drawing upon the other as resource. This is, of course, a partnership. Ultimately the professional dance companies are dependent upon dance educators and trainers for dancers and audiences. We outline here the contribution we think professional dance companies could make to British dance education and training.

16 Historical background

First, some history. The links between the dance profession and maintained schools date back to the earliest days of British ballet between the wars. The occasions were usually talks, lecture-demonstrations or small performances by dancers or dance students. After the second world war the Sadler's Wells/Royal Ballet School made a practice of responding to requests for lecture-demonstrations and the like from ballet clubs, arts societies and schools, provided there was no conflict with studies. In the early 1960s such lecture-demonstrations provided the foundation of what became the Royal Ballet's Ballet for All Company. Other schools have contributed to public understanding through lecture-demonstrations. The major examining bodies similarly organised lectures and lecture-demonstration tours. Sometimes these sporadic attempts at public education were complemented in the dance companies by special school matinées at which the performance would be introduced by a member of the company and the dancers would demonstrate a dancer's training or some selection from the performance to follow. Programmes of this kind regularly formed part of the work of the Sadler's Wells Theatre Ballet under Peggy Van Praagh at Sadler's Wells Theatre during the late 1940s and early 1950s. Today the idea is being developed by the Royal Ballet through the appointment of an education officer at the Royal Opera House.

17 Early educational dance companies

The first specifically educational dance company to be established on a regular basis was the Educational Dance Drama Theatre Company in 1957. This became a private touring company of between six and ten dancers presenting programmes based on the principles of Laban. Thus it provided support to teachers in the maintained sector teaching from the same principles. In complete contrast, and founded on very different professional principles, the next educational company to be formed operating on behalf of classical ballet was the Royal Ballet's Ballet For All company established in 1964. This toured Britain widely until 1979 with programmes which combined words, dance and music in special ballet-plays. Programmes described the history and background of dance training, of ballet at different historical periods, of choreography and so on. These ballet-plays, developed out of adult education lecture-demonstrations given originally for Oxford, Cambridge and London Universities, enjoyed considerable success. They proved that an educational company for classical ballet filled a considerable public need and could be viable* provided it balanced a measure of performance with direct educational work.[19]

18 Expansion
of educational
work

During most of the 1960s these two very different companies were almost alone in their educational task. The rest of the dance world showed limited understanding of the need to which they were responding and the huge potential of their work. For this reason, until recently, professional dancers have been involved in educational work in the maintained sector much less than professional actors, musicians, painters and sculptors. With hindsight, 1965 gave the first indication of a new influence. The year saw the first lecture-demonstrations of contemporary dance to a British public. The event at the Theatre Royal, Stratford East, London, was organised jointly by Ballet for All and Robin Howard, future founder of today's London Contemporary Dance Theatre and School. The programme compared the contemporary dance of Martha Graham with the classical dance of the Royal Ballet and was the first occasion dancers of both styles appeared in Britain on the same stage. The programme sold out for the week of its presentation.

19 The student
connection

Such public interest, encouraged by the pioneer activity of a few individuals and groups, brought about a slow change of attitude in the professional dance world during the late 1960s. From 1969 the number of new companies directly or indirectly committed to educational work increased rapidly, sometimes in collaboration with established companies and receiving support from the Arts Council of Great Britain. Liverpool University students organised the visit of an avant garde group of actors and dancers aiming to 'create a context for the development of a theatre language capable of expressing a range of ideas not accessible to existing forms of dance, theatre or event ...' This really marked the beginning of the involvement in dance of students in the tertiary sector, the beginning of the dance explosion in Britain. Other groups were established, particularly in the north of the country and in Scotland, with a brief to include educational work in their programmes. Today, all regional companies and most national dance companies expect to offer educational workshops, classes and residencies as part of their work. This rich and exciting outcome of the 1970s needs to become a principal concern of the 1980s.

20 Initiation of
residencies

While this expansion was taking place in the regions, and in those companies offering educational programmes through more or less traditional performance methods, an event occurred which transformed the educational service professional dancers might offer in schools and elsewhere. This was a pioneer series of residencies in Yorkshire and Liverpool initiated by the London Contemporary Dance Theatre in

---

*   In 1979 Ballet for All was the only section of Opera House activities to balance its budget, and in fact, show a small reserve of funds. Its final surplus on closure at the end of March 1979 was about £13,000, a remarkable achievement for a small touring dance company and proof of its considerable popularity.

1976. The idea came from the United States and was adapted to British conditions by Robert Cohan, artistic director of the company. The examples which he devised of lecture-demonstrations, talks, debates, classes, rehearsals and choreographic creation in public, set the relations between the dance profession and the education profession on a new course of closer collaboration and mutual respect. Soon afterwards, Scottish Ballet's Moveable Workshop, a small modern dance company separate from its parent, began doing much the same thing in Scottish colleges of education, anticipating Scottish Ballet's much larger later work. But this was not the only pioneer work of the kind. Two colleges in England appointed a professional dancer and choreographer to a residency spread over 2–3 years. In return for classes to students and other help, the colleges gave studio space and the Regional Arts Association gave a grant. Thus not only dance groups and companies could contribute to the educational process, but also a professional dancer, who happened to be a qualified teacher, could give and receive valuable experience in interaction with an educational institution.

21 Appointment of education officers

Within a matter of six years a dramatic change has taken place in the educational contribution of professional dancers. Although mostly inspired by contemporary dance and involving contemporary dancers, all the major classical companies have begun to revive earlier practices of school matinées and to introduce new practices. These developments have been strengthened in a number of companies by the appointment of a member of staff with educational responsibilities or by the specific appointment of education officers. The duties of these officers are to liaise with education authorities and to arrange master classes, lecture-demonstrations, talks and movement workshops whenever these are requested and schedules permit. Often the duties do not go beyond liaison and sometimes are closer to marketing than education. There is need for clarification of their roles and for more consultation between companies and education authorities. But the potential is there.

22 Link with community dance

The expansion of educational work is also a response to influences outside the theatre, dance and education worlds, in particular the development of community dance groups since the mid-1970s. These, and fringe theatre companies of all kinds increasingly use dance as one among several media through which to approach an audience. Dance, therefore, has begun to lose its rather specialist connotation. The community dance movement has been encouraged further in a number of ways. Sometimes a company is connected with a dance department in a college or polytechnic. Sometimes it receives support from one of the programmes of the MSC. We welcome these developments but think they can be extended to include more flexible use of other opportunities for support, such as association with further education provision, sport and recreation provision, and social service activities. In each case, however, any such extension should take place only after careful consultation with all concerned. This should include a rigorous assessment of local need and of the professional competence of the proposed artists.

23 Role of Regional Arts Associations	The growth of community and fringe theatre confirms the interest in dance which waits to be encouraged in the regions, particularly among young people. It is not surprising, therefore, that RAAs, which helped to initiate some of the expansion of the early 1970s, have provided not only further funds for experiment but also have taken tentative steps in some areas to act as a dance resource or co-ordination service for local education authorities, providing additional stimulus through companies and dancers brought in from outside. Often this is a result of the work of an officer whose main responsibility to an Association may be music or drama but whose interest in dance is strong enough to initiate projects; to nurture what is happening already in dance in the region; sometimes to set up a committee of dance advisers for the area. Further liaison between RAA officers responsible for dance, RAA dance panel chairmen, the Dance Director and the Education Liaison Officer of the Arts Council of Great Britain all help. The Arts Council's dance officers act as a link by attending dance meetings in the regions when required. As dance activity increases this liaison will be no substitute for a full-time dance officer in each region.
24 Contribution of television	The same growth of public interest has encouraged the BBC and IBA television networks to pay more attention to dance. For the BBC this revives an interest it showed during the 1950s and 1960s. BBC radio also has developed further its continuing series of informed talks on aspects of dance and music. 8,500,000 people saw BBC television's month of dance programmes in the spring of 1979. Even so, we are convinced that such a figure represents only a fraction of what could be achieved by television and radio given closer liaison between all concerned (including the relevant trade unions) leading to new forms of collaboration between media, educational and dance agencies. We emphasise, in particular, the need for carefully prepared educational programmes on all channels, including the new channel 4, to supplement performance programmes on both television networks. We emphasise also opportunities provided by the expansion of local radio and television to bring to microphone and screen dancers, teachers and the public to discuss and popularise the creation and appreciation of dance. We think also there should be immediate discussions to release and use for educational purposes the large amount of sound and visual dance archive material now available.
25 Where we stand now	To sum up. We have shown that most professional dance companies in Britain now offer their public educational experiences and that a number of companies specialise in this work. There has been, and is, a succession of individual foreign dancers, experienced in educational work, supplementing similar British initiatives with knowledge from abroad. The point is made in chapter 4, moreover, that much good school work exists in Britain as a basis upon which professional companies and individual dancers can build. Television, radio and regional arts organisations, too, have demonstrated their importance as channels for the dissemination of this effort, and for supplementing it in their own ways.

26 Where we might go	Development, of course, depends upon liaison and consultation between local education authorities, schools and dance companies to make greater use of the resources each can offer the other. We think, for example, that dance companies should consult more closely with educators about the precise needs of schools before a visit, during a visit and the follow-up. We recognise that the financial and touring pressures under which most professional dance companies work mean that time cannot be spared for preparatory visits by a company member before the arrival of a company, nor do most companies have the time, finance or expertise to supply teaching notes and other material about the visit in advance. We know, too, that it is difficult for discussion to take place between teachers and company members about the work at the end of a visit, if only because the company has to move on as quickly as possible. We think that some of the stimulus to resolve these problems must come from the Arts Council of Great Britain, or the Scottish or Welsh Arts Councils as appropriate, in concert with responsible officers and panel chairmen of RAAs. Other initiatives may come from local education authorities or RAAs themselves. We welcome unreservedly, therefore, two important initiatives by the Arts Council of Great Britain. One is the establishment of Dance Umbrella to serve small companies. The other is the launching early in 1980 of three pilot projects after the example of the American Artists-in-Schools Programme: Dance Component, described in chapter 5. We think, also, that there are two particularly important additional needs, at present undersupported, to which we draw the attention of responsible bodies.
27 Dance Umbrella	Dance Umbrella is an American idea introduced to Britain in the autumn of 1978 as a festival of small-scale dance companies — mostly contemporary — in which a number of visiting artists from the USA also participated. The first festival took place in London but an expanded second version, early in 1980, included three regional venues. Currently the organisation is introducing administrative services for small dance companies and artists, funded by the Gulbenkian Foundation. These services include the organisation of regional and foreign tours, publicity and applications for funding. Such an umbrella is much needed by small companies and we hope will continue to be supported and expanded.
28 Three pilot projects in schools	The Arts Council of Great Britain's three pilot Dance Artist-in-Education Schemes (based on the American example) each comprise a five week 'sandwich' residency. The residency is divided into three units. For the first two weeks a dance artist will go to the school which is hosting the project to explore and build upon the dance awareness which exists and prepare the way for a dance company. The company moves into residence for one week and is followed by another dance artist, preferably an experienced choreographer, who will spend a further two weeks in the school creating a work with and for the children. The culmination of the project is a performance of the created work. Thus the five weeks' work should have a linking theme and should be

11

devised as a complete project with the dance artist(s) present during the company residency. The purpose of the projects is to enrich the lives of the children involved by enhancing their powers of perception and ability to communicate creatively; to further the understanding of dance throughout the school community; to provide opportunities to dance artists to extend and develop themselves more fully as artists; and to give dance artists and companies a better understanding of education and the education world.

29 Provision for mime

The art of mime is, or ought to be, as strong an element of dance as of drama. As such it finds a place in training for both theatre arts. At the same time it is a theatre art in its own right, deserving appropriate support in funding and educational provision. For this reason of independence it was not included in our terms of reference and we have made no special study of its problems. We feel it right to emphasise here, however, its long tradition in Britain, its importance to dance, and the clear signs of a revival of public interest in recent years through festivals of mime, the initiation of training courses, and other events, as well as the following built up by distinguished individual mime artists, mostly from abroad. We conclude, therefore, that in the interests of the development of dance and drama as well as the art of mime itself, and to redress the balance, this revival of interest should be recognised by funding bodies and educational authorities as deserving a measure of priority in their allocation of resources, notwithstanding the difficulties of the present time.

30 Provision for archives

In 1980 the Imperial Society of Teachers of Dancing is 76 years old, the Royal Academy of Dancing 60, the Cecchetti Society 58, Ballet Rambert 54, the Royal Ballet 49, and London Festival Ballet 30. A number of established institutions of dance training are as old as, or older than, any of these. All of them must have records of value to the history of dance in Britain which are, therefore, essential resources for researchers, teachers and others concerned to study and disseminate the lessons of this history. Many of these institutions, as well as younger institutions like London Contemporary Dance Theatre, The Scottish Ballet and the Royal Ballet's former Ballet for All Company, have taken steps to preserve their records. A few have formed links with the British Theatre Museum. Some have taken no steps to safeguard their records, however, so that these are now at risk. Almost all those which have taken steps suffer from lack of space, funds and other essentials because companies and teaching bodies usually have to find the cost of upkeep, in competition with other needs, out of already restricted budgets. Nevertheless it is important to sustain these archives, not only for their own value, but for the documents, prints, slides and other teaching aids essential to the historical teaching which is part of all dance education and training. In all these interests we urge every dance institution to be aware of its archival responsibility. We think that a conference should be convened as soon as possible to concert and discuss the preservation and use of dance archives in Britain and that funding bodies should recognise the importance of this work by helping to implement the recommendations of the conference.

31 Need for partnership

Thus a considerable basis exists for further development. There is now a need for local education authorities, RAAs, the Arts Council of Great Britain and the Scottish and Welsh Arts Councils to review their provision and to stimulate not only greater financial support (possibly from a redistribution of resources), but greater support by way of the time of local authority, RAA and Arts Councils' officers. In the present period of restraint we believe that such activity is a particularly fruitful use of resources and preparation for the future. Indeed, it is a way to realise the close partnership between the dance profession and the education profession which we believe should be a priority for both during the 1980s.

3 Dance, Music and other Related Arts

32 Purpose of the chapter

One of the attributes of dance, which makes it both a rich contributor to the education and training of individuals and also a demanding area of study, is its inter-disciplinary nature. A comprehensive study of dance should include geography, history, literature and mathematics; some knowledge of anatomy, physiology and the technology of theatre; and the related arts of music, painting, sculpture, literature especially poetry, drama and mime. The great eighteenth century choreographer, Noverre, supported by many of his successors, included also geometry and architecture. We are concerned here with the education of young people learning dance as part of general education or as a vocational training. In either case the need for musical education is pre-eminent among the related arts.

33 Music in relation to dance

Music and dance comprise one of the creative partnerships to which we call attention throughout our study. In our various visits to different kinds of institutions in which dance is studied in both sectors, it was evident that many dancers and dance teachers seem to be aware of only one aspect of music, its time and rhythm. Such an attitude limits the creative partnership which composer, choreographer and dancer should labour together to create. Similarly, many musicians show little understanding of dance. Better musical education for dancers and dance teachers and better dance education for all musicians, instrumentalists, composers and music teachers, therefore appears urgent. We have found these needs recurring throughout both sectors of dance education and training and make proposals to meet them later in this chapter.

34 Mutual need for music and dance education

There are books available which discuss the nature of the music desirable for different kinds of dance. The problem for us is rather the way this music is selected, the manner of its reproduction in the classroom, and the way the teacher has been trained to make the best use of musical material. In practice, in Britain, the music to which a student dances in the general or vocational classroom is played on a piano or percussion instrument, or reproduced by tape or record-player. It matters very much that the pianist or percussionist should be a good musician with wide musical taste, have a feeling for movement and be able to improvise imaginatively within the framework given by the teacher. Equally, it matters that the dance teacher's musical education is such that she/he can communicate with the musician, be demanding of good musical standards and, if using mechanical reproduction, have the knowledge and library resources equal to the task of selecting music which contributes not only to the dance quality of a classroom, but to the musical education of the students. In our experience this combination of qualities is rare although, as we show below, teacher training institutions now seek increasingly to achieve it.

35 The
classroom
musician –
what is needed

The problem of music in relation to dance education and training thus has a number of aspects. There is, first, the quality of the classroom accompaniment to which we have referred. This has two aspects, the quality of the musician and the quality of the instrument, usually a piano. This implies a need to engage, and pay adequately, good musicians who will have had an appropriate training. The training involves more than adapting musical knowledge to classroom requirements. It is rather a training in the nature of dance; in understanding the teacher's approach to a dance class and the objective behind each activity; in understanding the difference between developing a musical theme and a choreographic theme; and in comprehending the physical limitations and needs of dancers in relation to music. The ideal should be a musician with a deep enough understanding of dance to be able to select from the wide literature of music that which is appropriate to a particular dance purpose, and an ability to improvise, so that the creative partnership of music and dance is translated into a creative partnership between musician and dance teacher. Such a partnership requires genuine motivation on the part of the musician and the dance teacher and an equally genuine recognition by young dancers of the status of music and musician in their studies. The musician is not a servant, but the teacher's ally and the students' friend. Dance teachers, therefore, should support their musicians in having instruments regularly serviced and in demanding a proper standard of all musical equipment. Otherwise a downward spiral is established. However well the musician plays, on a bad piano for example, the sound will always be unpleasant and unable to stir the imagination of dancers. The musician detects there is no response from the dancers, becomes discouraged and careless; the playing deteriorates.

36 The dance
teacher/student
dancer – what
is needed

To approach music in this way implies a wider musical education for dance teacher and student dancer than we have found is usually the case. First, dancers should be encouraged to enjoy music for itself. In this way they may become inquisitive and discover for themselves, new sounds, new sources and composers. Too often we have noted music considered as a tiresome but necessary tool. With sympathetic guidance and the help of tapes and records from libraries to listen to at leisure it can be a source of enjoyment. All aids to deepen artistic insight and experience should be encouraged. It is recognised that most truly great artists of the world, despite time-consuming commitment to their art, have a wide range of interests. Performing artists, to be of enduring interest to audiences, need to be interesting and interested people. The problem arises when artists have the technical ability to communicate to an audience, but apparently nothing to say. Musicians and dancers are especially prone to this accusation so that in practice, in staff rooms, for example, they seem sometimes unable to join in general conversations. This may be due to early specialisation and the physical demands of their art form. Such dedication is admired often as a virtue, but can produce narrow interests which stunt growth to maturity as

15

artists and people. A balance must be kept. The second need, then, is to acquire a sensitive response to music. The student dancer and dance teacher should be helped to listen, to sense or feel, and to respond in movement terms. This, of course, is not necessarily dance. As a musician moves — be it very slightly — and is moved by the music he/ she plays, so the would-be dancer or dance teacher should be moved, but with a fuller response of movement. This develops awareness of rhythm and phrasing, dynamics, the rise and fall of melody, recognition of repetition, patterns and so on. Third is a need to understand the relationship between dance and music. This has been well expressed by Stravinsky, 'choreography must realise its own form, one independent of the musical form though measured to the musical unit. Its construction will be based on whatever correspondences the choreographer may invent, but it must not seek merely to duplicate the line and beat of the music.' Fourth, it follows there is a need to appreciate music so that it is not misused, cut up, played with and treated as subordinate to the needs of dance. Part of the process of appreciation should be encouragement to collect a library of musical compositions.

Although we realise that percussion and/or mechanical reproduction very frequently have to be used in dance classes for practical or economic reasons, we think their use requires care and a full understanding of their particular value in the classroom. Too often we have seen and heard percussion used with such insensitivity that it helps neither dancing nor the students' musical education. Percussion is not a substitute for other kinds of music but a highly skilled type of music-making suitable for certain dance occasions and for dance lessons where it is appropriate. Percussion, therefore, should not be ignored, but neither should it be used all the time, nor always in isolation from other instruments. Dance teachers need to be aware of its limitations as well as its value. The same intelligent approach should guide the use of mechanical reproduction. Obviously this can assist musical education and understanding a great deal. The problem of its use in the dance classroom is not so much one of quality, but of response. A good accompanist can help a class by adjusting tempi and moods. Mechanical reproduction cannot do this and thus might be inappropriate to the particular level of a class. Its use can be beneficial because it enforces a discipline of timing, speed and rhythm. Our reservation, therefore, is that, like percussion, it needs to be used with care and sensitivity.

37 The student dancer There are, of course, a variety of ways in which the young dancer can acquire this attitude to music. Very often it is a question of providing opportunity at school. We think also there is much to be gained from the study of Dalcroze eurhythmics, not least because much of the Dalcroze approach to music is through the body. It is thus of value to musicians as well as dancers, a point to which we return in paragraph 41. Again, we think young dancers should be encouraged to make their own music. This may be through making their own rhythms, phrases and melodies in whatever way they wish, to be used as dance accompaniment. It may be through the study of a musical instrument. To

16

master a musical instrument, (required as a part of dance study by a few schools in both sectors) can assist the young student to understand better the task of mastering the body as the instrument of dance. It is also a desirable part of the acquisition of basic musicianship up to the maximum each dance student can manage. Basic musicianship in this context, we think, should require a balance of practical study (which may mean making music through singing or playing an instrument) with theoretical study, and linking dance history with music history. The object should be a co-operative approach so that the student, whether studying dance for general education or as a vocation, learns not just 'dance' or 'music', but 'musical dance' to the equal benefit of his/her dance and musical understanding.

38 Student dance teacher

Essential for this objective is the attitude and musical education of the dance teacher. A number of maintained teacher training institutions with significant courses in dance have faced this problem and produced solutions which suggest a rising standard of musical education in their course, (Dunfermline College of Physical Education in Scotland is one example). The approach usually seeks to provide a basic music training in the first two years of a three- or four-year course. This equips student teachers with basic music skills and a rudimentary knowledge of music form and analysis, music notation, score-reading and writing, and so on. At the same time rhythmic ability is developed and students learn how to use traditional percussion instruments along with a variety of other kinds of sound sources. An important element of this experience is the students' own musical composition for a dance purpose, using instrumental and electronic sound sources. In third and fourth year options practical work can be continued but supplemented by historical study and critical appraisal. There are, of course, many variations on this approach as well as restraints arising today from economies. A fundamental principle, however, is the need to equip the teacher with some musical skills.

39 Cultural education

An important element of musical education is its contribution to the young dancer's cultural education, as well as dance education. A study of music is a means of studying other cultures and dance forms. A study of music therefore is essential to any serious study of dance in its full context of movement, art and communication. Music, dance and song, for example, can be seen to be crucial factors in the development of new nations today. They are at once a process of personal communication available to each individual, an expression of nationhood and finally a means of international cultural communication which can enrich greatly the communicators. To study dance and music not only enriches individual students and the life of a school, but also an understanding of many other areas outside school.

40 Need for in-service courses

All this implies a considerable expansion of the role of dance teacher and musician beyond the usual boundaries. Music courses like those described in paragraph 38 will prepare future teachers for the possibility

17

of this larger role. The same can be said of courses provided by leading teacher training institutions of the private sector. Nevertheless it is true to say that a majority of dance teachers now teaching in both sectors — that is to say those qualified in the maintained sector through the three-year certificate course and those in the non-maintained sector who have obtained the diploma of a teacher training college — have received a more rudimentary education. We have heard and seen the results of this time and again during our study. Consequently there is an urgent need in both sectors for in-service training in musical matters for dance teachers and in dance matters for many of their pianists and instrumentalists.

41 Dance education of musicians

How ever one seeks the ideal of musically educated dancers and of a creative partnership between dance teacher and dance educated musician, it remains a fact that dancers meet music almost every time they dance whereas musicians rarely meet dance unless they seek it. Doris Humphrey, the great American choreographer, expressed the problem 20 years ago, and blamed the attitude of music schools, academies, conservatories. 'It seems to me that the attitude of most music schools is unrealistic and reactionary in regard to their young charges. The training is traditional in the concentration on pure music . . . I am sure it is unheard of for a young composer to be instructed to attend a class in choreography, or to learn about the theory and practice of movement, or to analyse the scores already composed for dance.'[21] The situation today is improved, at least in British music colleges, even though there remains much to be done. Composition courses, for example, now often include music for television, film and theatre as well as stylistic forms. Movement, which obviously includes some dance, is an obligatory part of the syllabus on some singing courses, and dance as well as movement, is a requirement on some opera courses. Dalcroze courses with lectures on dance and choreography appear in some syllabi. We hope that these are the beginnings of a wider recognition by music schools of the value of dance study to music students in general. Such study, even if begun only at tertiary level, clearly opens the possibility of a career link with the dance world, but dance study with its emphasis on the physical interpretation of music, the physical experience of music which it can give and its emphasis upon particular aspects of music, enriches in a unique way all musical studies whether or not the student later makes any special contribution to dance. We think, then, that some dance experience should be a part of all musical training.

Composers who wish to create music for dance need to maintain constant touch with choreographic developments and all composers need to have at least some exposure to dance during their courses, if only as a potential outlet for their work. Of musicians who play for dance in the classroom, dancers seek especially an ability to improvise so that they are given a greater freedom to explore moods, rhythms, melodies and so on. Musicians who play for dance and/or are musical directors for groups of dancers need not only to be aware of dance techniques but also to possess or acquire a special sensitivity for dance, a sense of being, as it were, on stage with the dancers. This applies particularly to conductors and is part of the special talent which can be observed in successful conductors of the ensembles and orchestras which accompany dance performances. It is another aspect of the creative partnership between dance and music. Tapes and records are unvarying from performance to performance: a good conductor, on the other hand, can strengthen immeasurably the musical element in each performance so that the whole becomes greater than its parts. Conversely, the special dance inspiration stimulated by sensitive conducting can be lost (at worst sabotaged!) by insensitive or unthinking conducting. Conducting courses too, therefore, need their element of dance study.

42 Areas of creative contact Musicians, particularly conductors, can play an essential role in the dancer's musical education and can help with advice about acquiring musical knowledge and the use of music. In return the musician can fairly expect that the dancer should not misuse music for dance purposes. There are two areas of musical study where this creative exchange is beginning to be explored and communicated to others. One is in the universities and in the maintained sector of tertiary education described in chapter 9. Here the flexibility of university music departments, the growing interest in dance on university campuses and, above all, the development of combined arts degrees at polytechnics and colleges of higher education provide new opportunities for closer creative contact between dance and music, dance and drama, or all three. The other initiative is the annual two-week international dance course for composers and choreographers described in paragraph 311. But this Course, whatever its achievement in the last five years, reaches only eight composers and a few musicians for a brief period each year. The proper answer to the problem must lie in a recognition by the music colleges that dance is a legitimate and desirable outlet for some of their students, requiring an appropriate preparation as a major option within the syllabus of one or more of the colleges.

43 Action needed At schools and colleges in both sectors we suggest four kinds of action to strengthen the place of music in dance education and training. One requires a continuing effort to raise the quality of musical education in dance courses, whether for general education, teacher training or vocational dance purposes. The second requires a similar effort to introduce dance education as an element of music training, again at all three levels. The third involves the development of more joint enterprises. In one private vocational school (pace Stravinsky's dictum quoted above) we saw fascinating experiments which sought to work out classical music forms in choreographic terms; at another we saw folk dance used as part of musical education. In a well-known music college we noted the creative interchange between parallel courses in music and drama and their use of dance. In maintained secondary schools we have seen specially devised projects involving music and/or drama to introduce dance to children, especially boys, who have missed an adequate primary school dance experience. We have seen, too, the

19

value of close-working teams in schools, combining the areas of dance, drama, music and design, or the alternative introduction of creative or expressive art departments. We think the development of such ideas could benefit everyone. Finally, the need to strengthen the musical sensibility of student dancers and dance teachers is sufficiently urgent to require discussions as soon as possible at local and regional level in both sectors between dance teachers who are interested in music and music teachers who are interested in dance.

44 Dance and other arts

Thus music is our paradigm for the relationship of dance with other arts. The links with these arts are obvious. The dance student needs the benefit of dramatic and mimetic training. Familiarity with literature — especially plays, short stories and poetry — may not only provide themes, but also give lessons in form and construction for choreographic work. Similarly, an acquaintance with painting and sculpture can help to educate the eye as music educates the ear. It can provide an introduction to the shapes and forms and history of movement which are the stuff of dance creation. Painting and sculpture are arts of space. So is dance. But dance, as we have seen, is also an art of time. It links the two, forming with drama and mime a strong creative centre. Thus a study of dance is incomplete without embracing its related arts and they, in turn, are assisted by an understanding of dance.

45 Value of studying related arts

To acquire and deepen this understanding of the relationship between dance and other arts, the role of the teacher is crucial. The training of the teacher therefore is also crucial. It may be that the contribution of related arts to dance study will seem different in the two sectors. The vocational dance student is bound to seek to draw from drama or fine art, say, elements of specific value to professional performance. The general dance student may draw other values according to interest. But the difference is one of emphasis or degree only, because the central value of a study of related arts has to do with extending communication skills, whatever the ultimate destination of the student. We have seen a number of syllabi of teacher training institutions in both sectors which concentrate on this point. The object cannot be to make the young dancer an expert painter, actor, mime. It can be to develop visual, verbal, musical, mimetic and movement communication skills; give confidence to draw on personal resources; extend a knowledge of history into other arts; and develop critical appreciation. This, we suggest, is the contribution, justification and value of a study of related arts as part of dance study and why dance teachers should be introduced to these possibilities during initial training, or through in-service training. The case applies, in fact, whether the basic study is music, drama or art no less than dance. The arts are interdisciplinary.

4 Dance and the State

Later, in Parts II and III, we describe the structure and organisations of the world of dance education and training. Here we relate to the larger world on which the dance world depends and with which it interacts – government at every level, the education system, national voluntary bodies like political parties and trade unions, other voluntary bodies, the media. We have developed many practical contacts with this other world in the course of our study, noting at first hand the nature of its help and influence. It is the framework within which the public and private sectors of dance education operate, providing thereby the principal link between these sectors. It represents the source of money, buildings, spaces and, therefore, power. Its philosophy conditions much of dance philosophy and so guides dance actions. It is one, but not the only, channel through which the dance world can reach the larger public we believe could and should be involved in dance. In the last resort it *is* the public. In our experience the world of dance education and training generally lacks understanding of this larger world so that dance development in Britain has suffered as a result.

The principal lesson we have learned from our discussions is the need to identify and understand sources of authority in relation to particular policies and projects. On the face of it these seem clear. There is the central authority of Parliament, the Government, Whitehall and so on – the State. Then there is local government exercising not only that authority which is devolved from the centre but also that which is conferred upon it by the local democratic process, and to which it is answerable. This is the local state. In the education world in which most of us move, however, things are not so simply divided between two powers. The central power is exercised by Parliament through the Department of Education and Science (DES) and Scottish Education Department (SED). The local power is exercised by the local education authority. But there is a third power, the head teacher, head master, head mistress. It is not always easy to know which authority might be most significant at any particular time. A head teacher, for example, is bound at the moment only to include religious instruction in the curriculum of his or her school. The rest, including dance, is the choice of the school. Local authorities are left by central government with powers to determine local priorities in the light of their perception of particular needs and availability of resources. These could be as decisive as any central government decision in determining how far dance receives support in any particular locality. Therefore the maintained and non-maintained sectors of dance education and training need to understand these power structures, to relate properly to them in order to obtain maximum support, a point to which we return at the end of this chapter.

48 Central *policy-making*	Government and the political parties are not monolithic. We have never failed to find some Members of Parliament and some Ministers from both sides of the House and in both Houses prepared to listen to us and to suggest an appropriate course of action. We in turn have something to offer them. Dance is part of the nation's cultural resources. These become more and more important as society changes the balance between the work and non-work periods of life. Indeed, the nature of this balance is likely to be a significant issue of the 1980s. Hence there is an increasing need for education to help prepare this change, and for educators and politicians in the cultural field to come forward with appropriate proposals. The dance world can provide unique expertise and should be able to formulate its own proposals to the policy-makers. In the past it seems to us to have lacked the means to do this, or to join with others having similar potential, or to understand the political system sufficiently well to make the best use of what it has to offer. The formation of national organisations of various kinds to represent the dance education profession in England, Scotland and Wales described in paragraphs 2–4, provides an opportunity to correct this imbalance. Through these national organisations and their activity it should be possible for the policy-makers to know the dance world and the dance world to know the policy-makers.
49 The *educational civil* *service*	Similarly, in Government departments and the Civil Service we think there is a need for more contacts. Obviously, support from the DES and the SED is crucial to the future of dance education and training. We have received from both Departments a great deal of encouragement as well as help in conducting this study. Bearing this in mind, we hope that they will feel able to develop further their support by implementing those of our proposals which are relevant to their functions. On their side, dance educators need to comprehend better the nature and organisation of educational administration and policy-making at national and local level so as to draw more fully on the resources administration can provide. We suggest later, for example, that insufficient attention to dance is given by the Schools Council in England and Wales and by the Consultative Committee on the Curriculum in Scotland, although proposals have been put forward to both bodies over the years. The creation of national organisations for dance education, funded by dance educators, and described in paragraphs 2–4 offers an opportunity to press the dance case more strongly. The same argument applies to the work of the Advisory Council for Adult and Continuing Education. If dance is to flourish in further and continuing education it follows that the dance world should know how to make its case with the Advisory Council!
50 Other *national* *administrative* *resources*	There are other departments in whose work the dance world is, or could be, involved justifying support and resources in return. The Scottish Office, for example, and the Department of Employment in England and Wales, through the MSC, has assisted the formation of a number of small dance groups in the social, community and educational

fields. Thus they have extended the employment of dancers in areas which are still relatively new. The problem is to find further funding once MSC support comes to an end, and therefore to make the initial selection with more care and advice. It is important to the funding of dance as of other cultural works, to counter the habit of looking for finance only to the DES, the SED, the Arts Council of Great Britain, or the Scottish and Welsh Arts Councils. Dance, like other arts, has a part to play in the increasing importance of leisure provision, one of the responsibilities of the Department of the Environment in England and Wales to which we return in paragraph 52 below. It has a growing contribution to make to therapy of various kinds under the Department of Health and Social Security (DHSS). More and more its value is recognised in social and community work for which responsibility is shared between the DHSS and the Home Office. Therefore we feel the relevant departments, including the Scottish and Welsh Offices, should recognise the value of dance to their work by including in their estimates an appropriate provision to pay for and develop this resource.

51 *Dance and local government*

Local government is the principal influence affecting the development of both sectors of dance education and training because it controls so many necessary resources at local level. It does this by operating usually through one or more of three departments: education; leisure and recreation; social services. Not all of these departments maintain an interest in dance in all authorities, though education normally must do so, and will be mentioned many times in this report. The department responsible for recreation and leisure (variously titled 'libraries and parks', 'recreation and leisure', 'entertainment' or some combination of these names) sometimes has an interest in dance ranging more widely than recreation. It controls many spaces, can take many initiatives to stimulate public interest and is often responsible for making staff appointments which draw on expertise from the private sector. The social services department may be concerned with the use of dance for community purposes, or the application of dance in other areas of social need. Thus local authorities have duties whose fulfilment either must include, or may include, dance. Their authority to make decisions about dance, even though they may not be experts, derives from their representative nature and their obligation to sustain appropriate standards. Success in enlisting their help depends upon a combination of these elements of authority.

52 *Dance and statutory bodies*

In the same vein we have noted moves towards greater flexibility by the Department of the Environment, national Arts Councils, Regional Arts Associations (RAAs), Regional Sports Associations and Local Authorities in supporting special applications of the arts, including dance, to new areas of activity. We hope that this flexibility will increase, building on initiatives already taken. Education liaison officers, for example, have been appointed by the Arts Council of Great Britain and Greater London Arts Association. One of their roles is to link dance art and dance education more closely. Some RAAs are supporting the intro-

23

duction of artists of various kinds to work in hospitals. Other bodies are establishing regional replicas of the national organisation, SHAPE, which seeks to encourage and relate the arts to social purposes outside the traditional theatre, in hospitals, prisons and rehabilitation centres. Of particular importance is the need for dance educators to grasp the significance of statutory provision to develop sport and leisure in the years ahead. A very wide range of statutory and voluntary bodies now contribute to this field offering opportunities for participation in recreational movement and dance which are used by a great many people. This should encourage the dance world by the demonstration of public interest in spending leisure time in this way. By and large, however, the private sector of dance training has been less adventurous — and perhaps less well-informed — in using opportunities available in the public sector. Each Regional Council for Sport and Recreation under the Sports Council has a movement and dance section, or a committee, or a panel each with functions which can promote specific dance and movement activities. This provision is almost unused by the private dance sector. We think it important that dance teachers and students should be aware of these developments and encouraged to participate in them under their own limitations, always pressing, where necessary, their local authority and the relevant statutory body for the means to do so.

53 Dance and voluntary organisations

The relation between dance and voluntary organisations sub-divides roughly into three areas. There is the relation with organisations like political parties and the TUC, discussed in the next paragraph; also relations with the dance world's own voluntary organisations and relations with other voluntary organisations. Other voluntary organisations cover a very wide range from women's institutes and working men's clubs, which sometimes act as sponsors, to organisations to help the disabled to which the dance world can contribute its special knowledge — for example the Imperial Society of Teachers of Dancing (ISTD) working with the Disabled Living Foundation. In a joint project supported by the Spastic Society, Gateway Clubs for the Mentally Handicapped and the Royal National Institute for the Blind, these organisations seek to provide dance for people with a disability. Other opportunities are provided by the important dance and ballet club movement in many British towns, cities and universities. They represent the amateur performance element in dance. They meet regularly to discuss and practise dance or see it through film shows or visits to live performances. Many ballet clubs are grouped into the Association of Ballet Clubs founded in 1947. It is our belief that the value of this amateur dance movement is underestimated by the professional dance and education worlds. Hence it deserves more support from these sources and from local government and statutory bodies to encourage its contribution to dance appreciation and the provision of opportunities for amateur performance. Finally, there are the voluntary organisations of the maintained and non-maintained sectors which aim to assist teachers and raise standards in various ways. These range from national bodies like the ISTD to regional bodies such as the Inner London Dance Teachers' Association. This association was formed and inspired mostly by students in the private sector training at the London College of Dance and Drama to teach in the maintained sector. It now has a very wide membership across both sectors. Other similar groups can be found in the dance education world, some of very long standing. Their purpose is to serve their members, provide a link between various interests and offer a forum for discussion. Collectively, this range of voluntary groupings provides a resource and outlet for dance educators to use if they wish. The need is for better liaison and exchange of information leading to clarification and redefinition of the links and possibilities for co-operation.

The same considerations apply to winning support from voluntary representative organisations like political parties and trade unions. Some trade unions, such as the entertainment and teaching unions, especially British Actors' Equity and the National Association of Teachers in Further and Higher Education (NATFHE) are directly connected with dance or dance education and have helped our study. Others, such as the National Association of Local Government Officers (NALGO), might be affected by our recommendations. The dance world should be concerned, however, to enlist the support of the trade union movement as a whole since so many of its members or their children are touched by dance in one way or another. The TUC has provided already a useful basis for such support in the report of its working party on the arts.[11] Here it argues, among other things, for more provision for arts activities at the work place and in the community; closer links at national level between the TUC, the Minister for the Arts and national arts institutions including the Arts Council of Great Britain; and more activity at local level by Trades Councils and County Associations of Trades Councils to press Local Authorities to increase provision for the arts. All this would benefit dance. In our experience, however, Trades Councils and County Associations have only limited knowledge of the arts and hence give the arts very limited, if any, priority. As in other areas, however, the initiative to promote dance interest among trade unionists needs to come from those concerned with dance. This implies study of the local trade union structure and invitations to individual trade union authorities to see dance events as a preliminary to seeking further support. At national level we think it particularly important to the cause of the arts, including dance education and training, that there is now an Arts Committee of the TUC as proposed in the working party report and by the Scottish Trades Union Congress (STUC). We think, though, that trade union education centres and related colleges, such as Ruskin College, Oxford, and the Northern College near Barnsley, should include in their curricula more consideration of cultural questions and funding for the arts.

54 The media The significance of the media at every level has been emphasised already in chapter 2. Television, the cinema, radio and the printed word help to create not only an audience but also an image for dance. It is in the

25

interest of dance educators, therefore, to see that the image-makers are as well briefed as possible. At national level this task falls probably to the larger organisations, to brief dance critics or writers and programmes dealing with aspects of dance education for national dissemination. At local level, however, the briefing falls to local schools and teachers or whoever is organising an activity. It should include not just the better known local newspapers, but the minority and community press. The growing number of local radio stations provides opportunities for news and features about dance. There is also the use of libraries and the possibility of using local communication centres. Local libraries are not only very important resources for books but valuable centres for discussion, meetings, lectures, and the presentation of films and video. Communication centres are a comparatively new form of community resource, usually established as independent, self-governing organisations on the initiative of a group of individuals or community activists in a particular area. They offer one or more of a number of facilities according to their success in raising funds and the interest of their members. Among these facilities might be a print-shop, useful for creating posters to announce local dance activities, meeting places for discussion or to see films, record and tape resources to hear music, and facilities for producing video recordings of local dance activities for showing around the area or dissemination outside. Communication centres, in other words, offer dance educators a valuable means of community communication and of educating the community about dance. Here again the dance world needs to understand and become familiar with these opportunities in order to use them.

*55 Using
resources*

Such is the context of power and resources at national and local level within which the world of dance education and training moves and which it needs to study and use. Knowledge is the key to this use. At local level, in particular, local education authorities and the local representatives of private dance teachers' organisations need to see that the dance teacher has the necessary knowledge and is made aware of how to obtain support which is usually there for the asking but often unsought. At the same time it is clear that more study is needed of dance in relation to society, what dance can do for society (its place in leisure provision for example) and how the State and its agencies should relate to dance. The satisfaction of this need falls properly to the institutions of higher education now beginning to embrace dance as a subject for study at honours level and to the teacher training institutions for dance in both sectors. It illustrates the importance of co-operation to create the future, nationally and internationally.

5 International Relations

56 Purpose of
the chapter

Like all arts, the art of dance is international and dance artists and educators need the inspiration which flows from contact with artists in other countries. Since the beginning of this century, for example, the impulse for dance change and development in Britain came very strongly from abroad. It is symbolised by the figures of Genée from Denmark, Espinosa from France, Pavlova and Diaghilev from Russia, Cecchetti from Italy, Duncan, Graham and Cohan from USA and Laban and Jooss from Germany, to whom we refer in Appendices B and C. Likewise the tremendous expansion of dance interest in the last 30 years is not a phenomenon confined to Britain. It is part of an explosion of dance interest among young people in all industrial countries – from the USA and Canada through Europe East and West, to Australia. In different forms it is manifest strongly also in the Third World, giving particular expression to new nationhood. It is not within our brief to describe this international scene in detail – another task, in fact, for dance researchers and historians – but since we in Britain are so much part of it, we sample and compare in this chapter some experiences which provide lessons for our own study.

57 International
consultations

As part of our study we made detailed inquiries in several European countries, assisted by government offices in each country acknowledged at the end of this report. Our vice-chairman visited Belgium, France, the Federal Republic of Germany, Italy, the Netherlands, Sweden and Switzerland in the course of a study commissioned by the Council of Europe. We made comparative studies in Australia and Canada through Government offices and visits by several members of our committee during the four and a half years of our study. We consulted with dancers, choreographers and directors from countries across the world, including the Third World, during four international conferences* and paid particular attention to experience in the USA appropriate to our study. From this we abstract below experiences and practices which, if they were introduced in Britain, might most help the cause of dance education and training.

58 Formation
of national and
international
organisations

We have noted a new tendency in the dance world to form national and international dance organisations for mutual support matching a similar tendency in other professions. Three years before our study began, the idea of an association for all dancers in Canada was born during a national conference on dance called by the Canada Council in 1972. This association was incorporated as the Dance in Canada Association at a second national conference held at York University, Toronto,

* The Cecchetti – Gulbenkian Commonwealth and International Conference, London, August 1976; the Dance and the Child International Conference, Edmonton, July 1978; the Commonwealth Cultural Conference, Edmonton, August 1978; and the Laban International Conference, London, July 1979.

in June 1973. It drew together for the first time dance companies and other dance interests in Canada. Our chairman attended and contributed to its meetings in Toronto 1973 and Montreal 1974. In Australia, partly as a result of proposals made by our chairman at the University of New England, Armidale, in January 1976, an Australian Association for Dance Education was established at a conference in Melbourne in August 1977 with representatives from all the States of Australia. A year later, in July 1978, an international conference on 'Dance and the Child' was convened in Edmonton, Canada, under sponsorship by the Dance Committee of the Canadian Association for Health, Physical Education and Recreation, Alberta Culture and the University of Alberta. As a principal speaker in Melbourne and Edmonton our chairman not only reported the progress of our study but gained in return experience which is woven into our conclusions.

59 Dance and the Child International

The 'Dance and the Child' Conference established an international interim committee to prepare the constitution of a permanent organisation. Today this organisation is in the final stages of formation. Called Dance and the Child International (DACI), it has entered the Conseil International de la Danse (CIDD) UNESCO, as an autonomous, fully constituted branch of the CIDD with the aim of promoting the growth and development of dance for children on an international basis. It will do this by promoting 'everything that can benefit dance and the child irrespective of race, colour, sex, religion, nationality or social origin ... in a spirit of peace and universal brotherhood.'[22] The practical measures proposed to realise this aim are listed at Appendix D.

60 Urgency of international co-operation

We are aware of the danger of too many new, possibly overlapping, organisations but it seems to us that these developments in general represent an important trend towards unity and co-operation in the international, as in the national, dance scene. They make possible, for example, consultation and potential action in response to research, showing the serious decline in the number of professional artists in employment in the consumer societies of western Europe during the last 20 years,* with consequent implications for the training and living conditions of all artists. These conditions in any case in many Western countries already 'give cause for concern'.[23] The problem is created not only by changing public taste and age, but by the spread of electronic entertainment, through radio, television and recording which paradoxically disseminate the arts to huge numbers of people never reached before. The problem seems to have been exacerbated in Europe by a provision of the Treaty of Rome which introduced the free movement of artists within the EEC. This has benefited a few artists of international quality with consequent reduction of opportunity for others. One result has been a catastrophic fall in the employment of singers, especially in France. We consider, therefore, that the national

---

* The trend is confirmed by the International Federation of Actors and by the European studies of our Vice-Chairman.

dance councils of England, Scotland and Wales should take notice of these plans for international organisation and assist and co-operate where appropriate.

61 Australia　We turn now to the experience of individual countries abroad, selecting those aspects which might be useful in Britain. We have chosen six countries — Australia, Canada, France, Holland, Sweden and the USA. Australia, of course, has its own structure of vocational training, mostly in the private sector, and a slowly growing dance element in the maintained sector. Our interest, however, centres on three factors which relate to experience in the UK. First, the formation of a national organisation, the Australian Association for Dance Education, almost at the same time as similar organisations in Britain, embracing the private and public sectors. This is now in its third year and already provides a forum within which differences can be discussed and through which communication can be sustained with federal and state governments in Australia and with organisations abroad. Second, the introduction of dance as a major subject within the Bachelor of Education Degree for the first time in Australia. This took place at the State College of Victoria, Rusden, in 1977 and established dance in the higher education system of Australia, though not without protracted discussion. The third factor is a joint study by the Schools Commission and the Australia Council (equivalent to the Arts Council of Great Britain) which has produced a national report, *Education and the Arts*, and corresponding state reports. It suggests the value of setting up a similar nationwide enterprise in Britain, supported by the relevant departments of state and the Arts Council of Great Britain.

62 Canada　In Canada the dance explosion has been in some ways more dramatic than anywhere else. In the decade since 1970, Canada's relatively small population of 23,000,000 has moved from a position where three established classical ballet companies dominated the national audience to one where small companies have developed in every province of this second largest country in the world. Modern dance has come to challenge classical ballet for the attention of young Canadians. This explosion has its reflection in new professional schools of modern dance, as well as classical ballet, in an expanding response of funds through the Canada Council, provincial and municipal authorities and private sources over the years, and in the establishment of two national associations embracing dancers of all kinds across Canada. The first is the Dance in Canada Association as a forum for professional and near-professional dancers. It is unique in the Commonwealth and is one of four elements of Canadian experience of possible value to Britain. The second, also of possible value to Britain, is the formation of a Canadian Association of Professional Dance Organisations. Representing seven professional companies and the National Ballet School, the organisation aims to handle problems of particular importance to the Canadian professional dance community such as government funding, immigration policies, domestic and foreign touring, and re-training

29

programmes for retired dancers. The third element of experience is the influence of the tertiary sector of education. The fourth element is the method of supporting specialist dance training in a multi-cultural society.

In 1970 York University, Toronto, became the first Canadian University to offer a degree course in dance. It is now the largest dance department of any university in the Commonwealth having added a graduate programme to its undergraduate beginnings. In the *York Dance Review*, sponsored by its Dance Department, are the beginnings of a much needed regular journal (with Commonwealth value) devoted to serious consideration of the historical, social, economic, aesthetic and technical problems of dance today. York, however, is not the only Canadian institution of the maintained sector concerned with dance education. There are now three other universities with degree programmes in dance — Waterloo in Ontario; Simon Fraser in British Columbia; and Montreal (Montreal Branch) in Quebec. Six other universities offer minor specialisations in dance and six offer dance courses mostly linked with their physical education schools. There are also three colleges offering diplomas in dance (one of them The Canadian College of Dance within Ryerson Polytechnical Institute, Toronto) and two Colleges of Applied Arts and Technology offering courses of dance. Much of this is of variable standard but the university lesson hardly needs underlining. University dance departments are an essential complement to any national development of dance education. University dance departments can make a contribution to dance learning which it is difficult for any other institution of higher education to make, particularly in the field of research and postgraduate study.

The fourth experience of potential value to Britain lies in Canada's method of supporting the private sector, having particular regard to the balance of interests in its multi-cultural society. Two leading classical schools, for example (the National Ballet School and School of the Royal Winnipeg Ballet) are funded in English-speaking Canada and one, the Ecole Supériere des Grands Ballets Canadiens,·in French-speaking Canada. Similar support is extended now to modern dance training. Funding for Canada's many individual ethnic dance groups comes mostly from provincial, municipal and private sources. Although the Federal Government's (ie Canada Council's) involvement in specialist dance training is thus limited to a small number of institutions, the involvement has significance for British Government funding practice. This is a recognition that the majority of dancers in major companies will come from a few vocational schools in the private sector. It is therefore in the national interest to fund these schools in order to protect the nation's investment in its major dance companies. One other Canadian experience also has significance for Britain. In Quebec, where a special support programme for dance is being developed by the Quebec Government, the Grands Ballets Canadiens (one of Canada's three major companies) has started a professional school completely within the maintained sector. It is too early as yet to assess results but the event provides useful support for Scottish Ballet's comparable development described in paragraphs 288–291.

63 France

Principal interest in France lies in the school of the Paris Opera Ballet. This sets a standard for dance in the French private sector of classical ballet teaching much as the Royal Ballet School does in Britain. This French private sector is orientated almost exclusively towards classical ballet. Within the Paris Opera Ballet School itself four elements seem to us particularly significant, always bearing in mind that it is a small school – only 59 girls and 49 boys at the time we visited it. First, the ballet school and its attendant educational school are entirely state supported. Second, the balance between boys and girls is better than any other ballet school. The recruitment of boys has been encouraged greatly through frequent television talks by Madame Claude Bessy about dance as a career for boys and girls. Apart from such television appearances, no other form of recruitment is undertaken. We in Britain, too, perhaps should look to television for more help in the projection of dance as a career. Third, the recruitment of pianists for class and rehearsal is carried out through a publicly advertised competition which gives status to the pianists. Fourth, retirement prospects are properly and reasonably arranged, an important consideration when parents have to make career decisions with their children. At the age of 40 for women and 45 for men, and after 25 years' service, a state pension of 50% of each dancer's highest salary level is paid. After 15 years' service a proportionately lower rate of pension is paid. In addition, administrative, supervisory or backstage opportunities for employment are offered in the first place to retiring members of the Company and School.

64 Holland

From experience in Holland one might conclude that for a dance student it pays to be Dutch. There are seven state dance academies in Holland spread throughout the country – located in Arnhem, Rotterdam, Tilburg, The Hague and three in Amsterdam – so that dance education is within easy reach of the majority of the population and free to all those qualifying for entry. The Royal Conservatoire of Music in The Hague, which concentrates entirely on educating and training dancers for the country's three major professional dance companies, accepts students between the ages of 10 and 12 (ie the last two years of primary education) and provides a combined general and vocational education to about the age of 18. The other six academies are all institutions of higher education, though in Rotterdam a High School specialises in combining general and vocational education at secondary level in preparation for entry into the Dance Academy which is part of the Rotterdam Conservatorium. In addition to training dancers for a professional career on stage, several of the academies also offer courses for dance teachers. A statistical comparison with Britain is instructive. A population of 13,897,874* in Holland is provided with six fully-financed state dance academies to train prospective professional dancers

---

* 1979 population statistics from the United Nations.

or dance teachers. In the United Kingdom, by contrast, the Royal Ballet School is the only institution even partly state-financed to serve a population of 55,521,534 . If state support for dance education and training were provided at the Dutch level in the UK, not only the Royal Ballet School would be placed on a more secure financial basis, it would transform also the situation of the London School of Contemporary Dance, the Laban Centre and half a dozen or so private dance schools we judge worthy to become regional centres. All would be able to audition solely on a basis of talent and so create a group of state supported institutions comparable with Holland. It is not, therefore, just a question of money, but of method and priorities. Dutch practice in the vocational sector suggests the value of re-thinking present British practice to create an organised relationship between important schools in major centres outside London and the Royal Ballet School and London School of Contemporary Dance as the country's two principal vocational institutions in London. The other example of Dutch practice important to British dance is the greater willingness of government to provide help from its central statistical services, a help so notably lacking in Britain. There is a permanent documentation division of the Central Dance Council Foundation in The Hague, roughly equivalent to the newly formed National Dance Councils. To this, and to research undertaken by dance companies themselves, the Dutch Government adds the resources of its Central Bureau of Statistics as well as research commissions through the Ministry of Culture, Recreation and Social Welfare, in order to study dance supply, audience composition and the social problems of retired dancers in Holland.

65 A Swedish Inquiry

From Sweden we have received the summary of a report by a Swedish Committee of Inquiry into Dance Education,[24] as well as other documentation. This report parallels our own study because it presents the Swedish study within the context of Sweden's state education system as a whole and within the context of a considerable debate on national cultural policy. The debate followed publication of a Government Commission's report and recommendations in 1973, followed by the establishment in 1974 of a National Council for Cultural Affairs to carry out the recommendations approved by Parliament, as well as to make further recommendations. The overwhelming emphasis of the debate, still continuing, and of the Commission's report, is on decentralisation, opportunity for all, practice by the many rather than the few. The Swedish method is to place the main responsibility upon municipalities, the local authorities. The general scheme of opportunity and training proposed by the Swedish Committee is also strikingly similar to our own. It suggests constructing a progressive system of dance education, available to the whole population starting at the earliest age. One major result of this would be a comprehensive provision for finding and developing talented children who might wish to become professional dancers. Recommendations are made, also, for in-service training and more specialist study, as well as regular free classes for unemployed dancers, or between engagements, when these dancers are not members of a subsidised company. A separate programme of training is proposed for retired professional dancers who wish to become teachers. A summary of the argument together with a review of what has been implemented so far is placed at Appendix I.

66 The United States of America

Dance education experience in the USA offers a contrast between success in the vocational and professional fields in higher education, but much less success in primary and secondary education. Across the United States there are between 300–350 professional dance companies, many of them world famous; a concentration of fine teachers, talent and experiment in New York; many good dance schools in other major cities; and a dramatic audience increase for dance in the 15 years following 1965. The most recent estimate* suggests that this audience now totals 30,000,000 spread across the country. It happens now that more people go to dance concerts than rock concerts on college campuses because there are more dance concerts. In 1975 the National Research Centre of the Arts (affiliated to the Louis Harris national poll organisation) conducted a survey of adult public opinion about the arts in the USA. This showed that 8% of the adult public – 11,600,000 Americans – had gone to a live ballet or modern dance performance in the 12 months preceding the survey and 4% of the adult population – 5,800,000 Americans – were frequent dance-goers. This does not include those under 16 years of age who comprise a substantial part of the dance audience. This same Harris study indicated that 77% of those interviewed thought that ballet or modern dance should be taught in schools. By contrast, the dance staffing ratios[25] in American schools, and the place of dance within the curriculum, are much less than that achieved in Britain. One report, summarising this difference, suggests that British schools are ahead of American schools in recognising the values of movement and dance in the educational process.[26] Certainly the Americans are still a long way from incorporating dance as a regular element in the school curriculum and even further from the kind of progressive system of dance education available to the whole population which is possible now in Britain and is advocated in the Swedish report above. What is useful to British experience from the USA experience lies in specialist areas; the link between higher education and vocational training across the country; and the Education Programme of the National Endowment for the Arts, especially its Artists-in-Schools: Dance Component.

---

* Based on the 350 weeks of National Endowment for the Arts Dance Touring in 1979–80. This represents about 10% of all touring and means there are about 3,500 weeks of touring. A further 4,000 weeks of home seasons make a total of about 7,500 weeks of dance. Estimating 4 performances a week this makes a total of 30,000 performances which, at an average of 1,000 in an audience per performance, amounts to 30,000,000 people.

67 Vocational links with higher education – USA There is no way in which we could or should reflect in this study the range of vocational training for dance offered across the USA. Of significance for our study, however, is the relationship between American modern dance training and American higher education. In the USA classical ballet companies and schools were established by private individuals and private money in much the way they were established in Britain, but the growth of all modern dance companies – Martha Graham, Merce Cunningham and Paul Taylor to give three examples – is rooted in the higher education system, particularly university campuses. It was the universities and training colleges, like Bennington and Connecticut Colleges before and after the second world war, which provided homes for the summer schools and courses where much of the early creative work and training were accomplished. No less important, it was these institutions and the adult and further education provision outside schools which often provided teaching opportunities for the members of modern dance companies who could rarely hope for more than seasonal employment on stage each year. This helped the young dancers' critical finances, but it also created today's modern dance audience across the USA. Today many dancers in American classical and modern dance companies hold university qualifications at BA or MA level. Many, indeed, started their training in the universities. The initiative for this movement in the early days came from professional dancers. It was the dancers who started working as teachers within some of the enlightened colleges and universities. The message to us to seek to establish similar links between our higher education system and performance companies seems very clear, provided we can adapt the experience to our circumstances.

68 Dancers in schools – USA The second message to us from American experience concerns the American Artists-in-Schools Programme: Dance Component of the National Endowment for the Arts. This is a nationwide scheme financed by federal, state and local funds to provide school residencies in strategic centres by individual 'dance movement specialists' and full dance companies. Begun in 1969 as a pilot project in six selected States by three companies and two teachers, the 1979/80 school year programme includes residencies in 29 States and special jurisdictions by 22 dance companies and 40 dance movement specialists.* The objects of the scheme are four-fold: to present dance as an art form; to begin to explore movement as a teaching tool; to employ movement as a means of encouraging self-expression and self-awareness in children 'through the revelation of their kinaesthetic sense'; and the continuation of dance activities in the schools concerned after the residencies are completed. Dance companies move into residence at each locale for a minimum of

---

* The Endowment's *1980–81 Directory of Dance Companies and Dance Movement Specialists* includes a total of 38 dance companies and 98 dance movement specialists but it is unlikely there will be sufficient federally-sponsored residencies to provide work for all directory listed artists.

two weeks; dance movement specialists enter residence in each selected school district for a minimum of four weeks to prepare for and/or follow-up the residence of the dance company. Both seek to work not only with the students and staff of the school, but with parents and community leaders, a method which has achieved significant changes in general attitudes towards dance. It is expected that federal funds will be matched by local funds, whether from the participating schools, other local authorities, or the business community. In addition, a 'summer workshop' of participating companies, teachers, school representatives and arts agency representatives is held for one week (with obligatory attendance) at the outset of the annual American Dance Festival, now held in Durham, North Carolina. Here mutual problems and plans for future development are discussed. One of the benefits of the National Endowment's programme has been the necessary co-ordination and co-operation of many agencies. Another is the projection of a vision of the arts as 'a better primer for our children',[27] assisted by clever use of the media to publicise the case much as we advocated in chapter 4. Let us learn from this. 'If we want our world to be still, grey and silent, then we should keep the arts out of school, shut down neighbourhood theatre, and barricade the museum doors. When we let the arts into the arena of learning we run the risk that colour and motion and music will enter our lives.'[27] We make no apology for this quotation. The involvement of dance companies in British schools, backed by individual dancers in residence or dance teachers with performing experience, is an important future development for the maintained sector, particularly building on the good school work which exists already — a point we developed in chapter 2.

PART II

The Maintained Sector

6 The Present Day

*69 A common
starting point*

The maintained and private sectors of dance education and training have common roots and possibilities of support in the British education system. They are linked through this system just as they are linked through their common interest in dance. The future professional dancer, like all other young people, will enter primary education at the age of five (six in Scotland) and will go to a maintained, voluntary or private school. It is appropriate, therefore, to review the education system which exists today, drawing attention to those elements which particularly affect our study.

*70 The
maintained
sector*

In 1978, the last year for which figures are available, there were just under 10,000,000 children[27] attending some 35,000 schools in Britain.* Of these, 8,912,684 children in England and Wales and 1,000,000 children in Scotland received education at Schools maintained from public funds under the control of 105 local education authorities in England and Wales and 9 regional and 3 island education authorities in Scotland. No fees are charged to parents of children attending maintained schools in England and Wales and books and equipment are free. Nevertheless as we shall see, equipment and other limitations reinforced by recent Government cuts very seriously affect the possibilities of dance education. In Scotland education authorities have the power to charge fees where this can be done without prejudice to the adequate provision of free school education. In addition, in 1976, 131,000 children in England and Wales and 20,000 in Scotland were attending schools receiving grants direct from the education department concerned. Collectively, therefore, schools fully maintained from public funds, plus the direct grant schools, cater for 94% of the school population of Britain. It is with this group of schools and children that we are concerned in this and the next two chapters. Independent schools, which provide an important category of dance education, are examined in chapter 16.

*71 School
management*

In England and Wales the management of schools in the public sector is of two main kinds. The greater number are those wholly provided and maintained by local education authorities from public funds. The lesser number comprise voluntary schools, mostly either 'aided' or 'controlled' by a voluntary body, usually of a religious denomination. Aided schools have more independence than controlled schools and

---

*   It should be noted that English/Welsh and Scottish statistics are not quite comparable. English/Welsh statistics are published in January, those for Scotland in September. Thus comparable Scottish statistics for January 1978 in England and Wales would be September 1977. The total school population for nursery, primary and secondary schools in all three countries will fall by about two million during the 1980s.

their governors are responsible for part of the cost of external repairs and of any building work. In Scotland by far the largest proportion of schools supported from public funds are provided by education authorities but in England and Wales about a third of the 28,329 schools maintained by local education authorities are voluntary schools. Of these 2,664 are Roman Catholic with smaller numbers belonging to religious bodies other than the Church of England, of which there are 5,862. It is not this duality in the management of the public sector which is important to our study, however, so much as the wide discretion allowed to local education authorities in discharging their responsibilities. For this reason our research has concentrated upon these authorities and the schools directly under their control. Here is the greatest possibility of development so far as dance is concerned.

72 Levels of education

The schools directly under local authority control are divided usually into nursery, primary and secondary schools. Compulsory education begins at five when children go to primary schools which normally have infant classes for children under seven. The usual age of transfer from primary to secondary school is 11 in England and Wales and 12 in Scotland. In England an increasing number of local authorities are establishing 'first' schools for pupils ages 5–8 or 10, and 'middle' schools covering various age ranges between 9 and 14. Leicestershire, for example, has a 3-tier structure 5–11, 11–14 and 14 onwards. The effect of this development upon our study is uncertain because the development itself is uncertain. There is no doubt, however, that the most important influence upon the quantity and quality of dance education in the public sector seems likely to derive from growth in the size of schools, large schools usually being co-educational and/or comprehensive.

73 Significance of comprehensive schools

In 1980 over 80% of the maintained secondary school population in England and Wales are attending comprehensive schools. These schools represent 82% of all maintained schools and take pupils without reference to ability or aptitude and provide a wide range of secondary education for all or most of the children of a district. The schools are organised by authorities in different ways. Some schools take the full secondary school age-range from 11 to 18; some have middle schools whose pupils move on to senior comprehensive schools at 12 or 13, leaving at 16 or 18; some serve the age range of 11 or 12 to 16 combined with a sixth form college for pupils over 16. The size of these schools allows them to offer a range of options, including dance, which smaller schools might find difficult. Most of the remaining children in England and Wales receive their secondary education in schools to which they are allocated after selection procedures at the age of 11+. In Scotland secondary education is organised already almost completely on comprehensive lines. Hence, by 1977, about 98.6% of all Scottish pupils were in some 440 education authority secondary schools, 99.8% of which (1977 statistics) had a comprehensive intake.

74 Teachers　Teachers and their training form such an important part of our study that we give them separate attention in chapter 10 below. Here we place them in the context of the system as a whole. In publicly maintained schools they are appointed by local education authorities or school governing bodies or managers. There were 515,000 teachers, full-time and full-time equivalent in England, Scotland and Wales in the academic year 1976/77 and it is estimated that this number will be reduced to 503,000 by 1981/82[28] — these figures are for nursery, primary and secondary schools. Such teachers, including dance teachers, must hold qualifications approved by the appropriate government departments of England, Wales and Scotland and will receive salaries determined by nationally negotiated scales taking account of qualifications, responsibilities and experience. In Scotland there has existed additionally since 1966 a General Teaching Council with which all certificated teachers are required to register. It is a quasi-governmental body answerable to the Secretary of State for Scotland and is concerned mainly with the standard of teaching in Scotland. Specifically it is required by statute to maintain a register of qualified teachers; to advise on the supply of teachers; to have oversight of standards of entry to the profession; to advise on the training and qualifications of teachers; and to exercise disciplinary power in relation to registration. The register now contains the names of 80,000 teachers, mostly in active service, and it is their annual fees which provide the greater part of the Council's finance. Of the 44 members of Council guiding its affairs, 25 must be practising teachers elected by their peers. This is the model we recommend to teachers of the private sector in paragraph 248 to do with the licensing of dance teachers.

75 Curriculum and inspectorate　In England and Wales the secular curriculum in maintained schools is the responsibility of the local education authority, or, more usually, of the schools' governors or managers. In practice, as we indicate in chapter 4 there is a very high degree of devolution to head teachers, particularly in nursery and primary schools, so that this is a significant factor in any development of dance education. Two groups of inspectors also report and advise on the content and value of the education provided. One group, Her Majesty's Inspectors of schools (HMIs), is responsible to the DES for the inspection of all schools in England and Wales, including independent schools. In Scotland the function of HMIs is in general the same, responsible to the SED. The other group comprises a variety of inspectors or advisers in all three countries employed by local education authorities to guide them on the work of maintained schools. Teachers' organisations and institutions concerned with the education and training of teachers are additional sources of advice. Further guidance and encouragement for school-based research and development is available to teachers and others in England and Wales through the Schools Council for Curriculum and Examinations. This Council, an independent body representative of most educational interests with functions recently reorganised, acts as an advisory body and carries out research and development work on curricula, teaching methods and examinations in primary and secondary schools. Unfortunately it has not yet initiated any research/curriculum development study into dance. Dance received only marginal attention in the Council's projects on 'Physical Education in the Secondary School' and 'The Arts and the Adolescent'. We recommend later in this report that research is urgent. In Scotland the content and balance of the curriculum is kept under continuous review by the Consultative Committee on the Curriculum,* which, with the Scottish Council for Research in Education, also commissions relevant research.

76 Curriculum innovation The schools' freedom to frame their own curricula has facilitated a rapid increase in study, experiment and curriculum innovation with consequent pressure to extend the curriculum. This has led to considerable thought being given to what is known as a 'core curriculum'.[29] The general purpose is to adapt the curriculum to changes in everyday life and needs of children and young people. The rapid advance of knowledge, social change, technical progress and new understanding of children's emotional and intellectual development, have encouraged changes in the content and methods of teaching which ought also to have encouraged the development of dance in education. Among the most clearly observable general trends, for example, has been the increased emphasis on 'learning by doing', particularly for younger children. Greater use of broadcasting — nine out of ten schools can receive television and almost all have radios — relaxation of copyright for educational purposes and growing resources in audio-visual presentation, have all enriched teaching and offer opportunities to dance education which can extend incomparably the range of learning, if the facilities can be made available to dance teachers.

77 Examinations The past decade has seen a large increase in the number of pupils in England, Scotland and Wales staying on beyond the minimum school-leaving age of 16. This tendency is stimulated further today by provisions made to combat youth unemployment. The result is an increase in candidates taking the Certificate of Secondary Education (CSE) or the General Certificate of Education (GCE) as well as in the status of these examinations among pupils, parents, employers and post-school education institutions. Over the last decade the number achieving the highest grade in CSE has increased steadily, while the number of school leavers obtaining two or more A-levels has increased by about 25%. 12.6% of all school leavers in 1978, for example, left with two or more A-levels and 9.3% left with five or more higher grade O-level/CSEs, but

---

* As an example, the Committee on Secondary Education of the Consultative Committee on the Curriculum in Scotland has just completed a review of the position of subjects and aspects of secondary education which at present are not represented by a Central Committee within the substructure of the Consultative Committee on the Curriculum. This includes proposals to which further reference is made in chapter 8.

no A-levels. This growth has affected also the status of dance, because dance, too, is becoming an examination subject up to and including degree level. We consider further the development of dance as an examination subject in chapter 12.

78 Provision of school facilities

Parallel with the formal development of education has gone development of its informal aspects, especially parent/teacher relationships and the growth of out-of-school activities. Two issues arise here of great importance to dance. One is the provision or availability of school facilities, the other the right to use them. There is a statutory provision, for example, that students educated through public funds *must* have the use of a playing field, and most secondary schools also have a gymnasium. No similar obligation requires a school to provide for the arts, although some authorities are beginning to do so. Dance has a particular need because it requires not just space, but its own space, a dance studio with a special floor, changing rooms and lighting. An area in which many kinds of movement activities can take place rarely meets this need.

79 Criteria for school building

Local education authorities and voluntary bodies are responsible, under the general supervision of central departments, for providing the schools and other buildings needed for public education in their areas. The central departments determine the maximum size of the authorities' individual programmes in the light of national priorities. They also offer guidance to authorities by means of building bulletins and other ways which are often difficult to resist. It follows, therefore, that the spaces provided and given priority in school building programmes largely determine what that school can and cannot do effectively in its teaching programme. More than this, the solid, immutable nature of buildings often makes it very difficult to introduce new priorities into a curriculum, even where experience shows this to be desirable. At the moment authorities have the triple problem of a great variety of buildings inherited from the past, general restrictions on new building so that very little has been constructed in the last ten years, and intense Government pressure to economise in every way. This surely compels a reconsideration of priorities to ensure a fair distribution of limited resources not only in terms of cash, but of space for which dance is unprovided in England and Wales. In Scotland, however, the policy appears to have been accepted already to include specially designed dance studios in Scottish secondary schools.[30]

7 Primary Level

80 Conditions for healthy dance life in schools There are 21,371 maintained primary and middle schools in England, 2,377 in Scotland and 1,959 in Wales. Notwithstanding a measure of central and local encouragement, the provision of dance in the curricula of these schools depends on individual schools. If it is included, a healthy dance life in the school depends on two main factors: first, the attitude of the school staff (particularly its head) towards dance; second, the effectiveness of the local authority in supporting the dance activities of a school by supplying appropriate resources. In primary schools this includes not only spaces and a music library of records and/or tapes, record players and tape or cassette players, but the advice and visits of specialist advisory staff to support teachers in the school. We have tried to consider these problems in this chapter by examining dance at primary level in three stages. First, what exists at the moment. Second, a brief summary of the evidence we consulted. Third, the main issues which arise.

81 How much dance takes place? How much dance actually takes place today in British primary schools? Neither time nor finance allowed us to survey every school but we commissioned the National Foundation for Educational Research to question a small sample of 1,336 primary schools during 1977, limited to England and Wales for economic reasons. This sample represents 5.7% of all primary schools so we treat the results with caution although our own experience confirms most of the findings.

Completed questionnaires were returned by 856 schools or 62.6% of the sample. Of these, 585 (68.34%) reported that some dance was taught often subsumed under 'physical education'. It has been useful, therefore, to compare and confirm our results through reference to the national survey of primary education in England carried out by HMIs between 1975–77.[31] The survey is the most comprehensive of its kind and covered the work of 7, 9 and 11 year olds in 1,127 classes in 542 primary schools in England. Here, too, dance was usually subsumed under physical education. The index to a report of 224 pages shows only one reference to dance as such. Nevertheless some idea of the incidence of dance at primary level can be gained from statistical tables in the report, and from reference to allied subjects in the text. Only 13% of schools, for example, had teachers with special responsibility for dance compared with 70% for music. Only 17% of all schools had written guidelines or schemes of work for dance. 'Movement with music was undertaken in four-fifths of the 7 year old classes and about half of the older classes. In dance, even in the 7 year old classes where this activity was most often encouraged, sensitivity in the use of movement was seldom achieved. About three-fifths of the 7 year old classes used radio programmes to supplement the work in movement and where these were followed up with appropriate practice and extension

42

of the ideas presented, they made a useful contribution to their work. There were also opportunities to link the experience of music and movement to language and art.' In other words the conclusions of HMIs are remarkably similar to our own detailed below, although our study was in greater depth.

82 Area distribution

From the responses to our survey the most dance activity appears to take place in the North West. Here three authorities (Manchester, Bolton and Knowsley) showed 100% of the sample having one dance lesson a week or more. After the North West comes the Midlands with four authorities showing more than 50% of schools offering one class a week or more. Areas where much less dance appeared in the replies were the North East, East Anglia, Wales and Greater London with the South East, excluding the Inner London Education Authority (ILEA).* We know from other evidence that the ILEA is a principal supporter of dance in education and education for the dancer, so were not too dismayed when postal difficulties disrupted the distribution of the survey in this area.

83 A composite picture

From the 585 responding schools can be summarised the incidence of dance in the normal curriculum. Just over one third of these schools are mixed Junior and Infant schools, the rest being Nursery and Infant, Nursery, Infant and Junior, Infant, Junior, First, Middle and 'other'.** On the school roll will be approximately 130 boys and 125 girls. In these schools female staff predominate and it is the usual practice for all class teachers — men and women — to teach all subjects to their pupils. This includes dance, almost certainly taught in the Assembly Hall. No primary teachers reported the use of a special dance studio. Dance will be taught probably once a week for 30 minutes. 89% of the schools use BBC Movement and Drama programmes, described further in paragraph 88, although they are questionable as dance. After this comes folk dance, taught usually in mixed classes by 77% of schools. We examine it further in paragraphs 86–87.

84 What is taught

Over the school age range there is a steady decline in the number of dance lessons given to mixed classes, from 47 a year to nursery age children to 29 a year for children aged 12+, where this age is retained.

---

* Compare areas of deprivation in *Primary Education in England*. (See note 31) The catchment area of the schools surveyed by HM Inspectorate were classified as inner city (17%), 'other urban' (45%) or rural (39%). The schools in rural areas were more likely than other schools to be small and to be combined junior with infant schools. Three-fifths of inner city schools were considered to be in an area of marked social difficulty. These areas, as a rule, also offered a smaller range of options including less opportunity for contacts with the arts.

** Compare school types defined by the Inspectorate. *Primary Education in England* (see note 31) covered combined junior with infant (49%), separate infant schools (19%), separate junior schools (19%), first schools (11%) and combined first with middle schools (2%).

Those who drop out are the boys, a point to which we return later. Where forms of dance other than folk dance are taught the sample shows these to be spread over creative dance, ballroom dance and classical ballet. By far the largest of these categories is creative dance, also called educational dance and dance drama. This implies today a very wide approach to dance teaching. In origin (to digress from our questionnaire for a moment) creative dance evolved from the work of Rudolf Laban and his associates who were a major influence in introducing a form of modern dance into schools, (see Appendix B). Subsequent development of the work has been carried out by individuals in schools, colleges and local authorities, often drawing on other outside influences. Hence a great deal of individual variation can be found now in teaching content and method. At best the work is creative, imaginative and incorporates a high proportion of skill in the form of dance technique. In schools where the work is of an advanced nature, the children acquire technical skills of movement and dance appropriate to their level and age, and the skills are increasingly available for use as a way through which creative work can be developed. At worst the work is no more than a free kind of self-expression with little skill and little development. Most of the work in schools, of course, is somewhere between these extremes.

85 Outside contacts

Answers to our questionnaire also suggest that primary schools have limited contact with dance outside the school and few out-of-school dance activities. The pupils are unlikely to have experienced any performance by a visiting dance group, any school dance display, day of dance, or performance during the year. They may have seen one professional dance performance during the year and one non-competitive dance festival and may have shared in one other miscellaneous dance event. No pupil has left the school to attend a full-time dance school during the last three years and there is no scheme to identify or help children with special talent for dance. 73% of the schools also reported no school club for dance. The other 27% reported one or more dance clubs typically numbering about 25 girls and 13 boys, averaging 9–10 years. Out of school dance activity since the survey was made would almost certainly, of course, include reference to disco dancing.

86 Use of country dance

It is appropriate here to identify more clearly the nature and role of folk dancing at primary level since this is the most popular form of dance. Our supplementary inquiries suggest that much of the dance taught is English country dancing, a tradition our historical outline in Appendix B shows has continued now for 70 years. This is confirmed by the English Folk Dance and Song Society (EFDSS) and by our visits to a number of areas. Folk dancing is sometimes a part of the school curriculum, sometimes done on a voluntary basis during the lunch hour or after school. Interest is stimulated by the widespread practice of holding area and regional festivals at which many hundreds of children can dance together in non-competitive events. Country dancing is also a popular item at school concerts and open days and received a special stimulus in 1977, Jubilee Year, when traditional dances were chosen to make an appropriate contribution to many local festivities. Within the curriculum, country dance most often forms part of the programme of the upper juniors (aged 9 and 10 years). For younger children most schools regard creative dance as more suitable. Dancing in any case is regarded as of far greater importance than the memorising of dances, though where the subject is well established the children master without trouble a substantial repertory. Country dance clubs offer the major opportunity for children to share regularly in the activity. Some schools also combine for folk dance parties and in support of the well run Hobby Horse Clubs introduced locally as the junior branch of the EFDSS.

87 Teaching country dance

Where country dance is well taught the children grow to appreciate its tunes and to dance with and not merely in time to the music. There is evidence of considerable helpful co-operation between the EFDSS and the physical education and dance advisers of some local education authorities. In-service courses are shared and there is general agreement that dance in the primary school should be informal in style, focusing on enjoyment, a sense of rhythm and the development of ease and skill in the performance of simple steps and patterns. In-service courses in folk dance give confidence to the primary school teacher whose college training may not have included dance, and offers also a means to prepare to teach a simple form of dance. While there is agreement among advisers that the main focus should be on creative dance where a good teacher is available, they recognise the value of folk dance carefully selected and skilfully taught.

88 Use of BBC Movement and Drama

BBC Movement and Drama programmes, although much used, are also among the most frequently criticised elements of current movement activity. 'Education requires a relationship on the spot between teacher and children', remarked one head teacher. 'The BBC is impersonal. It is a resource, not a substitute teacher.' But the BBC itself makes no claim to be a surrogate. A government publication *Movement: Physical Education in Primary Years*[32] suggests that the best results will be obtained if the programmes can be recorded on tape, studied by the teacher and then used appropriately. This is our conclusion, too, after seeing uses of programmes which were little more than fill-in periods and other uses which showed the value of this resource in intelligent hands. The BBC programmes can, after all, provide varied material and draw on a range of music far beyond the normal resources of a single school or teacher. The trouble is that very few teachers have the training to get the best from this material. In no way, therefore, should the programme be played direct to the class, but be used only as a resource for the teacher.

89 Primary dance in Manchester: an example

To complete this general picture of dance at primary level we offer the example of Greater Manchester, an authority where our questionnaire showed 100% of the sample taking one dance class a week or more. Dance in Manchester is part of the responsibility of the physical education adviser's department, as it is in almost every other authority throughout the country. The Authority tries to ensure that all its teachers have some creative experience in dance and feels that this has been achieved in all its infant and junior schools except two. Apart from these, all infant and junior schools in the city include dance in the curriculum and the subject receives a large measure of support from head teachers because so many head teachers over the years have actually *taught* dance! Our visits confirmed this claim. The classes we saw were almost always 30 minutes long, given in a classroom, the gym or the school hall. Sometimes there were interesting uses of words — a poem or a piece of prose as well as music to inspire movement. Several times we saw particularly stimulating work from teachers who had no dance training beyond the few hours given them in training college but who had developed the subject because they were interested, were good teachers and applied their imagination. On a number of occasions we found male teachers teaching dance, thus helping to establish the subject with boys as well as girls, though we never found any suggestion that it was more suited to girls than boys — as we have found in other areas.

90 Primary dance in Scotland

Dance at primary level in Scotland shows significant differences compared with England and Wales. As we have shown in chapter 1, our study helped to stimulate the first Scottish Conference on Dance Education to consider Scottish dance education problems. These included dance in primary schools where the conference confirmed that folk dances, including Scottish country dancing, are the most usual forms of dance. Conference also suggested that about 75% of Scottish primary school teachers have only between 21 and 60 hours to study the teaching of physical education, *including dance*, over the whole of their three-year training. Hence rather less dance and physical education appears to be taught in Scottish than in English and Welsh primary schools. On the other hand, rather more support is provided from visiting teachers in physical education, nearly all of whom have some dance experience. For this reason, perhaps, the time devoted to physical education in Scottish primary schools shows great variations between one school and another. In some it may not exceed one period a week; in others it may occur only when a visiting physical education specialist is available. There is continuing official pressure to correct the balance. For example, in 1968 a SED document was published to coincide with a specially produced film called *Into Action* aiming to enrich physical education programmes at primary level. Equal status was awarded in the film to games, swimming, gymnastics and dance, the last two defined as 'inventive movement' and 'expressive movement' respectively. As a result, it was hoped that the primary school teacher would be encouraged to complement the teaching of folk and Scottish dance with expressive dance movement.

91 Developing dance syllabi in Scotland

Obviously there is still some distance to go. Nearly all Scottish physical education advisers are convening panels of teachers to revise dance syllabi and prepare teachers' guidelines for dance appropriate to their regions. Development at the primary school level is in some aspects paralleling that at secondary level, due in part to the deliberate policy of extending resources and collaborating in dance events. The colleges of education are closely involved with primary school teachers in a variety of in-service courses constructed to meet specific needs. A particularly interesting example is the work on dance projects in areas culminating in festivals and days of dance: boys and girls of the complete school age range may be drawn from all schools in a district to share dance items of many styles. Peripatetic team teaching and the work of specialist principal teachers in dance are having an effect within the physical education programme of the primary schools involved. The Renfrewshire Dance Project, for example, noted that, at the commencement of the 1979 session, boys in the age bracket of 11–12 years were showing interest and that there appeared to be an improvement in the level of skill in dance.

92 Sources of evidence summarised

In addition to the surveys by the Inspectorate and our own study the evidence before us is derived from many visits, the advice or opinions of witnesses in written or verbal statements listed at Appendix K, and the collective wisdom of experts in conferences and seminars, usually convened specifically to assist the study and listed in Appendix A. One of these turned out to be as significant for our whole purpose as the Scottish conference was for our Scottish study. It took the form of a one-day seminar at the Institute of Contemporary Arts, London, on 3rd May, 1977. To it came head teachers and dance teachers from some 20 primary, middle and secondary schools throughout Britain where dance is a major subject. We felt that their experience could offer examples and answers to those who say that dance has little or no role in education and cannot, anyway, be timetabled. We describe this seminar more fully in paragraph 116 in the next chapter. We mention it here because it was instrumental also in framing our conclusions and recommendations in the primary field.

93 Major issues – variable standards

We try now to indicate the major issues emerging from all the evidence. Although dance in the primary school has developed as part of the 'primary school revolution', it seems clear that throughout Britain dance is still taught at very variable standards and with very uneven geographic distribution. Hence the child who receives continuity of dance education at infant and junior school is exceptional, while the uneven geographic distribution compounds the problem for those who have to move from one part of Britain to another. Therefore, in spite of good work by many teachers and some authorities, it is generally true that opportunities for an adequate dance education in British primary schools are still very limited.

94 Low subject status

Primary schools in Britain offer children the chance to participate in various physical activities such as games, swimming, gymnastics and dance. Considerable reliance is placed on the use of BBC Movement and Drama programmes for the younger children, a practice about which we have expressed our reservations in paragraph 88. Folk dance, maybe, is introduced for the older juniors. In many schools heavy demands on the use of indoor space, the multi-purpose hall, impose strict allocation of curriculum time. Frequently this amounts to only one single period per week for gymnastics and dance, which is inadequate. Since the class teacher has to choose how the time is used, the existence of gymnastic equipment all too often influences his or her choice in favour of gymnastics. This decision may result in many children being deprived of dance experience completely.

95 Teaching quality

Teaching quality is the next issue after the standards and status of dance in the curriculum. The evidence suggests that many young qualified teachers feel inadequate and insecure when asked to teach dance at primary level. Yet we have seen some very good classes given by teachers with a minimal dance training. More dance training would certainly help and we are critical of this aspect of training courses, as we show in chapter 10. Yet it does not appear to be inadequate training and the consequent physical problems of teaching dance which are crucial in sapping young teachers' self-confidence, so much as the teachers' lack of understanding of dance, the teachers' lack of imagination applied to dance, and the way these necessary qualities have been developed, or not developed, during training. Given better understanding of dance we agree with those who argue that dance in infant and junior schools should continue to be taught by a teacher within the school, provided dance has been a constituent part of the teacher's basic training backed by in-service training after qualification. The key to improvement is better understanding by the primary teacher.

96 Place of dance in primary education

An understanding of dance in the primary school would seem to rest on two points, firstly the nature of dance itself and secondly its place in education. Dance is, typically, a doing activity in which the making and performing of dances is central. Dances may be presented to audiences or danced solely for the benefit of the participants but in both cases the dance can be appreciated and valued for its own sake. Dance can explore and make statements about bodily rhythms, spatial tensions and relationships, as in the more non-literal forms of dance. Dance is also a means by which events may be described and commented upon and stories told as in dance drama. The fact that dance has many contexts — cultural, historical, social, artistic/aesthetic and so on — gives it traditionally a central place in human experience and, therefore, a relevance to education at all levels. At primary level, the central concern with the body, mastery of movement, using movement as a means of expression and communication, seem to us particularly valuable areas of experience. Through making dances, however simple, through performing dances whether alone or with others, through appreciating and commenting upon their dance experiences, primary school children can gain not only in physical knowledge and self-confidence but also in experience of themselves in various contexts which would otherwise be denied them. Thus dance in the primary school is, we believe, of value in its own right. When its links with other art forms, particularly music, and other areas of the curriculum, such as history and geography, are developed as suggested in chapter 3 it is difficult to see why dance is all too often accorded little or even no time in the school curriculum.

97 What to teach at what level

Dance in education, therefore, has a rationale in which the question of what to teach at what level becomes critical. Children seem to learn best when they are helped constructively to develop their vocabulary of movement and physical competence through simple movement explorations appropriate to their stage of development. They enjoy repetition and the creation of simple, individual dances, which may be enhanced by the use of mime, music, percussive sounds, words and so on. These 'dances' will have only the most elementary form: formations are appropriate at this stage. What matters is that children should have responsibility for their own choice of dance vocabulary.

98 Implications of more skill acquisition

We believe there is widespread agreement that for older children a higher level of skill acquisition is desirable, and that a more structured approach will not kill spontaneity but will increase the power of expression by widening the vocabulary of movement. This view was expressed frequently at the 'Dance and the Child' conference in Edmonton, Canada, in July 1978, described already in paragraph 58. There is a need to enlarge the child's vocabulary, it was argued, in order to enlarge the child's ability to discriminate, react with imagination, come face to face with feelings, thoughts and images. In general we underestimate the child's ability for hard work. 'Are not many children hungry for technique' asked one speaker, 'and become disappointed when insufficiently challenged, though frustrated when over-challenged?' The introduction of an element of technique, of more awareness of form and of a variety of relationships with others, would have as their aim not so much the introduction of a discipline (though this might be the case) as the extension of a child's movement possibility and hence the enlargement of its capacity for expression through acquiring a movement vocabulary and language. If this view is accepted, the implications of a more structured approach to dance teaching are three-fold. First, more time will be required on the school timetable* because classes need to be regular and consistent throughout the year. Second, there needs to be a logical progression of the dance experience. Third, some consensus needs to be reached among dance teachers and specialists about the meaning of technique.

---

* The amount of time each week has been much debated. Representatives of vocational training have argued that 'one class a week is not enough'. On the other hand, this is the norm for a majority of children in private studios, as we show in Part III. In the maintained sector we have been told that a practice of dividing classes into a number of activities during physical recreation periods can provide an element of choice. All the class cannot play hockey, netball or tennis at the same time. There should, therefore, be little problem in timetabling a dance class as an option for those who wish it.

99 Problem of technique	By technique we do not mean here the mastery of skill and accuracy in a particular vocabulary of steps and exercises in a particular style. Such a concept of technique is too narrow In any case, it is a point of debate whether classes to develop a technique of classical ballet, say, or modern dance, not only can but should be held in an ordinary school unless the school is prepared to give the necessary time on the timetable. Rather, we mean by technique the discipline of an art, something a child might acquire in three concurrent stages — personal development through movement; the acquisition of skill in movement; the bringing together of skill and personal qualities for an artistic purpose expressed through dance.
100 Need for co-operation between teachers and sectors	We have found a wish, among many primary school teachers, to develop dance in these ways and to liaise more closely with their colleagues in the private sector who represent a resource as yet largely untapped by local education authorities. It is not yet widely known, for example, that the ISTD, whose work is described in Part III, has taken the initiative to establish a research group to develop a 'fundamental dance technique'. There is, too, a growing amount of classical ballet, modern and national dance being taught in the maintained sector by the private teacher. All this represents a co-operation between the two sectors which needs to be encouraged. There is a questioning, a feeling, as one primary head teacher put it, 'that with dance we are in a workshop stage searching for ways to build and go forward.' Therefore it seems essential for dance teachers of all methods to come together to review the principles of their work. This review would embrace, particularly, differences of concept and philosophy and the value and nature of appropriate techniques at particular stages of development supported, where necessary, by relevant research such as that conducted by the ISTD.
101 Fuller use of teaching skills	If this could be done, we believe important modifications to traditional practice might emerge. Notwithstanding the usual primary school practice of one teacher to one class, we are attracted to the idea put forward in *Primary Education in England*[31] that staff members with a particular interest in dance might be given special responsibility for dance in each school. Where this is done, consideration should be given to providing time to perform their duties, to helping them improve their standing and in formulating policy.* Where schools are too small to appoint teachers with special responsibility, consideration might be given to teachers sharing skills in planning programmes of work, to more visits from specialist advisory** staff and to priority in in-service education and training to extend knowledge, skills and teaching tech-

---

* The views in this paragraph are based on conclusions of Her Majesty's Inspectorate in *Primary Education in England pp. 122–125.* (See note 31)

** Note the Scottish experience of visiting PE teachers already referred to in paragraph 90. These visits assist the general class teacher and are in no sense a substitute for his/her dance teaching.

niques. This concentration on staff development, nurturing teachers who have a particular ability, or the most experienced and able teachers, or those willing to increase their expertise in weak areas of the curriculum, should be a particular point of concentration during in-service education. The other point of concentration is to raise the expectations which teachers have of children in dance, thus helping to clarify the curriculum and raise standards.

102 The child as spectator

Although it might seem obvious that education in 'doing' dance should be balanced by education in 'seeing and appreciating' dance, we think that the child as spectator is generally more neglected in primary and secondary schools than the child as performer and creator. Not enough use is made of the opportunities for school performances – in school or in theatres – now provided by professional companies and described in chapter 2. Once again the issue requires collaboration between dance profession and education profession. Children do not watch in the way adults do. They participate as spectators, and this has tremendous implications for all performing companies concerned to reach them. Education in seeing and appreciating involves the whole visual experience of dancing; it is visual communication through dancing. Therefore children need to have first hand experience of all that is best in dance, first rate dancing performed by first rate dancers. To deny them the opportunity to see professional dance is to leave them with a very limited view of dance, as well as to deny them the inspiration and example to improve their own work. Such seeing is likely to be a significant educational experience because professional dance usually includes also drama, music and design. It is also an education of the eye, ear and imagination and therefore an important part of the education of spectator awareness. There is a need, therefore, indicated by our survey, for more regular opportunities for children to see professional dance of all kinds preferably through live performance, but otherwise through film and video provision. The first step towards this, at secondary as well as primary level, is greater use of the educational resources provided by professional dance companies.

103 Special needs

Finally, we draw attention to the duty upon education authorities to meet special needs. One kind of special need derives from children particularly gifted in dance who require vocational training. This demands special knowledge of the local education authority and imposes responsibility of a specific kind to which we return in Part III. Another special need derives from disabled children. The value of dance and movement training is recognised increasingly today in the education of the disabled. It requires of the teacher dedication and special knowledge fully comparable with the responsibilities of teachers in vocational training. We have seen striking examples of dance not only by blind, deaf and mentally disabled children, but also by the physically disabled. The education of disabled children, moreover, is an important part of the responsibility of the maintained sector, emphasised by the Warnock Report.[33] If dance can contribute signifi-

51

cantly in this field*, as we think it can, the case for dance in education is even stronger. Dance, as we point out repeatedly, is for everyone.

*   Appropriate contacts and further information can be obtained from SHAPE, 44 Earlham Street, London WC2H 9LA

8 Secondary Level

104 Background of change
Our approach to dance at secondary level has to start from an acknowledgement of the important changes which have taken place in secondary education during the last 15 years. These are substantial enough to require the stocktaking implicit in HM Inspectorate's survey of secondary education in England, described in paragraph 109 below. Like the Inspectorate, therefore, we begin with a summary of the changes, adding one item to the Inspectorate's list. During the last 15 years 'a large part of the secondary school system had undergone re-organisation; substantial curricula research and development had been sponsored, partly in direct response to comprehensive re-organisation planned or in progress, partly also in preparation for the raising of the school leaving age which occurred in 1973; a new examination, the Certificate of Secondary Education (CSE), had been introduced, styles of examining had been diversified and the proportion of 16 year olds entering for public examinations had markedly increased.'[18] We add, influencing the backdrop to all this, widespread changes in public and personal attitudes and teacher—student—parent relationships flowing from the cultural revolution of the 1960s/70s and the claims of young people generally for a greater say in shaping their lives including their education. Not just the structure but the climate of education has changed.

105 Looking to the future
Having sketched this background of change we think we should draw attention to our observation in chapter 1 about the nature of the education which might result from the general debate on education now taking place. Secondary schools and their curriculum are the focus of this debate. If the changes of the last 15 years do not seem to have advanced dance very far in today's curriculum, we should look forward to the next period of change, now upon us, to use better the opportunities it has to offer. The last 15 years were a period of relatively little economic restriction. The new period will be one of economic restraint with serious implications for the resources of schools, their staff and students, and the services which support them. It will also be a period of falling school population. This implies further re-organisation and change during which teachers will certainly continue to try to develop a curriculum more responsive to the developing needs of all children in a society coming to terms with new economic, technological and social imperatives. We have shown already that we think dance has a particularly valuable contribution to make to such a curriculum. This chapter is about the measures we believe necessary to realise this contribution.

106 Dance at secondary level
We emphasised in the last chapter the importance of the attitude of a school (particularly its head) and of the local education authority to a healthy dance life in school. What is essential at primary level becomes crucial at secondary level where there are new pressures and more intense demands for time in the curriculum. Dance at secondary

level also requires additional resources such as specialist teachers, spaces and appropriate equipment such as barres, music libraries of records and/or tapes, record players and tape or cassette players. It may also need special clothing such as dance shoes, tights and leotards. The results of our survey of dance in maintained secondary schools in England and Wales show how rarely this degree of support is available, although a number of physical education advisers in Scotland, England and Wales have begun actively to build resources for dance in schools at places like teachers' centres. Our survey indicates also that the problems and possibilities of dance in the maintained sector come together at secondary level. Dance at secondary level is a continuation, or not, of dance at primary level; it is a preparation, or not, for dance at tertiary level. Its study also acquires at secondary level a significance it does not necessarily possess at primary level. At primary level dance can be, and often is, studied as much for enjoyment as for any idea of improvement, even among older age groups. At secondary level the aim of improvement to become a better dancer guides the nature of study wherever dance is a curriculum subject.

107 Today's setting

There are 4,728 secondary schools in England, 438 in Scotland and 254 in Wales. Within these totals in England and Wales the percentage of students in comprehensive schools exceeds 80%. In Scotland, as we showed in paragraph 73, secondary education is organised already almost completely on comprehensive lines. This move towards fully comprehensive education is important to dance for reasons given already in paragraph 72 and 73, and developed in paragraph 114 below. As at primary level, we examine dance at secondary level in three stages. First, what exists at the moment, supported by two special surveys. Second, some general conclusions indicating areas of encouragement and important issues. Third, the resolution of these issues, often through successful experience.

108 Our survey

Our examination has been assisted, as for our study of primary schools, by a questionnaire compiled by the National Foundation for Educational Research. This questionnaire was sent to a sample of 347 secondary schools in England and Wales in the spring and summer terms of 1977. Completed questionnaires were returned by just under 70% of these schools. 61% of those responding (129) reported that some dance is taught.* Again we think it prudent to emphasise the limited nature of this survey. Nevertheless, as at primary level, its results generally are confirmed in England by an Inspectorate Survey.[35] Our own experience also largely confirms the findings. These findings show that dance is taught in only one third of our sample, that it is rarely taught beyond the first three years and is restricted almost entirely to girls. In Scotland our impression is that more secondary schools than this do

---

*   Our respondents interpreted dance very broadly. It can mean anything from a use of BBC Movement and Drama programmes through folk dance and forms of movement to music, to modern dance and classical ballet classes.

dance, perhaps because of the stronger tradition of Scottish country dancing.

109 The Inspectorate's survey

The report by HM Inspectors of schools is the outcome of a survey extending over the years 1975–1979. It concentrates mainly upon language, mathematics and science in the final two years of compulsory schooling, drawing upon a 10% sample of maintained secondary schools of all types and age ranges. It represents, therefore, a larger sample than we could cover. Its particular direction and purpose, however, make it less specifically useful to us than the primary survey. Even so, as much by what is not said as by what it says, its results and comments confirm our survey in the generally meagre and confused place occupied by dance in the British secondary curriculum. Dance, for example, does not occur in the report's index and is mentioned in the text only twice, in connection with a particular interpretation of giftedness to do with outstanding talent. It is so rare an option in the fourth and fifth year curriculum as to be omitted from all lists and tables, even when art, music and drama find a place. Yet we know from other sources of good dance work in secondary schools. Perhaps it is statistically too small for mention. More likely it is subsumed under physical education as it is at primary level. If so, there is opportunity for progress. At the same time there is the possibility of confusion because physical education figures regularly in the curriculum prior to the fourth year and is a candidate for 'core' subject up to and including the fourth year.

110 A composite picture

From the response to our survey emerges a composite picture of a secondary school in England and Wales in which dance *is* included in the curriculum. It is likely to be a mixed comprehensive school employing about 51 full-time and 6 part-time teachers with approximately 520 boys and 530 girls on the school roll ranging in age from 11 to 17 years. Dance is taught mainly to the girls and is the responsibility of the physical education department. The average length of lessons is 43 minutes including changing time and the number of lessons given in a year rises from 37 at 11+ age, or roughly once a week, to 45 at 16+ and back to 33 at 17+. The type of dance taught is folk or Laban-based creative dance. Two women full-time members of staff and two women part-time members teach dance, usually in the assembly hall although just under one third of schools reported using the gymnasium for dance teaching. Most responses considered this accommodation satisfactory. Only 2% of the sample reported the use of a special dance studio. Responses showing visits and displays during the year were so small as to be statistically insignificant, thus confirming the same deficiency noted at primary level.

111 School dance clubs in England and Wales

Half the schools where dance is taught regularly reported that the children wish to do more. This extra activity is reflected often in dance clubs meeting out of school hours. The clubs represent a strikingly positive feature, particularly in the interest of boys. The average number of pupils in regular attendance is 15–24 girls and 15–20 boys

55

in the age range 11–15 years. Thus, where facilities are offered it appears that boys will accept the opportunity. We have more to say about such clubs in chapter 11 where we look also at those catering for a slightly older age group, still at secondary level. Their growth is beginning to provide significant outlets for professional and amateur choreographers as well as performances of rising quality for their locality. The long term significance of such work cannot be over-estimated.

112 The picture in Scotland

We recorded above our impression that more secondary schools in Scotland do dance than in England. We did not have the resources for a separate survey but, to complete our portrait, we visited, interviewed, toured, consulted or wrote to 20 institutions and organisations connected with dance and/or physical education, and 34 advisers, school/college principals, inspectors, and dance and education administrators throughout Scotland during 1979. These are listed at Appendix K. Their responses show a considerable range of activity at secondary level. Many areas are preparing or revising teachers' guidelines in dance of various kinds, expecially Scottish, folk, social and modern dance. A variety of in-service courses for teachers are being organised within schools throughout Scotland in collaboration with colleges of education. Two areas have noted encouraging results from two specialist appointments of principal teachers in dance, while two other areas report similarly about their use of peripatetic team teaching. There were many reports of specially arranged festivals of dance in different regions and districts. 1,500 pupils from 30 schools contributed, for example, to five days of dance; 700 pupils from 20 schools contributed to one day of dance, culminating in an evening performance for the public; 1,300 pupils took part in one festival of dance, while at another 77 dance items were contributed from 30 schools. There was also a three day competitive festival of Scottish country dancing. An increasing number of schools report using groups resident in Scotland, like Scottish Ballet Workshop, Basic Space Dance Company and Dunfermline College's Dance Project 'Instep' to extend their students' appreciation and involvement in dance.

113 Dance clubs in Scotland

It appears to be an accepted feature of many secondary schools in Scotland that they maintain a performing dance club. This activity is finding outlets beyond the schools and thus parallels experience in England and Wales. An item contributed by a school, for example, took first place in the 1979 choreographic competition of the Scottish Dance Guild. In Renfrewshire the PEG Theatre has become established as an amateur dance group for students and ex-students of schools in the area. In Dunfermline College's '1979 Junior Dancescapers' – an Edinburgh Festival Fringe production organised by the College since 1977 – 130 students from 12 schools across Scotland took part for a week. The same year a conference organised by the College brought together professional and amateur dancers to discuss 'The Pupil as Performer and Spectator of the Dance.'

56

However tentatively we draw conclusions from these studies, including that by the Inspectorate, they suggest a rather patchy picture lacking any progressive, overall scheme. The achievements, welcome as they are, should not be allowed to obscure reality. This is that dance is taught in a relatively few British schools among which comprehensive schools, because of their size and/or philosophy, give it the best opportunity to flourish. 'Small schools,' note the Inspectorate, 'find difficulty in offering the range of choice . . . which is available in bigger schools.'[18] The Inspectorate confirms also our own experience in a number of areas at this level. First, more able fourth and fifth year students are likely to lose out on the creative/aesthetic area of the curriculum and thus are least likely to be encouraged to develop any dance talent they may have revealed earlier. Second, differentiation by sex remains prevalent in a number of subject areas. This, of course, includes dance. Third, as we argued in chapter 1, there is a need for a broader approach to curriculum provision 'to develop the potential of all pupils to enjoy a full personal life and to take an informed and responsible part in the adult world . . . Curricula provision, therefore, ought not to be such as to shut off any pupils from important areas of knowledge and experience.'[18] Our studies suggest that many students at secondary level, especially boys, are excluded from the areas of knowledge and experience represented by dance. This is a deprivation not only in terms of learning and possible career opportunity, but in terms of personal and social development to which the arts can be important contributors.

What then needs to be done before dance is accepted as a significant area of knowledge which can command a fair share of the curriculum? Nine major issues have arisen in discussing this question. They are: the particular and general contribution of dance to secondary education; arising from this, an appropriate curriculum for dance at this level; overcoming the low subject status of dance; improving teaching quality; how to involve more boys; how better to help gifted children; the needs of the handicapped; the special deprivation of inner city and rural schools; and what John Mann, Secretary of the Schools Council, has called the 'chasm between primary and secondary' education.[34] To consider these issues we began by reviewing successful experiences of dance in the curriculum at primary and secondary levels, approaching the two levels as a continuous process.

Our review took the form of a one day seminar convened at the Institute of Contemporary Arts, London. This brought together a selection of primary and secondary schools, listed at Appendix A, which had established dance as a significant part of their curricula. Their reports were, indeed, remarkable. One school will be known to many through a television programme for its incorporation of classical ballet training into the life of the school. What was surprising was to discover the number of other such schools around, not necessarily incorporating classical ballet, but all vigorously and with commitment giving to their own forms of dance that fair share of the curriculum of

57

which most dance teachers dream. Sometimes too, they draw on the knowledge of teachers in the private sector. These experiences indicate that there are no insurmountable problems once the will is there, and that there are a variety of ways in which dance can take its place in the curriculum. Some give dance full subject status alongside other subjects with its own full-time staff in a separate dance department. Some incorporate dance into an arts or theatre faculty structure for second and third year children, then provide opportunities for supplementary studies over the fourth, fifth and sixth years. Usually these studies are linked with other art forms and after-school 'workshop' sessions. Some have been particularly successful at capturing the interest of boys as well as girls. Some have formed youth dance groups, sometimes working with young people from other schools, and providing a valuable supplement for the training of the most talented dancers. All report that the influence of the dance work helps the life of the school. Many have introduced Certificate of Extended Education (CEE) and Certificate of Secondary Education (CSE) (usually Mode III) courses and some enter candidates for O-level ballet.[14] Very, very few of the students have any commitment to a career in dance, although this may arise as a result of the experience.

117 Contri-
bution of dance
to a school

Contributing to these experiences, one head mistress from a comprehensive school in a disadvantaged multi-racial part of London listed the reasons why she gave dance a regular place in her timetable. 'Dance helps the life of the school in five ways. First, it gives children an awareness and control of their bodies which Physical Education as such does not give completely. I would feel we had not done our job if a child left here less well educated physically than intellectually or spiritually. Second, because of the confidence gained in this way, there is a huge psychological benefit which can have very practical results, like self-confidence when entering a room to be interviewed for a job. Third, there is a community benefit because dance is a form of community education. Through dancing the children *must* relate to each other. Maybe that's why we have fewer community and vandalism problems here than other people round about, though I haven't done any research to prove it. Fourth, it provides aesthetic and emotional education. The children choose music and have to think about it. They have to think about costumes, colours, shapes and so on. They make up their own compositions, which express their feelings and deepen their knowledge of themselves. Lastly, we might, just might, spot a child with real talent — a potential Margot Fonteyn or a Martha Graham! In that case we'll pass her on to the right vocational school, and be proud. But talent spotting is not why we include dance.' Five reasons, given then, for dance in education — physical, psychological, community, aesthetic and vocational. Of course the five reasons are derived from the experience of one school but other schools responded during our seminar in similar terms.

58

118 Drawing on professional dance experience Another comprehensive school, in Cheshire, described a model experiment initiated by the Authority. An experienced dancer was appointed as artist-in-residence at the school with additional responsibilities in some of the feeder primary schools. Results were impressive, illustrating many of the factors we have stressed as important to success: the value of continuity, in this case a tradition of 15 years work on which the artist-in-residence was able to build; the support of the head teacher; the support of the Authority and its PE Adviser; the quality of the dancer, in this case not a qualified teacher in the educational sense but a professional dancer able to communicate her experience and enthusiasm to pupils, staff and parents; the support of other members of staff; the importance of a link between primary and secondary levels – another sort of continuity; the participation of boys through special classes, carefully devised, and through the encouragement of some male members of staff. In Strathclyde, Scotland, liaison of another kind with the dance profession took the form of a day seminar by The Scottish Ballet, sponsored by the Authority, to show teachers the nature of a professional dancer's work and way of life.

119 Conditions for success Collectively, these experiences suggest conditions for success in introducing dance into the curriculum. First, wherever dance is introduced in school on a significant scale, positive support from the authority is essential. Second, to achieve proper status the parameters of dance need to be more clearly defined. Third, in order to recruit a good dance staff there must be good facilities and internal support from head teacher and staff. Every teacher needs a secure base. Fourth, there needs to be a coherent programme of dance at each level throughout the school. Fifth, dance teachers need the status of having their own department as soon as is practical in the present economic situation. Where these conditions are met experience shows that dance becomes at its best a powerful force in the life of the school and of the students.

120 Resolving issues There seems no organisational or administrative reason, then, why dance should not occupy a significant place in the curriculum of British secondary schools. What is needed is conviction in the teacher, the head and the local authority. Given this, the consultations we have quoted show clearly that issues of status, time in the curriculum and so on can be resolved. Crucial, however, is the quality of dance teaching. As our survey showed, the dance teacher in a secondary school is probably a woman whose initial dance training was part of a specialist* course in physical education. The nature of this training is discussed in chapter 10. But three other factors affect the issue – scale of remuneration, opportunities for promotion and responsibility, and the amount of specialist support provided. These factors all depend upon the local authority.

---

* A survey carried out by the Inner London Dance Teachers' Association supports this conclusion. It shows that in the majority of secondary schools in London where a CSE examination course has been developed, the dance teacher was specialist trained.

121 Teacher *remuneration*	Qualified teaching staff in England and Wales receive salaries at one of seven levels: scales 1, 2, 3 and 4; senior teacher, deputy head, head. Scale 1 is the basic salary range, and probationary teachers begin at the bottom level of this scale unless they have a degree. Scale 4 is usually the top salary range of teachers who are heads of large departments in secondary schools. In other schools scale 3 is typical.* Most teachers in charge of a secondary physical education department are on scale 3 or scale 4 and a small number of these give particular attention to dance in their work. In very rare instances a head of physical education is in the 'senior teacher' salary range, although physical education teachers have quite frequently become deputy heads of comprehensive schools. These scales have been agreed by the Burnham Committee and are applicable to all qualified teachers in England and Wales. Scottish teachers' salaries are currently laid out in the Scottish Teachers' Salaries Memorandum 1978 and its amendments, and are, of course, constantly under review. A qualified teacher can be a graduate or non-graduate according to the training received, although the aim today is to make teaching a graduate profession. Clearly, however, while dance remains a minority subject the chances of promotion for a dance specialist will be limited. Yet proper remuneration is essential to recruiting and retaining good staff. The problem is linked to opportunities for promotion and responsibility.
122 Teacher *responsibility*	Promotion and responsibility, in turn, are linked with responsibility allowances. Within a school in England or Wales the allocation of 'responsibility allowances' among the teaching staff will be determined by the various needs of the school. The number of responsibility posts available to a school depends on its size, on the extent to which, for social reasons, the area in which it is situated is regarded as having special priority needs, and on the number of students. An appropriate balance between subjects is sought, and between the numbers of teachers in each subject department. Even with secondary or comprehensive schools of similar size, the number of teachers within the physical education department will vary from school to school and so will the responsibility allowances offered to the teachers. In Scotland, though the number of teachers in a department may vary in secondary schools of the same type and size, the number of promoted posts is statutorily determined by the work load (hours) of the department/ subject; the level of responsibility allowances is statutorily determined by the total school roll. Rarely will such responsibility allowances be exclusively for dance although there is a growing case for dance to take its place on an equal footing with other subjects.
123 Peripatetic *teachers*	The quality of dance teaching in a school will be affected not only by the quality of full-time staff and their position in the school, but also

---

* At the time of writing (June 1980), the Scale 4 salary range in England and Wales varies from £5,463 to £7,218; that for Scale 3 varies from £4,590 to £6,495.

by the number and quality of visiting teachers and the extent of local support, conditioned to some extent by geographical location. The ILEA, for example, has appointed annually since 1974 an advisory teacher of dance. This is not a dance adviser but a teacher seconded from a school to work with the Authority for at least a year, thus communicating school experience. In Leicestershire there are five peripatetic dance teachers. In Northamptonshire, Manchester, Wolverhampton and a few other authorities there is one each. The Calderdale Education Authority runs a Peripatetic Dance Teachers Centre. In Scotland we reported in paragraph 112 the successful use of peripatetic team teaching. Peripatetic teachers are usually teachers employed on a permanent basis and recruited as if to become teachers in schools, forming the nucleus of a specialist teaching force. If qualified, in England and Wales, they receive the appropriate Burnham rates, holiday pay and superannuation benefits. If unqualified they may receive 'instructor' rates of pay, although in Leicestershire they receive Burnham minus £50, thus giving parity with music peripatetics. As a matter of principle, in fact, authorities employing dance peripatetics should surely consider provision for them on a parity with their colleagues in other subjects. In Scotland 'instructors' may only be engaged for special visits and paid instructors' hourly rates. All others employed to teach school pupils must be qualified teachers registered with the General Teaching Council.

124 Visiting teachers

A few authorities now provide visiting dance teachers along the same lines as for other arts. This means the employment of outside dance teachers on an hourly basis to teach their specialisms in schools. Such teachers are usually restricted in the number of hours they can work each week (often ten hours) and need not be of qualified teacher status. The local authority negotiates its own hourly rate but the teachers receive none of the security of a salaried post. Usually selected by the adviser, they are sometimes used to operate an 'award' scheme supervised by the adviser and his or her staff. Pupils showing some ability are auditioned for individual lessons paid for by the authority. These lessons may be given by peripatetic teachers, or by visiting teachers in addition to their normal work, or by private teachers. They can be given at school, at some local centre, or in the teacher's own studio. The authority usually pays an hourly rate it has itself decided. Some authorities will extend their award scheme to paying for advanced pupils to receive occasional lessons from distinguished teachers outside the area of the authority, or for paying the fees and expenses of promising pupils to attend Saturday morning schools run locally. No authority, however, yet runs dance centres like the centres for music, art and drama which a number of authorities operate on Saturdays, or after school, or on half-day release from school, although a number of authorities had hoped to do so before cuts in the Government's education budget.

125 The ILEA: an example

It might be useful to instance what one authority, the ILEA, admittedly the largest, provides for dance in a programme which is by no means unique in Britain as a whole. As soon as facilities become available it hopes to establish a pupil centre for dance. In this way it aims to help those pupils who are in schools where physical conditions make dance difficult or in schools where there is no teacher able to teach the subject. The Authority is continuing to arrange special ability classes at the London School of Contemporary Dance in Central London and at the Laban Centre in South London. It assists the Royal Ballet School's liaison with schools to encourage and discover talent. It is sustaining, too, an Inner London Schools Dance Group meeting each Saturday, working towards performance. One of the schools organises an evening of dance each year when secondary schools in the neighbourhood gather to show work at lower and upper secondary levels providing valuable opportunity for teachers and pupils. Apart from the school clubs, which continue to flourish after school hours, a few schools have groups which perform outside London and in some cases abroad. One encouraging development is the fact that more boys are now being involved in performing groups. Other provision for dance includes: opportunities for dance in education which include both school visits to dance companies in their own setting, and dance companies performing in the schools; grants to support various projects, usually by providing tutor hours or premises; links with the EFDSS enabling teachers' courses to be held each term, and providing opportunity for schools to meet and dance together. Apart from the work in schools, there are also many opportunities for young people to dance within the Youth Service and Adult Education. The Authority has a scheme for providing a limited number of places at dance schools for pupils between the ages of 11 and 16, and grants a number of awards for further study in dance.

126 Local authority support

Thus, much of the quality of dance and dance teaching in individual schools has to do with the nature of the support, or lack of it, provided by the local authority. In particular it is dependent upon the vision, energy and expertise of the local authority adviser. Most local authorities have special subject advisers, including physical education advisers and music advisers, sometimes known as 'organisers' or 'inspectors'. These advise the local education authority — that is, the education committee of elected representatives, co-opted experts and the chief education officer — on policy to do with their subject in all places of education maintained or aided by the authority. The adviser also advises schools on matters concerning the subject in question, including the appointment of subject staff, help for probationary teachers and other in-service training, new approaches to the curriculum and the provision of specialist teachers and equipment. The adviser is responsible for the administration of any budget allocated to the subject, possibly including the building or equipping of special accommodation in new or remodelled schools, the provision of specialist teachers, the supply and purchase of special equipment lent to schools or provided for special activities within the authority. The adviser also interviews or auditions candidates for discretionary awards for vocational training and advises parents about their children who seem to have a special gift for their subject. In this the adviser will usually be assisted by a team of specialists.

127 Dance advisers

Clearly, the role of the adviser is crucial to the development of any subject within an authority's schools. For dance this would involve standards, teaching problems, subject status, resources, balance between boys and girls, and special needs. There are no dance advisers as such in British education. Dance usually comes under the remit of advisers in physical education, some of whom have served dance very well. The nearest to a separate dance adviser in England is the kind of appointment made, for example, in Oxfordshire and Leicestershire. Oxfordshire's Advisory Teacher for Dance is responsible not only for dance teaching in primary and secondary schools but for in-service training of teachers; arranging liaison between visiting dance companies and schools for workshops and theatre visits; arrangements with local art and community centres for on-going dance experiences; and for interviewing applicants for discretionary awards for vocational courses. In Leicestershire the development of dance is under the guidance of an Adviser for Drama and Movement, assisted by the team of five dance specialists already mentioned. In Scotland there are the examples of Ayrshire and Renfrewshire, where the physical education advisers are each assisted by a qualified teacher who has undertaken an additional study of dance, and who has a responsibility to develop dance. In each case the teacher's status is neither that of specialist adviser nor of a peripatetic teacher, but rather that of staff tutor. There is ample evidence that in all four authorities dance has developed dramatically as a result of their efforts.

128 Boys in dance

We direct attention to three other problems raised above before attempting to draw conclusions from our study: boys in dance; gifted children; and particularly deprived children. The successful involvement of boys in dance has been quoted several times in this chapter. Nevertheless, our statistics and all other evidence demonstrate the traditional view that dance is taught by women and is for girls. It is thus a single sex, female activity. The prejudice is profound and automatic. 'Right!' said one headmaster of a mixed school after the director of the Royal Ballet's Ballet for All company had been speaking to an assembly of boys and girls in the late 1960s, 'hands up those girls who would like to see the performance.' Nowadays, that headmaster, and any other schools which discriminate, albeit unthinkingly, against boys in the allocation of dance opportunities, could be a target for the Equal Opportunities Commission under the Sex Discrimination Act (1975). But the vocational sector reflects the same prejudice no less unthinkingly with equal damage. The logos of the Royal Academy of Dancing, Imperial Society of Teachers of Dancing, British Ballet Organisation and International Dance Teachers Association all have a dance theme illustrating girls only. For them it seems that dance is a single sex sub-

6

ject.* Thus the problem is how to change traditional, entrenched ideas of this kind. But ideas *are* changing and there is experience on which to draw. Hence one can list a number of points born of experience. Wherever possible there should be a comprehensive programme of development for dance training in mixed classes from infant school through to higher education — thereby reducing the alienation boys feel from what often becomes a female orientated activity. Where boys are introduced to dance at a later (eg secondary) age range, they need to gain confidence in their own movement ability before being set alongside girls who have been studying for a number of years; this can be achieved either by giving separate boys classes for a period prior to introducing mixed groups, or by taking a new direction with the dance work, which will be new to boys and girls alike. In the latter the teaching and acquisition of specific dance skills can provide a solution; the forms and ideas selected for dance interpretation need to reflect the different interests and experiences of boys and girls at particular age levels; special benefits in involving boys with dance can be achieved through establishing links with their other creative work such as drama, music, art and extending their creativity into a kinaesthetic awareness and appreciation; boys have been shown to be as responsive as girls to technical dance styles such as classical and modern techniques, where a definite objective is in view, such an objective might take the form of performance work; there is ample evidence to show that boys who have worked in mixed dance groups respond in a more mature and sensitive way to girls. This important benefit is, of course, only an extension of the point already made that dance has a community benefit. Lastly it should be noted that, in the non-maintained sector, the Modern Dance Branch of the ISTD has been working for some time on a course of movement for boys. This has proved popular and successful so that it would be valuable if its details could be disseminated alongside other successful experience of the kind we have quoted in the maintained sector.

129 *Gifted children*

Gifted children — the potential professionals — are rare. Many others, who also need special opportunities for dance, will have a particular talent which deserves encouragement even though it may not lead to a career. Facilities are needed for all at many levels and in the process this will enable the gifted and talented to benefit too. Like our colleagues on the committee of inquiry into the training of musicians,[2] we stress the need to pay more attention to the identification of giftedness and talent in dance. We believe that this applies in equal measure to all schools and local authorities throughout the country. Advisers responsible for dance, in consultation with representative bodies of the private sector, should draw up guidelines to help alert primary school heads and their staff to what may be real dance talent in a child, and

---

*   All these organisations, of course, acknowledge the male dancer and provide for his training. It is inexcusable, however, that they should perpetuate the single sex image.

then make provision for it to be encouraged at secondary level. It should be borne in mind, particularly, that children gifted and talented in dance, as in music, need special facilities and support at a much earlier age than is the case for any other subjects. This need is recognised in the Education Act, 1976. We return to its financial implications in chapter 16.

130 Helping
giftedness

How best to help giftedness in dance? We have benefited from the studies of the National Children's Bureau,[35] the National Association for Gifted Children,[36] the report of a working group[37] set up by the SED in 1973 to consider the general and specialised education of gifted young musicians and dancers; and a paper for guidance, *Find the Gifted Child*,[38] published by the Devon Education Department. From this evidence and our own discussions we make two observations. First, in the words of the Devon Study, 'There is a responsibility for the Authority, together with schools and parents, to review the way in which highly gifted children may be identified and the manner in which their level of achievement might be evaluated. It is expected that the majority of schools will already have their own way of noting and providing for children of exceptional gifts. It is hoped that practices and policies will be reviewed and defined in such a way that all teachers and particularly new teachers, together with parents and governors and managers, can be clear about the direction from which they may, if they need it, seek help and guidance. The task of the Authority is to ensure that the level of concern and care for highly gifted children is neither so high as to be divisive nor so low as to lead to waste.' Our second observation is to emphasise how much can be learned from experience in other areas — not just in the arts or languages or the sciences but also, because performing skill is closely associated with physical development, in non-academic areas such as sport and physical achievement of all kinds. Here the need for special coaching and other kinds of selective attention are completely accepted and have been available for many years without any charge of élitism. The skills involved may be different but the nature of the gift itself — and its importance to possessor and onlookers — are the same.

131 The
handicapped

There are three aspects of help for the handicapped to which we draw special attention. First, dance is a legitimate and helpful activity for very many handicapped students of all kinds, whether or not it has therapeutic relevance to their condition. Handicapped people have as much right to dance as their more fortunate companions. Second, dance has a therapeutic value to particular conditions. The same responses are necessary to these needs by committed and trained teachers, as we indicated at primary level in paragraph 103. We have seen remarkable and moving dance creations by handicapped people, all entirely acceptable as dance. We think, though, that this, like other aspects of help for the handicapped,[39] is an area of provision often overlooked and undersupported by authorities. Therefore it is a field worthy of further exploration and study by dance specialists. This usually means an appropriate teacher training course in dance at a maintained or non-maintained institution followed by a diploma course (normally for one year) to be able to teach in a specific area of handicap. There are, however, other methods and approaches from which we have seen notably successful results. The third aspect of help makes an opposite approach. Many schools, as the Inspectorate points out in their report, now provide opportunities for at least some of their pupils to engage in community service, '. . . some schools had established close links with school or hospitals . . .'[18] We already have examples of performances by school dance groups to handicapped people and we hope many more may develop. It is a special kind of community service already pioneered by community artists, particularly enriching to both performers and audience.

132 Deprived children

Our travels and school visits make us draw special attention finally to the cultural needs of children in the deprived areas of inner cities and in rural areas, just as we do to the needs of the handicapped. In the inner cities and rural areas, what we have seen convinces us not only of the loss of the enrichment dance can bring to children generally in these areas, but the loss to dance of potential artists. The loss occurs in and out of school where there are not enough facilities in spaces and transport to organise opportunities for dance outside school through classes and evening clubs, even where an authority is willing to accept this commitment. There seems to us a real need here for priority treatment so far as arts provision is concerned. In a similar context we draw attention also to the need for more use in these areas, and by all secondary schools, of the educational dance performances now made available by professional companies, large and small. The same point was made at the end of the last chapter, but performances at secondary level are an essential complement to impressions at primary level and an essential preparation to the enjoyment of dance seen in adult life.

133 Conclusion

We return to the theme with which we opened this chapter, the need for dance to be part of a broader curriculum which prepares young people more fully than now for a world likely to be very different from ours. The Inspectorate has made a convincing case for a broader approach, 'the curriculum in this context may be seen as all the experiences that have been planned and organised by the school, whether for groups or individuals, inside or outside the classroom . . . The overall curricula programmes . . . therefore reflect the values of those responsible for the curriculum'.[18] We think the relatively low status of dance in today's curriculum perhaps reflects not only a low esteem of the arts generally, but a deficiency in thinking of values in the framing of the curriculum. It underestimates the way a curriculum, rather than pastoral care alone, contributes directly to social and personal development as well as to preparation for a career. Therefore we have tried in this and the last chapter not only to review existing practice and experience at primary and secondary level, but to offer ideas which authorities can develop according to their own resources. The aim should be simply to provide for every child in an authority the opportunity to study dance in his or her own school as an integral part of the curriculum at primary and secondary level. However this is achieved, the essentials of such provision are: continuity of teaching and dance experience in and between school; quality of individual teachers regardless of background; adequate support at every level.

9 Tertiary Level

134 Definition   In this and the next chapter we interpret higher and further education as covering full- and part-time advanced courses in universities, including the Open University, polytechnics and other maintained grant aided or assisted institutions of higher and further education. 'Advanced' courses are broadly those which lead directly to qualifications of a higher standard than GCE A-Level or its equivalents. To comprehend the various elements of this sector of education more clearly it will be helpful to illustrate its elements statistically, particularly in view of the emphasis we place in chapter 11 on the importance of developing opportunities for the 16–19 age group of young people who do not move into universities, polytechnics and colleges of higher education.

135 Some statistics   In 1977/78 there were about 1,813,000* total student enrolments in major establishments of further education in England. Of these 472,400 were on full-time and sandwich courses, 24.5% of which were in polytechnics. 676,200 students were part-time day courses and 664,400 on evening only courses. In addition there were 280,500 full-time students in the universities of Great Britain and 66,100 students enrolled at the Open University. Projections for the future are uncertain, but it seems probable that numbers will not increase. By 1981/82, therefore, almost the only change now projected, in spite of the 'bulge' in the 18+ age group, will be the planned reduction in teacher training to be compensated by the provision of other advanced level courses. To accommodate student needs there are now 35 universities in England, including the Open University; 8 universities in Scotland and 1 federal university in Wales; 29 polytechnics in England; 14 central institutions (the polytechnic equivalent) in Scotland and 1 polytechnic in Wales. In England and Wales there are 621 major establishments of further education including former colleges of education. There are also many diverse further education institutions combining more limited provision of full-time advanced courses with other works such as part-time advanced courses, non-advanced courses or a combination. In Scotland the bulk of higher education courses outside the universities is provided in some 24 institutions and colleges of education. In addition, full-time advanced courses in Scotland are provided in 20 further education colleges, although again for the most part on a more limited scale.

136 Dance as an academic subject   Where dance is part of degree studies there are certain requirements. Degrees are predominantly concerned with the conceptual frameworks of a subject and students are led to an understanding of the methods of

---

*   Latest statistics available from the DES Statistics Branch summarised in *Trends in Education* Spring 1980

working within a distinctive area of knowledge. In the case of dance these frameworks are still in an early stage of development, hence the reluctance of some validating bodies to accept courses in dance. Training for professional standards of performance in any art form has been predominantly the concern of specialist vocational training schools which award diplomas.

'In American universities' Robert Cohan emphasised to us in committee, 'nothing changed until the teachers changed, becoming either professional dancers or trained in a professional studio. As long as dance stayed theoretical nothing happened. It is now generally accepted that a student goes to university to major in dance in order to join a professional company. University dance students should have the same opportunity to become practising artists as have students of the other arts.' The American experience has great relevance but it should be noted that dance studies in this country have not been purely theoretical because dance students in the maintained and private sectors have been training, respectively, to teach and to perform. Thus while the performing aspect of dance is central to its existence and might form the focus of a degree course, experience of dancing without the development of theoretical studies is unlikely to meet the requirements of a degree in the UK.

137 Educational value at tertiary level Since dance is, by its nature, choreographed, performed and appreciated, some awareness of this totality seems essential in degree studies, although specialisms might develop within degree studies. Courses of study which approach dance, for example, from a sociological or historical standpoint are valid in their own right and contribute in a particular way to an understanding of the subject. Similarly, courses which emphasise performance of modern dance forms and choreography are valid although distinct. The total range of provision over the UK as a whole ought, we suggest, to reflect the variety of ways of approaching the study of dance in order to provide an eclectic programme rather than a concentration in all institutions on the same form of dance studied in the same way. We accept, therefore — as do our colleagues in drama[1] and music[2] — the educational value of dance as a subject on a par with many other subjects traditionally regarded as a means of acquiring a trained intellect at tertiary level. This conviction may not yet be widely held in universities or in general educational thinking in this country but it is becoming increasingly accepted in polytechnics and colleges of higher education.

138 Dance in the universities We have identified seven universities in England, Scotland and Wales* where dance studies are undertaken in a significant way. The seven may be further sub-divided into those where undergraduate study occurs and those where post-graduate study is pursued. At Hull dance is well

---

* Although Northern Ireland lies outside our terms of reference it should be noted that dance is studied in relation to anthropology at Queen's University, Belfast.

established at undergraduate level in a drama department while Birmingham, Glasgow and Bristol are developing courses which link dance with drama. Glasgow has developed also a link with Scottish Ballet as a result of which movement classes, open to all students, are organised on campus and workshops are given by visiting companies. At post-graduate level Leeds has a well established MA course, while those at University of London, Goldsmiths' College and at Manchester are of more recent origin. Dance is accepted as a research area for MPhil and PhD degrees at Leeds, Goldsmiths' College and at Manchester. We are aware, of course, that in most drama departments, as in most vocational drama schools, dance and/or movement is a required subject, and we have been introduced to a considerable amount of student and extra-mural dance activity, some of it overlapping recognised studies to sustain a performance group, as has happened at Hull. One needs to distinguish therefore between the few universities where dance is part of the curriculum and those where dance is an extra-curricular activity.

139 Extra-curricular dance in universities

Three kinds of extra-curricular dance activity can be distinguished in British universities. There are student dance clubs financed by the students themselves, such as the ballet clubs of Oxford and Cambridge, often combining appreciation with the possibility of practical classes; extra-mural classes, usually in history and/or appreciation, organised by university extra-mural departments, like London, open to the public and to students; and recreative dance classes financed by university authorities or student unions. These are usually taught by outside teachers and are open to students as part of the campus facilities. In England and Wales such classes are usually in classical, modern or ballroom dancing. Leeds University is exceptional in having a hall of residence, Sadler Hall, which has an international reputation in folk dance. The Sadler Hall Folk Dance Group tours abroad regularly to participate in international festivals. In return, folk dance groups of many nationalities take part in an annual folk dance festival at Leeds University. Such activities indicate how firmly and successfully dance can become established within a university. In Scotland extra-curricular dance activity tends to concentrate on folk dance through Scottish or country dancing, which is also encouraged in the curriculum under the umbrella of Scottish studies. Indeed the practical study of Scottish dance is surely inseparable from Scottish studies wherever these take place. Edinburgh University has an active modern dance group and Glasgow University has a Mediaeval and Renaissance dance class organised by the Department of Adult and Continuing Education in association with the Drama Department. All this enriches university life and often places the student body ahead of staff and administrators so far as dance interest is concerned.

140 Dance development in universities

Thus there is a great deal of dance of one kind or another taking place in a number of British universities, suggesting untapped resources and possibilities in the university sector as a whole. Dance has not yet, however, gained widespread acceptance as an academic subject in its own right, although a case for dance in universities (see Appendix J) was generally well received by senior academics when presented by our chairman to a recent conference on universities and the arts.* Whilst the total number of university students has changed little in recent years, dance studies have continued to expand. There is, too, a growing amount of post-graduate study, including some at Leeds University which has proved very useful to this inquiry, as well as an amount of original research.[41] Finally, we know at least two universities which would have moved to establish a chair in dance had it not been for the current freeze on new appointments. We think that, ultimately, separate departments of dance, each with their own direction and character, will be as necessary to the proper development of dance in British academic and cultural life as they are already for the development of drama, music and fine art. Indeed students who opt for dance at a university will do so for reasons similar to those who opt for music and drama. They discover they are interested in dance and wish to pursue it further, as they would any other subject. Or they have pursued vocational study for some years to a point where physical development persuades them it would be better to look elsewhere than performance to continue their interest. Others will have a research, historical or literary objective. A few may have failed to make any contact with dance at school until discovering, almost too late, that it is a subject of consuming interest. For them, dance in one or other form of higher education is their only chance of catching up. It is reasonable to assert, however, that for the time being the number of performers entering the dance profession from universities will be small; that universities are likely to attract those with a wider motivation and those more academically minded; and that the broader educational base of university study could make a significant contribution to a deeper understanding of the nature of dance and its many manifestations in the theatre, in education and society in general.

141 Validation of courses in the non-university sector

However positive, if slow, might be the development of dance in universities, the real pace for change has been set by the polytechnics, by former colleagues of education merging with polytechnics, and by colleges of higher education seeking to diversify courses from a predominantly teacher training role. The polytechnics, urged Anthony Crosland in 1965, then Secretary of State for Education, should be distinguished by their 'social responses'. So far as dance is concerned, social response has provided the principal impetus. At the time of writing, dance is a *major* study at, for example, Middlesex Polytechnic, Leicester Polytechnic, Worcester College of Higher Education, Crewe & Alsager College of Higher Education, I M Marsh College in Liverpool Polytechnic and Dartington College of Arts. It is a *minor* study in a larger number of institutions. Some of the new courses have been validated by the Council for National Academic Awards (CNAA), some by universities. Some were validated in 1975, some will start only this year.

---

* Convened by the Arts Council of Great Britain at the University of East Anglia, 14–16 September, 1979.

All are diverse in character. Most of the major studies, for example, are for Creative or Performing Arts Degrees approved by the CNAA. But Worcester's course is for a Combined Studies Degree covering a wide range of academic subjects. At University of London, Goldsmiths' College and at other colleges such as the Roehampton Institute, undergraduate courses have been approved by the university. These lead to the BEd degree and to combined subject degrees, like the BHum. Similarly, courses at Bretton Hall and Trinity and All Saints' Colleges are approved by the University of Leeds. Account must be taken also of other new degree proposals, such as Recreational Studies, where dance has an important place as it does in older degrees like the BEd.

142 Evolution of CNAA courses

These developments have come about as a result of the contraction of teacher training; of the Government's demand to diversify courses referred to in the White Paper *Education: A Framework for Expansion*, December 1972, following the James Report;[42] through the example of liberal arts degrees in the USA;* and by the demands of students and teachers. Since the changes must influence significantly the status of dance in secondary schools and the further involvement of the dancing profession in higher education, it will be helpful to review their evolution. In 1974 the CNAA established a Creative and Performing Arts Panel to validate degrees in the perfoming arts. The following year the Panel was enhanced in status by becoming the Combined Studies (Creative and Performing Arts) Board. It is this Board which has validated the various creative and performing arts degrees which include dance as a major or minor subject of study. At the same time the Council also established a Movement and Dance Panel to validate degrees in dance and to be a point of reference for the validation of the dance element of combined degrees. In 1978 this became the Dance Board. It was the Dance Board which validated Britain's first BA Honours degree in dance at the Laban Centre for Movement and Dance.**

143 Purpose of degrees

The first honours degree in dance is only five years old so it is too soon to comment. It is possible that this kind of degree may be particularly suited to professional dance institutions aware that the teachers, or even some of the performers they produce need academic recognition. The aim is to provide a broad experience and additional opportunities to those whom the profession can accept on their merits as performers or teachers. Ultimately, professional dancers might take some kind of degree course as part of professional training, as is often

---

*   Courses including dance have developed at North American universities since the middle 1920s. Today at least 26 American/Canadian universities offer Master of Fine Arts and MEd in dance and at least 40 offer dance at BA level.

**   Chairman of the Combined Studies (Creative and Performing Arts) Board since its inception has been John Holden, and of the Dance Board, Peter Brinson. Membership of the Boards is reviewed and reconstituted through a 'rolling annual review' system.

the case now in the United States. The purpose of combined degrees is different, more resembling the experience of combined degrees involving dance in universities. To begin with the Combined Studies (Creative and Performing Arts) Board emphasises that these degrees are strictly 'academic', although it uses that word in a non-traditional manner. The Board is agreed, for example, that any course must contain a rationale and enough practice in at least one art for the student to gain an authentic experience of that art. The first requirement represents a large part of the course to which can be added options in support of the main study or studies. Thus what the Board looks for is a course structure in which the whole becomes greater than the sum of its parts. It is not a performance degree but a degree in the understanding of performance arts. It does not seek to produce performers, although some may emerge.

144 Staffing the new courses

The problem in developing these new courses is that staffing resources may not be available at the required level. In the former colleges of education, for example, expertise has been developed in teaching to honours level in dance as part of educational studies, but the growth of dance studies in other contexts requires rather different skills and experience. Undoubtedly dance staff resources could be strengthened in the polytechnics and colleges by drawing upon relevant expertise in other departments, but the most significant resource for the development of dance courses must lie within the dance teaching and dancing professions. Two conditions seem to be crucial. One is adequate and regular in-service training for existing dance staff, including further study and research opportunity; the other is the recruitment of tutors from the whole spectrum of the dance profession particularly for the choreographic and performance studies. This is why we have emphasised that the introduction of degrees involving dance would benefit from the experience of the dance profession. It is evident that dance in the theatre is playing a greater role in education, especially in higher education; and education, especially higher education, is taking a greater interest in the performing professions.

145 NATFHE's Dance Section

Linking dance staff in many of the higher and further education institutions discussed in this and the next two chapters is the Dance Section of the National Association of Teachers in Further and Higher Education (NATFHE). NATFHE itself has over 70,000 teacher members and one of its important functions is to provide opportunities for the pursuit and furtherance of academic and arts subject interests for its members. Most subjects taught in further and higher education have their own sectional membership and executive committee. The Dance Section like others is a recognised body directly accountable to its parent body through the Association's National Executive Committee. During the past six years, under the chairmanship of Gordon Curl, the Dance Section has set itself a number of published priorities. These include: to provide occasions which would forge links with artists in the professional world of dance — dancers, choreographers, dance adminis-

73

strators, critics and the like; to promote within schools and institutions of further and higher education the concept of dance as an art form in both its appreciative and participatory aspects; to search for the most appropriate means of initiating children into dance experience by harnessing creative and educational techniques with genuinely aesthetic aims; to encourage research and scholarship in the many allied aspects of dance — its criticism, history, philosophy and notation; to publish conference papers and seize any opportunity to contribute to national journals concerned with dance education; to lend active support to other bodies concerned to promote dance in education; to promote as far as possible some insight into the potential and practical problems of audio-visual media in film, video and other resources of benefit to dance education; to work towards the eventual publication of a Dance in Education journal which would lend some cohesion to all the activities of educators and administrators concerned with promoting dance as an art form. Many of these aims have begun to be realised and some indeed are reflected in our recommendations. Two of the most valuable developments have been the Section's growing contacts with the professional dance world and its many conferences, some attended by over 350 delegates. Conference reports have been published and distributed widely and many of the Section's members have undertaken research in dance leading to valuable new findings. There is little doubt also that during this period of drastic change in higher education the Section's work has served to provide a focus of continuity and a sense of direction for the future so far as dance is concerned.

146 Concerns for the future From this summary of dance courses in universities and those in the non-university sector we see four principal concerns about the future of dance in higher education. Our first concern is for a measure of rationalisation and co-ordination of new courses. Already, there is an imbalance between supply and demand in some of the merged colleges in the non-university sector. Complete rationalisation is probably not feasible nor even desirable, but there is need to avoid under- and over-provision of dance courses and to make effective use of limited resources of skilled and talented people. Second, we think there is need for those with professional performing experiences to be drawn into the higher and further education system for purposes explained above. Third, is the need to assess the structure and qualities of the new degrees involving dance and the direction in which they might best be developed. Following from all this evolves, fourthly, a need for continual consultation between degree-giving bodies and the dance profession as a whole.

147 Some implications In Britain many dance students in higher education may be primarily interested in the academic study of dance or have physical or technical limitations which may preclude a performing career. Nevertheless, any department whose dance syllabus includes a performance element is bound to require that all candidates for the course should have attained a reasonable performing standard on entry. This has significant implications for dance and dance teaching in secondary schools. Second, whether the course is a single honours degree involving dance or a combined honours degree course where dance is one of two, three or even four subjects studied, the result could lead to career opportunities in teaching, publishing, administration, management, criticism, dance journalism, dance direction or dance research, as well as performance. This will strengthen the world of dance in many areas where it is weak today and extend the study of the arts in higher education into areas where it was previously neglected. It follows that a major justification of higher education departments of dance, or departments involving dance, is their role as a forum for specialised work leading to research, performance and publication. This specialised work may well include work by former dancers who have entered as mature students without formal qualifications in the manner encouraged by the CNAA. Third, an examination of university and polytechnic prospectuses in dance indicates a great widening of the concept of dance. It includes now, ethnic dance, historical dance and the philosophy and aesthetics of dance as well as maintaining a proper balance between theory and practice. Hence there is a growing need for more specialists within dance. It follows they will require initial entry standards, unobtainable unless there is more attention to dance as a curriculum subject in primary and secondary schools. Fourth, the development of higher education studies in dance, music and drama carries further the pioneer work of the Summerson Committee[43] in gaining acceptance for visual arts degrees based on performance — as painter or sculptor for example — without course modifications or concessions in the cause of academic 'respectability'. Fifth, we think that higher education institutions, where dance is a major study, should consult and combine with colleagues in the dance profession to produce a journal for dance in higher education. Sixth, we believe it essential that these advances in the maintained and university sectors should be supported by research and study at post-graduate level. Therefore it is crucial to safeguard the few institutions and courses where this can take place in the present period of economic restriction. In England we identify especially the work being done at Leeds University within the Department of Physical Education and the Faculty of Arts Workshop Theatre MA Course in Drama. In Scotland we think Dunfermline College of Physical Education could become a centre for dance studies at tertiary level and explain our reasoning in the next chapter.

10 Teacher Education and Employment

148 A background of change

Our studies have had to take into account the general move towards a graduate profession as well as the widespread re-organisation in England and Wales, following reduction of teacher training to less than half that of the late 1960s. This re-organisation did not affect Scotland. 'The new system', observed our colleagues in the Gulbenkian Music Inquiry about the changes in England and Wales, 'is not the old system writ small'.[2] Some of the colleges which are being closed are known for the quality of their dance teacher training. The greater part of the remainder have merged with polytechnics or with other colleges of further or higher education to become institutes of higher education, or in a few cases, merged with universities. Over the next decade there will be at most about 17,000 new teachers a year entering the maintained sector in England and Wales compared with 30,000 to 40,000 a year during the decade 1965–1975. A quarter of these new teachers will be graduates in the traditional sense and the remainder will hold a Bachelor of Education degree or equivalent. During the next ten years the number of newly trained teachers will rarely reach 1 in 30 of the total number of teachers. For example, a large primary school with 10 teachers may get a newly trained teacher possibly once in three years. Thus any change in the quality of the teaching of dance in the maintained sector must depend largely upon an extension of the range and competence of existing teachers through induction and in-service training. This is why we identify initial teacher training followed by adequate in-service training as the key to the future of maintained dance education in Britain.

149 Our method of analysis and supporting research

To analyse this teacher training is not easy because of the process of re-organisation still taking place. We present it, therefore, in five stages. First, as it was before re-organisation – that is, the training with which the majority of dance teachers today are equipped. Second, as it is becoming since re-organisation – that is the training this new generation of graduate dance teachers will acquire. Third, a correlation between this teacher provision and the pupil needs we have described in previous chapters. Fourth, the nature of induction and in-service training as we see it. Fifth, our conclusions. In examining the maintained sector of teacher training we have been fortunate to be able to supplement helpful publications from the DES[44] and SED and our own survey of dance teaching by the National Foundation for Educational Research with a timely private study by Janet Adshead. Undertaken at the University of Leeds for the degree of Doctor of Philosophy (submission 1979), this private study examines the changing nature of dance in higher education and, in particular, changes in the curriculum in teachers' education. Janet Adshead's work has saved us much extra research since it is the most recent in its field and refers also to results from a supplementary investigation initiated during 1976 by the Dance Section of NATFHE in response to our appeal for evidence. We are grateful to the Dance Section and its Chairman, Gordon Curl, for this response.

150 The training of most dance teachers today

In 1975 there were some 170 colleges of education and physical education in Britain, 32 university departments of education and 8 specialist colleges of music, dance, speech and drama. These numbers include the 9 Scottish colleges of education, Dunfermline College of Physical Education and the Scottish School of Physical Education which is part of Jordanhill College of Education. Within these 212 institutions students could pursue studies leading to a Certificate of Education (conferring qualified teacher status), a diploma or a degree. The emphasis of the teaching qualifications could be towards primary, secondary or further education. In addition there were, and still are, special qualifications for teachers of certain categories of pupils such as the mentally or physically handicapped. Under this system the most usual training pattern for teachers of dance in maintained primary and secondary schools would be a three-year course in a college of education or college of physical education leading to the award of Certificate of Education. In the years following the Robbins report it became possible for students who had two GCE A-level passes on entry and/or who did well in the three-year course to continue for a fourth year of study for the award of BEd. This would be an honours degree in most instances. A small number of dance teachers will have attended one of a number of colleges concerned totally with the arts and offering two or three-year courses in dance and/or one of the other arts. These might be colleges in the maintained sector or colleges in the private sector described in chapter 18. These students would normally transfer for a fourth year of study in a college of education if they wished to qualify to teach in the maintained sector.

151 Dance in the Certificate of Education

Within this maintained teacher training system before re-organisation, most of today's teachers of dancing in the maintained sector will have studied dance in the colleges of education. Here it featured in varying amounts depending upon the particular strengths and interests of the college and its staff and on the place of dance within the awards offered. It could be a main subject for the student's own personal development for which the hours allocated in the colleges varied from 300–700 in the three years of the course. Or it could be a component of a Physical Education course with hours ranging from 22–300. As a curriculum subject within the professional courses concerned with preparation for teaching, the allocation of time to dance for the primary school course was 4–60 hours in three years, and for the secondary school course the average was 30 hours. Additional subsidiary courses of an optional nature were offered by many colleges, and in some colleges, dance clubs and dance circles operated in the evenings.

152 The re-organisation of teacher training

This maintained teacher training system has contracted as a result of the falling school population and has now been re-organised. The main effect of contraction on entry routes and training institutions is a reduction of the estimated number of places required for teacher education in England and Wales from 100,000 places in 1975/76 to 45,000 places at most by 1981. Of these, 35,000 will be for initial training and 10,000 for in-service training. Although this process has led already to announcements about the closure or merging of a number of colleges well known for training dance teachers, it is difficult as yet to estimate exactly what the current re-organisation of colleges will mean in terms of future places for dance training in England and Wales. The position in Scotland is much the same, although less complex, because there are only two specialist institutions of physical education. Even so it is very difficult to predict numbers reliably because unit systems are still developing and their effect on under-graduate choice is not altogether certain.

153 Possible need for further rationalisation

In all three countries, therefore, there is a need to obtain information which would relate demand and supply in the maintained sector taking into account whatever remains of the places now available in the non-maintained institutions of the private sector, described in chapter 18. Some process of further rationalisation may be necessary taking into account two trends already visible. First is the influence of falling school rolls. A reduction of 2,000,000 children in the next decade and a half suggests that demand for dance teachers, even if the amount of dance in schools increases, is unlikely to rise above 1976 levels. It may well fall, whatever the path of entry into teaching and wherever the place of training. Second is a change in the nature of training institutions due to mergers, federations and associations. The traditional monotechnic college of education or college of physical education, concerned solely with teacher education, will largely disappear, replaced by the multi-purpose college of higher education or polytechnic. In particular the traditional link between colleges of education and universities for validation purposes is being replaced in many instances by validation of courses through the CNAA. The impact of this validation upon the nature of courses needs to be monitored and evaluated.

154 The new training of dance teachers

With the disappearance of the Certificate of Education (as a consequence of the move to an all graduate profession), a variety of other awards and courses are coming into existence, offered by the new training institutions described above. These new degree and diploma courses have, as a principal feature, a greater flexibility within the structure which allows students a wider choice than before. In addition, commitment to a profession may be delayed or changed during higher education. This makes an estimation of the number of future dance teachers and the depth of their experience particularly difficult. The three and four-year BEd courses allow a student to select a greater or lesser emphasis on different subjects, but within a framework of three main areas: education; professional studies and teaching practice; and other subjects. Specific preparation for teaching dance occurs within professional studies in varying amounts according to the age range and degree of specialisation. Sometimes the study of dance as a subject in its own right occurs under the broad heading of Human Movement Studies. In relatively few cases does it appear within arts-based courses. In direct contrast, new diploma and non-teaching degrees tend to locate dance within the arts. These are the courses described in the previous chapter leading to Combined Subject degrees or degrees in the Performing Arts, usually validated by the CNAA.

155 A wider notion of dance

Interviews conducted by Janet Adshead with college dance tutors, and information derived from course syllabi, reveal that with the restructuring of courses there has been an opportunity to extend from the Laban-derived modern educational dance, which was the basis of teaching before the re-organisation, to a wider range of study. Although the aims of various courses (eg BA or BEd) may differ fundamentally, yet, at the level of a student's personal education, the main objectives are seen to be the development of a sympathetic attitude towards dance, involvement in the activity of dance and in creating dances, appreciation of dance and the understanding of its structure. Nowadays the dance taught is more clearly identifiable as an art form. Modern dance constitutes the core of practical and theoretical study, supplemented in some instances by other forms of dance where these can be seen to contribute to a convincing whole.

156 The main curriculum areas

The main curriculum areas identified by Janet Adshead are: movement studies; observation, recording and notation; dance technique; choreography; aesthetics; dance and the arts; history of dance; dance in society; dance in education. The extent to which these aspects are studied in each institution depends upon the time available and the strength and interests of staff and students in relation to the broad aims of the course. Of considerable concern in all courses, however, is the lack of suitable scholarly texts and resource materials of every kind at all levels. Slides, video and film material are inadequate. One way to improve the situation might be to establish selected institutions as resource centres for their regions, giving them help to duplicate slides and other material and, of course, the appointment of appropriate technicians. This service would need to be supported by a national resource centre operating in consultation with dance teachers in both sectors. The establishment of some such centre is a matter of urgency.

157 Problems of courses and standards

The place of dance within institutions primarily concerned with teacher education has changed considerably during the period of this study. The number of institutions with separate dance departments has been reduced as the result of pressures for viability. Increasingly dance is to be found within arts departments or broadly based human movement studies. While many dance lecturers seem to welcome the move to the arts, the new courses do not seem to have been able to resolve three areas of weakness we have observed and our inquiries have confirmed.

7

These concern the diversity of course content and the widely differing standards of achievement; the amount of time allocated to practical training; and the relationship of courses to the needs and expectations of the schools where the students will later be employed. To combat these weaknesses there is need, we think, for a clarification of aims, for the establishment of a common basic structure to courses, including an agreed minimum practical component, and for the opportunity to make the comparison of achievement necessary to the raising of standards. The nature of the training should be correlated with the variety of needs which have emerged from our study of primary and secondary levels in chapters 7 and 8. The range of preparation which teachers require today to meet these needs implies a corresponding rise in the calibre of lecturers in the training institutions to achieve a raising of standards throughout the profession.

158 Dance training of primary and middle school student teachers

We have shown in chapter 7 how teachers in primary and middle schools are required usually to teach all subjects. In their training, therefore, much time is devoted to the demands of teaching for literacy and numeracy. It is evident that many future teachers of these age groups are given little help in relation to the teaching of dance and/or movement. If dance is to be improved at primary level it should receive more attention in the training of the general class teacher. It is desirable that such teachers should have had some dance experience while themselves at secondary school, and that more time should be devoted to dance during training and in induction courses, to build confidence as well as knowledge. Some middle schools, on the other hand, are recruiting teachers with expertise in a related group of subjects such as dance and drama, as well as the class teacher who covers all aspects of the curriculum. Since such teachers often take a central and initiating role in team teaching and may be responsible for the dance component of school productions, their training should take account of the extra knowledge required to fulfil these functions adequately.

159 Dance training of secondary school student teachers

Secondary schools, senior high schools, and so on are characterised by their specialist teachers. Therefore, any student training to teach dance at this level should have a highly specialised education in dance. As in other subjects in the curriculum, it might be, for example, that in future, students wishing to train as teachers of dance should provide evidence of appropriate dance education before acceptance on teacher training courses. There is some evidence that entry requirements are beginning to reflect this new thinking, which is in line with the wider notion of dance courses referred to in paragraph 155 above. The new thinking, however, carries a number of implications for the training of dance teachers at secondary level which we would like to see embodied in training courses. First, future dance teachers, being specialists, need to be seen to have mastered their instrument (the body) just as a teacher of music is expected to have mastered the piano or violin. This can be achieved only if more time is given to practical work than is usually the case now in training. Complementing this requirement is a need to master theory and history, to acquire a wide dance culture as as performers and spectators and to become expert as teachers able to educate young people in dance. This requires more time as well as more instruction in the methodologies of teaching dance and the construction of dance curricula. Teaching dance at secondary level includes, in our view, an ability to apply elements of dance composition, to identify and know how to help talented children and inspire children in their class by communicating relevant dance experience and explaining the value of what they are doing. It follows that the teachers need to be reasonably expert in at least one dance form and, know something of others selected from modern, classical, ethnic, folk, historical and popular dance.

160 Involving professional dancers

One way to strengthen the practice of dance in teacher training institutions is to develop more regular contact with the dance profession during the process of training. We know that regular contact is not an easy matter, but we think it essential in order to raise practical standards. It can be done in two ways. First, is the exposure of student dance teachers to many more professional performances of all kinds of dance. This can be done through visits to outside theatres where possible and/or the visits of professional companies to training institutions. Financial arrangements to make this possible can be made to link with other activities of the company in the district during a visit. The other way is to develop the practice of professional dancers-in-residence. In short, we think the raising of standards throughout the dance teaching profession requires a regular contact with the dance profession which ought to become a continuing concern for those who organise the training of future dance teachers.

161 Need for re-thinking

We realise that the suggestions offered so far in this chapter imply considerable, even radical, re-thinking of the training of teachers of dance at primary and secondary levels in England, Scotland and Wales. This is not a criticism of existing methods. It is a practical, pragmatic conclusion from the tremendous changes taking place in all teacher training and in the non-university sector of tertiary education. The changes require as much response from teachers of dance as from teachers in every other subject area. They provide, therefore, an opportunity for re-thinking within the general context of teacher training such as has not existed for many years, and which ought not to be missed. Such re-thinking, we feel, must be initiated at the highest level and involve the dance teaching profession alongside those responsible at the DES, the SED, the Schools Council, the Consultative Committee on the Curriculum and the Local Education Authorities. It should range over long and short term policies which take into account proposals already made in this chapter, especially in paragraphs 158 and 159, and which embrace additional considerations below.

162 Long term policy for courses

The range of courses now available suggests that certain criteria should be met if courses are to be successful. First, where dance is part of a degree course — a BEd, BA, BHum and so on — it should be available as a study in depth as well as one among two or three other arts, whether combined or integrated. If dance lies at the core it will become inevitable that knowledge of dance will deepen an awareness of its relationships to other arts. The same is true, of course, of any other art taken as the core. Second, emphasising a point made several times already, the practice of dance is essential. Third, with the increasing knowledge which a three or four-year course can give, further aspects of dance can be introduced giving students opportunity to follow individual interests, including dance composition. All this requires time, making it important that opportunities should be provided for students to extend their knowledge and experience in extra-curricular dance activities of all kinds.

163 Need for post-graduate qualifications

With the development of courses it follows there will be a need to foster the growth of scholarship and professional expertise especially in two areas: among those who are training new teachers in colleges and polytechnics, and among institutions of training. We think it should become established that lecturers in colleges and polytechnics will need to have had all the experience as teachers outlined above and also hold a post-graduate qualification. The possibilities for acquiring this qualification now exist, for example, through the post-graduate work of the Department of Physical Education at Leeds University. This University has developed post-graduate studies in dance since 1972, mostly for students who are lecturers in colleges and institutes of higher education, although some students proceed straight from first degree to the MA course. Of the 48 students entering the course between 1972 and 1979, all with good honours degrees or equivalents, 28 were college of education lecturers or senior lecturers, 4 were principals or heads of departments and 16 were students or school teachers. On leaving, 13 went into schools, 29 went into colleges of education as lecturers, senior lecturers, heads of department or, in one case, deputy principal, one to be local education authority adviser and the remainder into research or university lecturing. This includes a number of students from overseas. The possibility is well established in Britain, therefore, to acquire a post-graduate qualification in dance, and strengthens our arguments in the previous chapter to support this work at Leeds University.

164 Long term policy for institutions

We think the aim in each institution should be to create a team of dance tutors, each having a particular expertise in dance, able to offer a variety of dance courses at least to degree level. To make this more possible we think that, in co-ordinating plans for future provision in consultation with the DES and SED, each region should ensure that it retains in its local institutions an adequate source of expertise in subject areas such as dance; and also that existing provision of specialised or expensive resources and facilities is not dissipated but concentrated in particular institutions and used as fully as possible for these subjects.[45] We believe, however, that such centres should develop from local strengths rather than be imposed from outside and that they should consist of a network of co-ordinated provision rather than a simple list

82

of individual institutions. Little or no extra expenditure will be involved. A large number of colleges are being closed or merged. There exist, in relative abundance in buildings up and down the country, special studios, theatres and halls, lighting equipment, sound equipment and technicians. At a time of cuts and economies it is essential that these resources be identified as rapidly as possible so that the specialist institutions can be maintained, or created, and designated so that dance quality and geographical spread are taken equally into account, and the interests of dance are treated fairly.

165 Illustration of a regional centre

We believe the development of such regional centres is important and so ought not to be too long term an objective. They will be realised in different ways according to local possibilities. Therefore an illustration of what we have in mind might be helpful. Dunfermline College of Physical Education, near Edinburgh, has manifested for some time a growing role as a focus for the development of dance in Scotland in a number of directions. It has always been a major influence for dance in Scottish education, providing regular in-service courses in various styles of dance related to primary and secondary education. At tertiary level it offers a dance specialism under the CNAA, following its BEd degree course in physical education. During the last decade it has broadened this work by developing connections with a wide range of organisations such as Scottish Ballet, the Theatre Workshop in Edinburgh, Basic Space, the Academy of Ballet, Strathclyde University and the School of Scottish Studies, Edinburgh University. This ecumenical approach has led students and staff of the college into community dance — a two year project, funded by MSC, to work with adults and children in schools, hospitals, community centres, universities and the like; encouraged special study and research projects; created many performance opportunities for members of the college and students in schools; brought about close and continuing contacts with professional companies from Scotland, England and Wales; and stimulated combined studies with other departments, resulting, for example, in the production of two films.* Among current special projects is research into the dance of the people of Barra and a study of the dance and dance music of the Faroe and Shetland Islands including a conference at the College in collaboration with the School of Scottish Studies.

166 Need for development

It is not surprising, therefore, that there has been a marked increase in recent years in the number of appeals to the College for information and advice on dance matters. There appears to be a need for a consultancy service and/or a resource centre. With this in mind the College has begun negotiations with the Scottish Arts Council, the Sports Council, and District and Regional Authorities to strengthen its facilities and capacity to provide the help which seems to be needed to assist

---

* One film on the Billingham Folk Festival with commentary; the other a tribute to Rudolf Laban using biographical and archival material including an interview with Lisa Ullmann and a performance by final year students.

dance in Scottish society generally, as well as dance in Scottish education, at both amateur and professional levels. It feels there are two needs in particular to be met. One is to extend provision for modern and indigenous dance in Scotland to balance Scottish achievements in classical ballet. The other is to develop a resource centre of visual and other teaching aids of all kinds to assist teachers and encourage dance study and dialogue. Such ideas illustrate the service one kind of regional centre might provide. Others may do things differently to meet varying regional needs. Nevertheless the experience of Dunfermline demonstrates powerfully, we think, the possibilities within the idea of developing regional centres out of existing local centres of quality.

167 Short term policy, in-service education

Short term training policies will concentrate naturally on in-service education. This is for those who already have experience of teaching and can concentrate upon developing and gaining further dance knowledge. Pre-service training really has two elements: personal education in the discipline, in this case dance, and professional education, that is, pedagogy. Logically, these two elements should be continued in in-service training but at present this is not done with enough consistency in any of the three countries. This is especially important for the arts where participation is vital. Development is necessary, therefore, and should take into account the changing requirements of schools, changing ideas of dance among young teachers and their students and the desirability of closer links between professional dancers and dance educators to help meet these changes.

168 Need for expansion

Authority to make provision of this kind exists in the relevant Education Acts, but much more is needed for dance teachers so that some structure will be needed to make the best use of expert resources. This is essential if the standard and quality of the teaching of dance is to be improved at a time when the teaching force is relatively static. Proportionately greater resources need to be directed to this end, including greater willingness to grant secondment and to use the experience of professional dancers. There is scope both in teachers' mode of attendance for in-service education and in the type of institution providing in-service courses. Whatever method is followed, however, we think it should be supported by regular seminars on dance for head teachers. In this connection we welcome particularly the development of dance centres as a valuable resource and stimulus for improving the quality of dance teaching and discussion, provided the courses for teachers can be related to the needs of their schools.

169 Importance of adequate resources

Lastly, we wish to emphasise the importance of adequate facilities and resources at every level of teacher training if standards are to be raised. Not only should these be of a high standard, but the institution should offer a genuine example of the dance atmosphere it is hoped the students will create once they become teachers. Assuming adequate classrooms for pedagogic training, the facilities should allow, as a minimum, regular dance technique classes throughout the course;

frequent choreographic opportunities; significant study of music with choice of instruments; study of dance theory, dance history, aesthetics, and consequently a wide dance culture. Dance teachers, after all, will help create the dance atmosphere of the schools; they will provide the means by which the talented will be identified and helped; it will be they who liaise with the advisory teachers, the peripatetic teachers, the dance centres, Saturday dance schools, youth dance groups and other ventures disseminating ideas and experience. It follows, therefore, that while most, if not all, colleges where teachers of any kind — especially primary school teachers — are trained should be able to provide dance 'minor' options (since many non-dance specialists will rightly want to 'do' dance as they do drama or history or mathematics), a small number of institutions must specialise in the complex and difficult task of training dance teachers through major options.

170 Special nature of teachers of dancing

We realise that even if what we suggest were to be implemented at once and to the letter, gifted teachers of dance would not thereby be created in large numbers. To be a gifted teacher is difficult enough; to be a gifted dancer no less so. To be a gifted teacher of dance is especially difficult because such teaching requires at least some ability as both teacher and dancer. The degree of dance ability needed will vary with circumstances, but the minimum is to know the nature of the body, how it works/dances, and how to move and motivate it. This experience cannot be acquired except by doing. Thereafter the teacher of dancing has to communicate this bodily knowledge and arouse a motivation to acquire it. It is the extra dimension of the body which makes the good teacher of dance so special, so difficult to train, and so worth the effort to re-think and improve our methods so as to produce teachers who can help children acquire the qualities of movement, art and communication which come from dancing.

11 Full-time and Part-time Continuing Education

171 Arts and education linked in continuing education

'The test of education', said a Government Report in 1919, 'is not what children do in school, but what men and women enjoy out of it'.[46] A quarter of a century later the 1944 Education Act required local authorities not only to provide education for persons over compulsory school age but also to provide 'organised cultural training and recreative activities'. 'The language is unfortunate' remarked Sir Roy Shaw, Secretary General of the Arts Council,[47] 'but the intention is clear'. He went on to show how 'the great spur to closer co-operation' today between the arts and adult education comes not from the Russell Report of 1973[48] but the Redcliffe-Maud Report of 1976.[13] 'We must reject the long-established fallacy' wrote Lord Redcliffe-Maud, 'that 'arts support' and 'education' are two separate things. More positively, we must insist that those responsible for them are natural allies and see to it that they collaborate at national, regional and local levels.'

172 Dance and 16–19 year olds

This view of the interdependence of arts and education is one which we accept and apply to dance in this chapter. It is supported not only by the Russell and Alexander[49] Reports, but by those responsible for developing adult and continuing education,[50] community education,[51] and education through broadcasting.[52] Together they illustrate the growing public pressure to offer all people, young and old, through further education, the opportunities which the Robbins Report opened to those qualified for a university education. We are concerned particularly, of course, with ensuring for the 16–19 year olds a proper provision of dance within the broader range of courses now argued in many quarters for post-16 education generally.[53] The needs of the 2,000,000 young people in this age group in Britain are naturally diverse. The range of provision needs to be equally diverse 'so that no one group should suffer from a lack of suitable opportunity'.[54] For dance training the age of 16 can constitute a vital last opportunity for anyone coming late to dance, or deciding to pursue more intensively an interest aroused at school.

173 Three aspects of continuing education

In considering the extension of educational opportunity to dance in this way, therefore, we need to approach the problem through its three currently accepted aspects of further, adult and community education. The aspects are linked, as indeed they should be, with tertiary education. They are linked, too, in common adversity arising from cutbacks in education. To prevent these cutbacks endangering future development, particularly of adult education, we have kept in mind two courses of action necessary to the achievement of all we argue in this chapter. The first is to impress upon local education authorities, who have discretion in this matter, the increasingly significant role of continuing education in shaping the future of our society and therefore the need to sustain it at a level comparable with other education. The second is the benefit which can come from co-operation between relevant bodies and from the re-deployment of available resources. This last is a part of the remit of the Advisory Council for Adult and Continuing Education with whom dance organisations should press their case. Help can come also from co-operation between dance institutions of the maintained and non-maintained sectors.

174 Dance in full-time further education

The most rapidly developed of these aspects in recent years is that of further education, particularly in relation to the Training Services Agency. We have noted that it is possible in some instances today to pursue an interest in dance from primary school through secondary school to degree study at tertiary level. While the possibility is real, if still exceptional, it is certainly a happy extension into dance of the guiding principles of the Robbins Report. It applies, however, only to the 14% of 18 year olds who move into higher education. It does not apply to the remaining 86% among whom are the part-time students who comprise the vast majority of students in post-school education today. Since interest in dance is growing among young people, there needs to be provision even in the present economic climate for students in post-school education who wish to continue an interest in dance or who acquire that interest after leaving school and cannot afford private lessons. This provision needs to be supported by better information than usually exists today from local education authorities and Schools Careers Services.

175 Main institutions

The most numerous of the institutions able to make this provision are the 600 or so major establishments of further education in England and Wales, and the 100 similar institutions in Scotland, responsible for the development of non-advanced further education. Together they illustrate the extraordinary diversity of the further education sector, both in level of studies, courses offered, modes of attendance and in the opportunity to develop a dance interest.[55] It is important for the dance teaching profession in the maintained and non-maintained sectors to continue pressure to ensure that this range of non-advanced further education includes adequate provision of dance opportunities in each local authority area, with properly qualified teachers. Such opportunities are most likely to be developed through the initiative and pressure of local teachers of dancing and their organisations according to local circumstances, or through collaboration between the maintained and non-maintained sectors. An example is to hand.

176 The Rambert Academy scheme

In the autumn of 1979 the Rambert Academy was launched as a special scheme in conjunction with the department of movement studies of the West London Institute of Higher Education. The scheme is thus a collaboration between the Institute and Ballet Rambert offering courses designed for gifted young people, aged 16 to 20+. The courses will provide an opportunity, not before available in the maintained sector, for a professional training in dance combined with opportunities for study to A-level standard, giving rise to the possibility of a graduate and/or other professional qualifications which may lead to a variety of career opportunities. Professional dance training will be provided through a two-year foundation course in dance. Entry to this will be by audition and interview normally supported by at least 5 GCE O-levels. It is estimated there will be a maximum of 30 students in each two-year course. This foundation course might provide the opportunity of a professional career in dance for at least some students. For others it might offer the basis for expression in one of two directions. Either, a three-year degree course in dance combined with one of the subjects available to the Institute for a BHum degree or as part of a programme for a degree in Performing Arts. Or, a three-year degree course in dance combined with a professional course available in the Institute such as business studies, secretarial, and the like.

177 Significance of the Rambert scheme The essential element here is collaboration between a professional dance company able to provide expert dance tuition and/or guidance, and an institute of higher education in the maintained sector able to provide academic tuition including, where necessary, courses leading to A-level qualifications. The advantage to the company is the possibility of recruiting a gifted student educated and trained in a style the company has helped to form. The advantage to the West London Institute is an extension of its movement studies in the area of the performing arts and an increase of its contribution to Government plans for helping talented young people aged 16–19. The advantage to the student is the possibility of a professional training in dance combined with other options, albeit not as yet with the help of a mandatory grant. The advantage to dance in further education and dance in Britain as a whole is a significant model for the development of training for professional dance within the maintained sector. Significant, too, is the demonstration it provides of a way in which further education can involve professional vocational teachers to help late starters, particularly important at the present time.

178 Need for a broader conception Underlying this Rambert experiment is a broader than usual conception of further education. The post-school situation of young people today plainly requires such a concept. Indeed, we argued it in chapter 1. But the Rambert experiment is only one solution. There can be other strategies. A specific private dance school of good repute could be designated as a regional centre in the way we suggest in paragraph 275. There could be co-operation between this school, providing dance training, and schools or colleges of the region providing academic subjects. There is, too, a case for using spare physical capacity in the education system to develop previously under-supported subjects such as dance.

179 European example The case for a broader approach is strengthened through the experience of some West European countries quoted in chapter 5. Clearly, any strategy which faces up to the structural nature of unemployment must of necessity include extensive re-education and training schemes throughout major sectors of the economy. During the last five years

West Germany, France, Sweden and Belgium have all responded to this problem through legislation which guarantees paid educational leave. The precise nature of the entitlement and provision of leave varies from country to country. In West Germany it is seen as an introduction to social, civic and cultural education; in France as an instrument for achieving full economic growth. More significantly perhaps, West European legislation has given access to education for the working population to an extent more than twice that of the United Kingdom. In the United Kingdom total provision for adult education and training, including industrial training through the MSC, reaches no more than 6% of the population. In West Germany 18% of the work-force enjoys paid educational leave; in Sweden 25%. It is hard to believe, then, that Britain will not need to move in some similar direction in its fight against structural unemployment. When it does so it will be important to include the arts within the legislation, partly for those who wish to seek their livelihood in this field, partly for the many more whose personal lives and leisure will be enriched through the experience. We believe, therefore, that the MSC, the Training Services Agency and their related schemes should broaden their definition of training in or through further education to include training for the arts and arts related careers. Such training should include helping young people to acquire a critical framework through which they can formulate better their aspirations and understand their own career potential.

180 Expansion of dance to include ethnic dance

If further education is extended in directions indicated by European experience, there will need to be consultations between dance organisations in the private sector, the DES, the SED, local education authorities and other bodies,[56] supported by exploratory studies and pilot schemes. By 'dance' we do not just mean classical ballet, forms of modern dance, jazz or tap. We mean all the dance which pertains to a multi-cultural society. Therefore ethnic dance study, with its potential for fostering racial understanding, should form an especially important part of dance in further education involving collaboration between the dancing profession and teachers of dancing in the maintained and non-maintained sectors. We are glad to note a development in recent years of ethnic dance classes among physical education courses, provided, for example, by adult colleges; also more specific studies at some maintained institutions of higher education.*

181 Dance in adult education

The second aspect of continuing education is adult education.[57] Today, adult education** has expanded beyond concern for teaching a subject or acquiring a skill for its own sake or for the purpose of getting a job. Adult education provides now a wide range of personal and social education. It is an essential part of continuing education likely to exert

---

*   Such as the work of the Academy of Indian Dance at the Polytechnic of Central London. See paragraph 303.

**   We are especially indebted in this section to a paper by Derek Buchanan, deputy director of the National Institute of Adult Education (England and Wales). The conclusions and recommendations, however, are our own.

growing influence from the 1980s onwards. 'Research shows that about 6% of the adult population is likely to be following adult education courses at some time or another.' Much of this opportunity, moreover, is provided not in the ad hoc manner of an outdated adult education image, but in adult education centres offering many courses identical in all respects to those provided in further education colleges. The ILEA's adult education centres, for example, employ a relatively large number of teachers of dance for whom minimum qualifications are laid down in various forms of social dancing such as Latin American, ballroom, sequence (Old Time) and other styles.

182 Need for review of dance in adult education

We need, therefore, to review the possibilities of dance in adult education. What kinds of dance should be provided and what resources will be required? There are still negative attitudes to dance which need to be overcome. These are the results of an education which in the past has tended to devalue the arts, giving expressive and creative activities low priority and status. On the other hand, social dancing classes maintain their popularity and offer the opportunity to meet a variety of people, to gain competence in a simple dance style and to enjoy an active response to the popular music of the day. For women, in particular, there is great and increasing interest in the movement and dance classes which form part of the programme of almost every evening institute in the country. Classes are taught by teachers trained in the methods of the Medau Society, the Keep Fit Association, Margaret Morris, the Women's League of Health and Beauty and the Dalcroze Society, as well as those trained in classical ballet, modern dance, jazz, tap and folk dance. Of particular importance, we believe, is the recreational value of such activities. This is often underestimated or ignored by administrators and funders. Yet figures show that a very large number of men and women – in excess of 2,000,000 a year – choose to participate. These figures indicate the very real deprivation which would result if recreational and non-vocational courses of this nature are withdrawn as a result of educational cutback. It is important, therefore, for organisations concerned* to come together to protect the considerable contribution made by movement and dance to the cultural life of the community. They need especially to disseminate[58] more information about the range of disciplines subsumed under movement and dance. The Sports Council has given a valuable lead in such dissemination, but much more remains to be done.

183 Dance appreciation

A number of adult education classes are offered in dance appreciation – particularly through university extra-mural departments – often coupled with theatre visits, live demonstrations or the viewing of films

---

* Organisations we have in mind, besides the Sports Council, are the Movement and Dance Committee of the Central Council for Physical Recreation, the Keep Fit Association, the English Folk Dance and Song Society, Medau Society, Margaret Morris Movement, the Physical Education Association, and the Women's League of Health and Beauty in their English and Scottish versions.

or video tapes. The style and form of the Royal Ballet's Ballet for All company, for example, arose out of such dance appreciation classes, sometimes using live demonstrations, sponsored by the Oxford University extra-mural department in the early 1960s. Adult education can encourage this kind of experience particularly well, provided there is proper preparation and follow-up, a sufficient availability of dance to be seen, and/or an adequate provision of films and video tapes with appropriate exhibition facilities. Preparation and follow-up would benefit, of course, from live demonstrations if only by one or two dancers. This is where the education world again needs expensive visual resources best provided through the central teaching resource centre suggested in paragraph 156. Films, videos, books, slides and notation, constitute an essential literature of dance education needed at every level and enriched through international exchange. Such education is threatened, like so much else, by educational cutback, yet it is an important means of realising the full value in audience terms of subsidies to the performing arts. It needs to be protected, therefore, not only by some redeployment of educational resources, but also by some redeployment of the educational activity undertaken by professional dance companies. Professional companies are as concerned as anyone to develop the educated spectator whose characteristics are discrimination, judgement and the ability to interpret with imagination, feelings, thoughts and images on stage. To know how to watch is to learn to be involved and stimulated throughout life.

184 Need for teachers

Possibilities in adult education, given the will and imagination, show dance taking its place within a range of subjects any of which may be the means to personal and social development through an increase in self-confidence (from mastering a skill) and therefore an improved self-image. Thus dance has its own valid contribution to make to the broad purpose of personal and social development which is the aim of adult education today. It is a contribution often underestimated by those responsible for providing courses and therefore under-funded and under-resourced. Often, too, it lacks teachers whose own dance experience enables them to link theory with practice, the appreciation of dance with its performance. Teachers able to teach dance in this way in adult and further education will emerge, we hope, from the new courses in performance arts and combined arts in universities and polytechnics described in chapter 9, or from teaching courses for professional dancers in the private sector described in chapter 18. Because of lack of adequate provision in the past, however, dance will need to receive particular attention in any development plans arising from the recommendations of the Advisory Council for Adult and Continuing Education. Extra provision is needed not only in teachers but in space and visual aids.

185 Dance in community education

Community education encompasses adult education and the youth service, co-ordinating the work of the statutory and voluntary bodies, working with all ages in their leisure time. 'Community' remarked the chief education officer for Birmingham, 'is a useful descriptive word which says no more than that people come together and find personal satisfaction and fulfilment through group activities with the strong implication that this will include the acquisition and development of skills.'[59] This area has a tremendous potential for supporting opportunities for the continued development of people of all ages and so complementing the work of the schools and colleges and for making 'second chance' opportunities possible for those young people who have not continued to further or higher education. The best kind of provision, in our view, would be within continuing education whereby the experience of dance, whether gained in full-time education or newly acquired in further education, could be complemented and continued through recurrent opportunities to practise and study during the rest of life. Essential would be provision to *see* dance of as many different kinds as possible and to experience dance at whatever practical level is appropriate. This would include opportunities for performance.

186 Importance of the 'second chance'

Already a variety of initiatives have been taken by voluntary and statutory organisations, combining private and statutory youth service funds. From a request to find finance for a promising young dancer in classical ballet, the Inter-Action Centre in North London has developed the idea of the Weekend Arts College offering tuition in classical ballet, mime, jazz and contemporary dance, leading eventually to other arts such as music and drama. The Weekend College offers opportunities for serious study to children and teenagers and is already over-subscribed. Similar ventures in London are the Islington Dance Factory and London Youth Dance Theatre. The Islington Dance Factory was created to give children in a deprived area the opportunity to study classical dance, and has developed classes in a variety of dance styles, creative workshops and performance experience for people of all ages. Members are involved in local festivals, national and international dance exchanges. The London Youth Dance Theatre was initiated by the dance department of the Tower Hamlets School in East London to provide serious performance opportunities for dedicated teenagers. They now offer a wide variety of classes of all grades and styles to children and teenagers; create their own new dance works as well as those commissioned from professional choreographers; work closely with professional and school orchestras; and have created a dance ensemble of impressive standard able to give seasons of public performance. These are but a few examples of initiatives made possible by the collaboration of voluntary and statutory effort they also rely heavily on the time and expertise of interested, enthusiastic professional dancers and teachers of dance.

187 Role of weekend arts colleges and community arts projects

Clearly these initiatives are applicable to all inner city areas and might help to mitigate the lack of dance opportunity suffered by children in these areas. This lack of opportunity does not mean necessarily a lack of dancing time in maintained comprehensive schools. It *may* mean dance opportunity for those who have never danced before. It *can*

92

mean also an opportunity to develop special skills which cannot be developed in schools which have to cater for the majority of average ability pupils. Weekend arts colleges and community arts projects, publicly or privately funded, can provide the professional atmosphere, techniques, discipline and private tuition which are now the prerogative of youngsters from richer families but which are essential to any young person seeking vocational training or further education in the performing arts. Thus community education and the community centre are seen to be a vital part of all continuing education.

188 Provision
of resources

Extra dance opportunities, however, whether in weekend arts colleges or elsewhere, require resources. Available resources, in fact, are considerable. They include the further and adult education structures to which we have referred. Supplementing these structures is growing provision by the Sports Council, especially through its new Regional Councils, and by enlarged local government departments of social services, and recreation and leisure, as well as education. Since the reorganisation of local government these enlarged departments have had more opportunity and more resources to appoint dance teachers and introduce dance classes for recreational and community purposes. Sometimes, though not always, the problem is lack of facilities or lack of know-how by the departmental officer concerned rather than a lack of willingness to make such provision if the demand is there. Within the Youth Service and voluntary youth organisations we have noted, too, encouraging signs of a growing interest in the arts to supplement more traditional provision of various forms of physical outlet. The National Conference on Youth, held at Wembley in 1977, gave significant impetus to this movement, but, even before the Conference drew attention to the importance of the arts for young people,[60] the National Association of Youth Clubs, the National Association of Boys' Clubs, the London Federation of Boys' Clubs and the London Union of Youth Clubs, as well as other youth organisations and the statutory Youth Service, had begun to appoint arts specialists or advisers of various kinds. A number of youth dance groups have begun to appear, equivalent to the youth orchestras and youth theatres now established in many areas. It follows that local authorities should give every encouragement* to youth dance groups, matching that given to youth orchestras and theatre groups, including professional advice and help in production skills.

189 Teaching
needs in youth
and community
education

If this movement is to flourish, it will require not only local authority encouragement of a very practical kind, but also new programmes of challenging in-service training for established youth and community workers and officers, together with special preparation of dance specialists to play their part in expanding provision. In-service training will need to provide some exposure to the possibilities of experiential

---

* An important development is a Festival of Youth Dance organised by the Leicestershire Education Authority and Gulbenkian Foundation for September 1980. It is hoped this will inaugurate such festivals as an annual event.

and enactive learning, to broaden the consciousness, attitudes and sympathies of community workers and youth leaders to understand the challenge and opportunities the arts can offer. Dance specialists will need to be drawn either from dance teachers with special aptitude for this work trained within the maintained system, or from private teachers with production experience, or from former professional dancers trained on professional dancers' training courses. In the last case these courses will need to be broader than they are now to embrace knowledge of the needs and methods of youth and community services. Supporting these teaching needs, local arts associations and committees need to reconsider their often limited views of the received arts and consider helping and encouraging youth and community arts, in which dance, of course, will figure. Individuals with an understanding of the arts in an educational context need to be elected to local youth committees[61] to influence attitudes and grant allocations for the provision of resources and the payment of visiting arts teams to clubs and centres. Within this general framework each area or region will need some co-ordinating dance organisation to provide information about local dance resources and to provide a local voice for dance. This would provide a national, as well as a local, means of collaboration and co-ordination to strengthen the place of dance in our national education system at all levels.

190 Some conclusions

Drawing together the needs of this diverse field of continuing education leads to three conclusions. First, continuing education is of particular importance in establishing the climate, a community belief in dance, within which the rest of our proposals can flourish. Second, the further, adult and community education systems have aimed traditionally at responding as closely as possible to locally expressed demand from all sections of the community and for all types of courses. Therefore this area of dance education, so important to dance education as a whole and so rich in possibilities, will not realise its potential unless local initiative and demand provide the principal stimulus. Third, the development of continuing education on a mass scale in Britain demands the closest collaboration with the mass media, especially broadcasting through television. Therefore we devote our final remarks to broadcasting.

191 The importance of broadcasting

We are guided particularly by the response of the Advisory Council for Adult and Continuing Education to the Government's White Paper on Broadcasting.[52] We endorse the views of the Advisory Council because it seems clear to us, as it does to them, that the necessary scale of provision needed for large scale expansion of continuing education in the arts through broadcasting is insufficiently appreciated by the Government, the broadcasting authorities and the Annan Committee.[62] This will affect dance, in particular, which is still a minority among minority arts in this field. To enhance this provision for dance we add to the recommendations of the Advisory Council[63] particular recommendations that liaison groups should be established at national and local level between broadcasters and dance educators to identify opportunities to develop dance education, to consider and promote schemes of collaboration and strengthen the work of existing advisory machinery in all networks at all levels; that this collaboration should include collaboration with other media, especially to provide better follow-up material; that the Advisory Council's recommendations for a new form of artists' contract in relation to copyright to enable general output to be used for educational purposes be strongly supported as in the best interests of dance and the artists concerned;* that a focal point of collaboration between dance educators and broadcasters might lie in the National Councils for Dance formed by the private sector, and/or in the National Resource Centre for Dance Teaching which forms one of our principal recommendations. Finally, we emphasise the special opportunities created by a fourth television channel and the growth of local broadcasting of all kinds. We believe the fullest response to these opportunities will depend upon an effective collaboration between dance interests in the maintained and non-maintained sectors to achieve adequate and regular representation of dance through all these channels.

---

* When we represented this point to British Actors' Equity Association they responded: 'Our present agreements allow very great flexibility of use of television programmes and there are special provisions for the making of educational programmes in our television agreements. What is lacking, perhaps, is the desire on the part of those who run the television companies to use the facilities they have already in the service of dance. That is not to say, of course, that we would not be willing to consider proposals which might extend the use of dance programmes in education.'

12 The Assessment of Standards

*192 A contri-
bution to
national
discussion*

We have conducted our study at a time when the assessment of performance of students in schools is under discussion and review by students, parents, teachers, administrators, the Inspectorate* and politicians. This chapter is our contribution to these discussions. We recognise the practical need for some means to assess the performance of students in dance as much as any other subject. Such assessment 'is important for the pupils themselves to know how well they are progressing, and for their parents. It is important for teachers to know that their pupils are learning effectively and that the teaching material and approaches adopted are suitable. It is important for employers, particularly those who must look for certain aptitudes in those they employ.'[64]

*193 The
problem of
formal
assessment*

Since teachers all the time assess their students as part of the process of teaching, we have no doubt about the value of assessment in the classroom. Our concern is rather with the relevance and validity of formal assessment through examinations. What are the attitudes and skills amenable to measurement or evaluation in dance? If dance examinations spread, will it not become true that dance in schools will suffer as other subjects have done, because students will study to pass dance examinations rather than study dance? To answer these real problems we outline briefly the general situation of examinations and assessment today in relation to dance, and then turn to what we think is the central issue, the question of 'examination' or 'assessment'.

*194 Pressures
for assessment*

We belong to a world which lives by, and demands, examinations. The annual turnover in fees for CSE and GCE O- and A-levels is approximately £15 million, a sizeable industry in itself. As the Secretary of the Northern Universities' Joint Matriculation Board pointed out '. . . on the three occasions when attempts have been made this century to curb the growth of public examinations the public had responded with an even more luxurious demand. Examinations are something the British love to hate.'[65] This being so, it is hard to resist pressure to include dance more firmly and formally within existing examination systems. Pressure flows partly from a need for status to gain full recognition in the school curriculum, and for other advantages felt to belong to a subject which yields GCE and CSE results; partly from the demand of parents and children themselves; and partly from a reasoning which argues that not to examine in present circumstances is to discriminate against those who teach and study dance.

---

* We are indebted, for example, to chapter 10 on public examinations in the Inspectorate's *Aspects of Secondary Education in England.* (see note 18)

195 The *present* *system*	At present dance examinations at secondary level in the maintained sector of England and Wales relate to three national certificate examinations — the General Certificate of Education (GCE); the Certificate of Secondary Education (CSE); and the Certificate of Extended Education (CEE). The GCE examinations in dance are conducted by the Associated Examining Board (AEB) and the University of Cambridge Local Examination Syndicate, both in classical ballet. Both favour the traditional written paper although the AEB paper includes also a practical element. All the dance submissions for CSE and CEE so far have been in Mode III. This is an examination set and marked internally by a school, or group of schools, moderated at each stage by the Board. All such examinations in CSE and the comparatively new CEE increasingly use continuous assessment and practical work as a major part of examination. They can be in any dance style but so far have been mostly in modern dance forms.
196 Continuous *assessment* *and/or* *examination*	In considering these examinations in the maintained sector we have been able to draw on a special investigation[66] undertaken by Joan White, Senior Lecturer in Movement Studies, Roehampton Institute of Higher Education — Southlands College, London. This study concentrates upon public examinations available in maintained secondary education in England and Wales. It has proved invaluable to us particularly for its evidence of the existing situation and its analysis of syllabus submissions within two regional CSE examining boards. In comparing the methods of GCE, CSE and CEE, Joan White quoted preliminary research which indicated 'no evidence to show that standards were different for candidates awarded grades by continuous assessment and by examination in any of the following subjects studied — English, history, geography, technical drawing, biology, chemistry, physics and mathematics'. There is no reason to suppose a difference, either, for dance although the CSE/CEE Mode III syllabi with their combination of practical and theoretical abilities and interests seem to us to demonstrate qualities particularly desirable in dance assessment.
197 What can *be assessed* *and how*	That dance of all kinds can be assessed formally is no longer in doubt. Experience over many years at secondary and tertiary level* has shown what can be assessed in dance, and how best this might be done. The three areas which characterise dance**— choreography, performance and appreciation — can all be examined practically and theoretically.

---

*   We have found a widespread assumption that formal dance assessment is still new and experimental. Experiment is needed continually, of course, but we can draw now on some decades of assessment experience in colleges of education and in the non-maintained level particularly related to teacher training; on GCE, CSE and CEE experience; and on CNAA experience of the new combined and performance arts course.

**   We have drawn again in this section on Janet Adshead's research 'Dance as a Discipline: an examination of the nature and study of dance and an analysis of its viability as a distinct discipline.' PhD thesis submitted November 1979, University of Leeds.

Practical choreographic ability can be assessed by reference to the students' choice and manipulation of thematic material, use of choreographic devices, techniques, artistry and so on. In the theoretical aspects of choreography, students' knowledge and understanding of the works of various choreographers, the salient features of compositions, the relationships between form and content can be examined. In the performance of dance, the students' own technical ability, as well as the interpretation of the performed work is assessable. Similarly, the theoretical aspects of performance can readily be examined, such as the evaluation of interpretations of roles and dance works together with a knowledge of different dance techniques and their relation to performed works. Appreciation of dance through active spectator involvement in its many forms can provide the basis for critical analysis and is another well established area in which students' knowledge can be examined. In addition it is evident that anthropological, cultural, historical and sociological aspects of dance as well as the study of dance notation and dance production can be examined in a variety of ways. It is important, however, that in the examination of dance the relationship between practice and theory is recognised and continually maintained.

198 Need for
O- and A-level
assessment

We believe the time is ripe now for dance to gain full recognition in the national assessment system at secondary level and that it is well placed to be included in new examination proposals, including the single examination system now under discussion. We draw attention, therefore, to anomalies at secondary level in England and Wales which affect entrance to higher education. Students intending to study dance at tertiary level cannot, as their colleagues can in other subjects, study dance for one of the O- or A-levels needed as an entrance qualification. There are no O-level examinations in dance, only O-levels in the narrower field of classical ballet, and there are no A-levels of any kind in dance. The recent submission of an O-level Mode II in dance to the University of London School Examinations Department is still under discussion and may take some time to reach a conclusion. Thus English and Welsh students entering dance courses in higher education are penalised by being unable to qualify by virtue of O- and/or A-levels in their subject. The present O-level examinations in ballet, offered by the Associated Examining Board and the University of Cambridge Local Examinations Syndicate are too narrow in scope, however significant their pioneer value. Although as we noted in paragraph 195 the AEB'S examination does include a measure of practical ability, the level demanded is far below the ability of pupils taught in specialist schools and outside the dance experience of pupils in most maintained schools. O- and A-level qualifications in dance, as opposed to ballet, would match the trend of interest in dance observable in secondary and higher education and would fulfil an obvious need. Furthermore, the development of dance as a subject for GCE could greatly improve the quality of entrants for dance study at tertiary level. In Scotland, by contrast, the opportunity to develop O- and A-levels in dance does not exist because there is no comparable examination, only O- and H-grades, a situation we deplore.

199 Reservations *about the* *present system* We argue, then, that dance *can* be assessed formally and that it ought to be included in the formal examination system to confirm its place in the school curriculum. The fundamental issue, though, is the nature of the assessment to be used, and its purpose. Here, some of us have reservations about the adequacy of formal examinations to assist and measure the contribution of dance to a young person's development. Our first concern is the effect of the existing examination system on the arts in schools, generally, especially dance. The syllabi of the 8 GCE and 15 CSE examination boards in fact provide a broadly common curriculum throughout England and Wales. A similar provision derives from the Scottish examination system. Hence the status need for dance to be examined and examinable. These examinations condition every school timetable from at least the third year onwards even though, for one reason or another, there may be pupils who do not take an examination at the end of the school course. In human terms this means every school is biased towards academic study and academic achievement. Tragically, therefore, the non-academic students are placed in unreal competition with academic students, while students having creative ability in either category tend to receive least attention of all. A system is needed, reflected in assessment methods, whereby different aspects of schooling and achievement can be recognised equally — the academic, creative and practical. Within such a system dance would take a natural and necessary place in the assessment of each student.

200 Problems *of formal* *examination* Our next reservation, then, concerns the adequacy of formal examinations in dance. Accepting that a method of assessment is necessary to measure ability, inform parents, teachers and students of progress, consolidate learning and sustain standards, some of us feel that formal dance examinations are inadequate for these purposes in ways which may apply also to other subjects. First, recalling the argument of the preceding paragraph, such examinations tend to benefit academically-minded students against those with a greater bias towards practical or creative abilities. Elements of competition and stress are introduced which are foreign to the study of dance as part of the learning process. Indeed, they are contrary to much of the spirit of dance which requires co-operation rather than a process of selection. Second, such examinations tend to distort motivation. They measure a student's ability to cover an examination syllabus rather than a student's personal ability in dance. They induce students and teachers to concentrate on the examination syllabus to achieve success rather than on dance in whatever variety or form best suits the students. Third, formal examinations, in any case, tend to be inefficient at revealing a student's full ability. So much cannot be revealed, has to be omitted, in the comparatively short period of examination time. Consequently students are tested more in what they do not know or cannot do than in their actual ability.

201 Continuous assessment As a committee we neither sought, nor arrived at, a consensus around these problems. We agreed that the most desirable forms of assessment are those which measure significant achievement and enable students to demonstrate the range of their abilities in dance. Encouraged by Joan White's preliminary research in paragraph 196, some of us feel that there should be a substantial school-based element in assessments, as there is in CSE Mode III, and that continuous assessment provides the best opportunity to develop dance curricula in the interests of students and subject rather than the examination. Continuous assessment seems to us to be a method which can help to increase the self-awareness and self-confidence of students whereas formal examination tends to sap these qualities, at least for the majority. Continuous assessment also offers opportunities for co-operative working, project work, experiment and self-expression and therefore seems more suitable as a method of dance assessment than once-off formal examinations. It is facilitated now, moreover, by the development of educational technology. Through video cameras in schools it becomes possible to view the best of dance students' work done during the period of a course, ie while they were creating at their best, as it is possible to view art students' work through photographs and slides. This new technology can help also in training teachers for continuous assessment as well as help students' own self-assessment and learning. Clearly, more study, research and experiment is needed into all methods of assessment. Whatever is decided, the most important element of assessment is surely that which fulfils the accountability of teachers to themselves by allowing teachers and students together regularly to assess progress and decide which teaching materials and approaches are relevant and appropriate.

202 Assessment at tertiary level Similar problems and needs can be found at tertiary level. We have discussed formal assessment at this level already in chapter 9, but add here two observations which have relevance also to secondary level. First, since assessment at tertiary level often influences career directions, the purpose of a course needs to guide the nature of assessment. We have noted some confusion on this point although the guidance seems to us simple. If the object of a course is performance, the priority of assessment is to measure performance. If the object is understanding, the priority is to measure understanding. We are aware that the issue of understanding, especially in relation to appreciation raised in paragraph 197, is contentious among those responsible for advising on the assessment of the arts. We believe that dance experience contributes much to the cognitive development of young people at all educational levels* but we can see for assessment purposes a difficulty in identifying what constitutes the knowledge component of an art, and the distinction

---

*   It has been brought to our notice frequently during our study visits that students applying themselves more completely than others to dancing classes and examinations are often also those most academically able in other subjects and examinations.

between content and critical appreciation. Nevertheless, assessment surely needs to be guided very much by the rationale and purpose of those who devise and lead a course. Consequently the purpose of a course and the nature of its assessment need to be made clear to students on entry.

203 Need for a university contribution

Second, the presence of dance in the university sector, which is minimal, needs to be increased. British universities as a body have always proved resistant to dance as a subject for study, notwithstanding the pioneer work of London in this field and the example of universities in the United States. It is significant, perhaps, that it was the AEB, the only Board not associated with a university, which pioneered GCE Ballet. At present it is the polytechnics and colleges of higher education who lead in the dance field and open the way for exciting developments in assessments. We are hopeful, however, that this situation is coming to an end and that dance will be seen more and more to take its place in British universities as a subject in its own right rather than linked as now with teacher training.

204 CNAA growth and dangers

By the terms of its charter the CNAA degrees have to be, and are, comparable in standard with those awarded by universities in the United Kingdom. The particular contribution of the CNAA dance assessment, however, has been its flexibility in face of dance change and in using non-traditional forms of examination which include most, if not all, methods additional to the formal unseen written examination. Expansion nevertheless carries with it inevitable dangers. Many of us have served on the Council's boards and panels and acted as its examiners. We have seen, in the course of our duties, the threatening shortage of experienced examiners in the dance field, of insufficient polytechnic and college staff able to carry the subject to honours standard, of inadequate physical facilities and other resources. These and other problems were the subject of a special conference organised by the CNAA and Gulbenkian Foundation, at Stratford-upon-Avon, in November, 1978. It concluded that in spite of the CNAA's great pioneering successes in the arts field, it risks losing impetus unless it can continue to apply pressure for the improvement of standards both in resource terms and in the evolution of the courses themselves. At a time too when it is reconsidering its methods and structure with a view to allowing the more mature institutions greater freedom from control, it needs to ensure that courses in new areas such as dance are properly monitored. It should be added that the CNAA's subject board system, represented here by the Dance Board, provides in some ways a unique forum for the discussion of matters relating to the assessment and evaluation of courses.

205 Role of the Inspectorate

There are, of course, methods of assessing the performance of the education system nationally and regionally, and the performance of individual schools, other than by examination. Principally these are through HM Inspectorate and the local authority advisory services.

Supplementing these means in England and Wales is the work of the Assessment of Performance Unit of the DES. Already we have shown how much the development of dance in maintained and non-maintained schools owes to the encouragement of individual inspectors and advisers. There is scope, however, for further development of this system so far as dance is concerned, for a critical appraisal by the Inspectorate for the guidance of dance teachers, perhaps within the HMI series, *Matters for Discussion,* and for greater concentration, in particular, on ways by which the maintained and non-maintained sectors might work more closely as resources for each other. We appreciate that the Inspectorate places no pressure to favour one method or form of dance beyond another, but the Inspectorate draws from school experience the information necessary to the formulation of policy. This information is translated into policy recommendations for the Minister, who decides. The views of the Inspectorate are, therefore, significant for the future and provide always a valuable basis for discussion.

PART III
The Non-Maintained Sector

13 The Present Day

206 A time of crisis

We begin this part of our report with three emphases which we think are fundamental to understanding the present situation and objectives of the non-maintained sector, but whose importance we think is underestimated by those outside the sector. The first emphasis is the nature of the sector's economic base. Traditionally, this comprises two sources of income: fees paid by parents, and fees paid by local education authorities through discretionary awards or grants. The first source is threatened by the general rise in the cost of living. The second source is threatened by cuts in discretionary grants as a result of the Government's economic policies. Therefore the private system of vocational training for dance is now in danger from the way cuts in discretionary grants are being applied. These training institutions, created often with much sacrifice, are at risk and, with them, not only Britain's pre-eminent position in theatrical dance but much of the present vocational training system for all the performing arts. We issue this report at a time of the greatest crisis facing vocational training for the performing arts, and dance in particular, since the second world war.

207 Two philosophies

Our second emphasis is the need to distinguish between the work of teachers of dance in the maintained and non-maintained sectors, and therefore between their different philosophies and approaches to their responsibilities. We do not wish to over-emphasise this distinction because all teachers of dance are involved in forming minds and bodies. Nevertheless, the distinction is important to a fair estimate of teachers in both sectors and, especially, to an understanding of the role of the private teacher. The teacher in the maintained sector sees dance as a significant resource in forming and developing minds and bodies, whether or not this involves an element of public performance. The teacher in the non-maintained sector is concerned mainly with forming minds and bodies for dance as a vocation or for those young who are able, for one reason or another, to study dance in a private studio. The teacher of dance in the maintained sector earns his or her living by providing an experience which the child receives, as in the rest of education. The teacher in the private sector earns his or her living by providing an experience which the child buys. The private teacher, therefore, is totally dependent on being able to sell expertise on an open market. Thus the maintained sector provides dance *education*; the non-maintained sector provides dance *training*. This is not to say that dance training cannot take place in maintained schools and dance education cannot happen in private dance studios. Our third emphasis, therefore, is the interdependence of the two sectors. Increasingly, as we shall see, there is a need for collaboration or even for some merging of the two sectors. Teachers in both sectors, like many other teachers, are moved by a passionate commitment to their subject and to their students. Here is the common ground between them for the give and take which is essential to the future.

208 1939/1979 Teachers of the private sector work within a system they themselves have helped to create. By 1939 today's pattern of the private sector had largely been established. Forty years later 'today's pattern of the private sector' remains that of 1939, but writ large through growth and significant innovations such as dance notation and opportunities for choreographic experience. The private sector of dance training can demonstrate now, and draw upon, an authentic professional background consolidated out of tradition, which deserves full acknowledgement for its achievements from teaching colleagues in the public sector, from educational administrators, and from educational policy makers in central and local government. This professional background guides the standards of excellence the sector has established, the nature of theoretical understanding in its teacher training institutions and in its learning structure for students as well as its methods of assessment. All these are comparable with the public sector, but different. They constitute Britain's entire vocational training provision in dance of many kinds. They provide a wide range of dance experience outside the public sector available to many thousands of young people who have no career ambitions. They are a very important resource of dance teaching public sector available to many thousands of young people who have no career ambitions. They are a very important resource of dance teaching expertise. Increasingly, though, it has become clear that the pattern and many of the assumptions of 1939, however embellished, are inadequate to today's opportunities and the changes which are taking place in British society. Since the middle 1970s the need for change has become generally accepted. This chapter sets the scene for succeeding chapters in which we recommend a new pattern of the non-maintained sector for the 1980s onwards.

209 Wartime legacy The first period of expansion of the private sector came as a result of wartime initiative by the Council for the Encouragement of Music and the Arts (CEMA) now the Arts Council of Great Britain. Through the Council's work the nation's best cultural products were seen throughout the country. From 1940–1945 dance companies appeared regularly in factories and hostels as well as theatres of all kinds. This constant wartime touring by Ballet Rambert, the Sadler's Wells Ballet, the Ballet Jooss and other companies, no less than the large number of servicemen and women who saw the companies in London, created a new interest in dance, especially classical ballet. Consequently the post-war world offered classical dance teachers in Britain wholly different opportunities from the world between the wars.

210 Expansion of private dance Developing from this new interest the last 40 years have seen, in particular, a steady expansion of the work of private studios teaching classical ballet described in chapter 15 and of the number of candidates entering

104

for classical ballet examinations each year, discussed in chapter 19. Other forms of dance, too, have developed. The teaching of national dance has grown throughout the whole of this period, in some ways matching the expansion of classical ballet. Various forms of modern dance have evolved their own teaching systems, organisations and examinations. Ethnic dance is nourished and growing today through the increase of Britain's immigrant population of many nationalities, including Poles, Ukrainians and Cypriots as well as Africans, Asians and West Indians.* We believe it is important to encourage and provide for the dance of ethnic minorities as much as possible, partly for the way it enriches the dance culture of Britain itself, and partly for the sense of identity and cultural roots it can strengthen in the ethnic communities.

211 Growth of independent schools and private teacher training

The immediate post-war period into the 1960s saw the development of the idea of independent schools combining general education with classical ballet and stage training. The idea had been introduced before the war as we show in Appendix C. Its development was a part of the post-war boom lasting two decades. Then, as inflation brought rising costs, some schools closed and many faced difficulties. Those which remain constitute important centres whose contribution is discussed in chapter 16. In a similar way private colleges for training teachers for the non-maintained sector have developed also since the war, sometimes on earlier foundations. All these institutions, described in chapter 18, run three-year courses and some issue a diploma or certificate of qualification. For them, the contraction of teacher training in the 1970s and the introduction of graduate qualifications for all teachers in the maintained sector have compelled a re-thinking of the present and the future.

212 Development of dance notation

One of the most important post-war innovations for dance of all kinds in Britain has been the development of movement notation systems. These enable dance movements to be recorded on paper in the sense that musical sounds can be recorded. Methods of dance notation have been in use for nearly five hundred years. Earlier systems were invented in relation to particular dance styles and thus had severe limitations for broad practical use today. The implications go beyond dance to embrace all forms of movement and therefore have validity across both sectors covering all education, sport, therapy and other activities where movement is involved as well as dance. The two systems gaining widest acceptance since the second world war are Kinetography Laban, for which the Americans coined the title Labanotation, and Benesh Notation. We describe them here, rather than in Part I, because they were evolved on private initiative and remain sustained by private institutions. Nevertheless we emphasise the importance of students in both sectors learning about notation as a significant contribution to the greater part of their curriculum. Such a tool is essential, equally, to a study of the

---

* For example, the Academy of Indian Dance described in chapter 17 and the Aklowa Centre for Traditional African Drumming and Dancing which introduces British audiences to Ghanaian music and dance.

history of human movement, human culture and human communication recommended in chapter 1. Notation should become a necessary element in all movement study, dance teacher training and dance courses in the vocational sector, as we believe it should be also in the maintained sectors.

213 Labanota-
tion

Kinetography Laban was copyrighted in Germany in 1928 after which Albrecht Knust established the Dance Notation Bureaux in Hamburg and Berlin. Kinetography Laban was introduced into Britain in 1934 by Sigurd Leeder and in 1952 The Dance Notation Centre, founded by Sigurd Leeder and Lisa Ullmann, was registered in London. Ann Hutchinson, who had studied notation in England, together with two colleagues trained in Germany, established the Dance Notation Bureau in New York in 1949, consolidating the work of Irmgard Bartenieff begun in the States in 1936. In 1957 an International Congress of Dance and Movement Notation was held in Dresden. The recommendation made by the Congress delegates 'that Kinetography Laban be adopted as the international means of communication in the field of movement research, dance training and choreography' was unanimously accepted. Laban authorised Lisa Ullmann, Albrecht Knust, Sigurd Leeder and Ann Hutchinson to have custody of his notation system. After his death, the custodians, realising the need to unify the differences which had arisen in the system, established the International Council of Kinetography Laban in England in 1959, with the support and financial assistance of the Laban Art of Movement Centre Trust. The Council, the only organisation of its kind with a world-wide membership including countries of Eastern Europe, meets biennially. England has been frequently the host country for this conference. Today this system has widespread acceptance and use in education; many ballets have been notated by its method on both sides of the Atlantic, as are all the dance studies of Sigurd Leeder referred to in Appendix C. A library of notated works has been created. It is a comprehensive system and can be used for any type of human movement. In Britain it is taught at the Language of Dance Centre, the Laban Centre and a number of other institutions.

214 Benesh
Notation

Benesh Notation was copyrighted in 1955 as the creation of Joan Benesh, then a member of the Sadler's Wells Ballet, and her husband, the late Rudolph Benesh. The same year it was adopted by the Royal Ballet and Royal Ballet School. Today it is used internationally to record and reproduce the dance works of many professional dance companies. The Beneshes defined the writing down of movement and ballets in their system of notation as choreology. With the help of the Pilgrim Trust, the Leverhulme Trust Fund and the Gulbenkian Foundation they established an Institute of Choreology in 1962 to train teachers and to record ballets and other aspects of movement. As a result, choreologists are attached today to more than 20 professional dance companies across the world and the system is in international use. A growing library of notated works, and a growing number of choreologists and dancers educated in notation, facilitate the exchange of ballets, the study of choreography and, with Labanotation and other systems, the analysis of all forms of movement for athletic, industrial and medical purposes.

215 Dominance of classical ballet   By the middle 1960s the dominance of classical ballet in the private sector of vocational training in Britain seemed complete. Its system was based firmly on a wide distribution of private studios across the country, supported by a number of large independent dance schools. It produced its own teachers, its own examiners and examinations and, finally, even its own system of notation. At its pinnacle was the Royal Ballet and the Royal Ballet School which had risen to become a world centre of professional classical training. Collectively this system produced the dancers who made and make British classical ballet one of Britain's great cultural achievements this century.

216 Challenge of modern dance   Barely more than a decade later the unquestioned dominance of classical ballet in Britain no longer exists. Among those who least regret this change are classical dancers and teachers themselves. The reason is the tremendous extension of dance and dance interest represented by three events. First, the growing popularity of modern and contemporary dance. Like many phrases used to describe dance, modern dance and contemporary dance have a number of different meanings. For the purposes of this report we use modern dance,* wherever possible, to describe all or any styles of performance dance, excluding classical ballet, national, ethnic and tap dance. (The remarkable growth in recent years of the modern theatre dance branch of the ISTD suggests that an important change may be taking place in what private teachers of dancing now feel they should offer their students.) Second, the change of Ballet Rambert in 1966 from being a classical ballet company to become a modern dance company. Third, the emergence of the Contemporary Dance Trust in the mid 1960s, guiding the London Contemporary Dance Theatre (LCDT) and the London School of Contemporary Dance (LSCD). Students were sent to study in New York in 1964; regular classes were started in London in 1965; LSCD officially opened its own premises in 1966; and LCDT gave its first performance in 1967.

---

*   In Britain the term 'modern dance' is sometimes employed in another sense to describe styles established before modern dance began to develop separately in the USA and Europe. In this sense 'modern dance' often describes the later European styles particularly associated with artists like Jooss, Leeder, Wigman and Kreutzberg whilst 'contemporary dance' describes Graham, Horton, Humphrey and later American styles. In this interpretation there was no significant contemporary dance in Britain before 1965–66. Today the styles are beginning to relate to each other and the emergence of contemporary dance has enormously strengthened modern dance.

217 Significance Such developments added greatly to Britain's cultural achievement in
of modern dance. They embrace a wide range of dance styles, all of them looking
dance for their students, not to the private sector, but to the maintained
sector and to the dance taught there. This has begun to change the
relationship of the two sectors, as well as the attitude of young people
in the public sector towards dance. The change has gone farthest in
England where the two national modern dance companies have their
base, plus a growing number of regional companies. In Wales and
Scotland these new companies have built an interest through visits.
There are also possibilities for locally-based modern dance companies
or centres, pioneered by existing institutions such as Moving Being in
Wales, and Basic Space in Scotland, neither of them indigenous.

218 Develop- The growth of a variety of modern dance styles in Britain has stimulated
ment of also a new range of choreography. This brought a reconsideration of the
choreographic opportunities which ought to be provided for choreographic develop-
opportunity ment. Historically, the provision of choreographic opportunities was
pioneered in the 1930s by the Camargo Society and the Ballet Club
staging the first works of Frederick Ashton, Antony Tudor and Ninette
de Valois among others. After the war the pioneer role was assumed
first by the Royal Academy of Dancing's Production Club in the mid-
1940s, giving early opportunities to John Cranko. After that it was
sustained by Ballet Workshop at the Mercury Theatre and by Sunday
Choreographers at Sadler's Wells Theatre (a first chance for Kenneth
MacMillan) in the early 1950s, then by the Sunday Ballet Club, then
Ballet Makers, during the late 1950s and early 1960s. This was followed
by the development of choreographic workshops attached to individual
companies. In these workshops, however, there was no attempt at
choreographic training as such until in 1966 the Contemporary Dance
School and Company began to develop methods already tried in
America. Presently these ideas were supported by the Gulbenkian
Foundation which then encouraged similar developments in the classical
field, especially at the Royal Ballet School. Ultimately the Foundation
established a National Choreographic Summer School which has become an international dance course for the advanced study and practice
of choreography and musical composition for choreography. All this is
discussed in greater detail in chapter 17, but it is important here to note
the new balance and profound shift in British vocational dance education
wrought by the change in Ballet Rambert and the arrival of the LSCD
and LCDT during the last ten years.

219 Problems So much, then, for the achievements of recent years. These achieve-
of the system ments, however, have revealed problem areas, five of which especially
disturb us. They are to do with the effectiveness of the private vocational training system in relation to: its standards of dance teaching; its
own organisation; the young people it serves; the professional dancers it
produces; and, the central and local government structures with which
it must work. Standards of dance teaching are discussed in chapters 15

108

and 16. We turn, here, to the organisation, or lack of organisation, of the dance teaching profession in the private sector. In spite of recent moves, a substantial gulf still separates one kind of dance in the private sector from another. These tragic divisions have done infinite harm in the past and are illustrated by the proliferation of teaching and examining bodies described in chapters 18 and 19. The plethora of organisations, and the rivalry between them, gravely hinders the creative partnership which ought to exist between the dance teaching profession and the professional dance theatre as well as confusing the larger world of public education authorities. Considerations of this nature led the Royal Academy of Dancing (RAD) and the ISTD to initiate discussions in late 1968 to explore the possibility of establishing a joint organisation with the International Dance Teachers' Association (IDTA). These discussions did not prosper but were revived in a different and broader form in 1974 following the Action Conference on dance education described in chapter 1 and Appendix A. As a result three national bodies have been formed to which reference has been made already – in England a Council for Dance Education and Training with offices in London, in Scotland a Scottish Council for Dance with offices in Glasgow, and in Wales a Welsh Dance Association with offices in Cardiff, soon to become the Dance Council for Wales. The two last named organisations bring together teachers from the maintained and non-maintained sectors so that we hope it may not be long before the English Council does the same.*

220 The system and the once-a-week child

How effective is this present system of private dance teaching for the young people it has been created to serve? Or was it created more to serve their teachers? For whom, in fact, does the system exist? There are three groups of young people it might serve – those we shall call the once-a-week child; the talented child; and those at present unserved and unidentified. Within its own limits and under good teachers the system seems to serve the general child fairly well, so much so that we would like to extend the service to the areas described in paragraph 222. The general child or young person is one who attends a studio class probably once a week and does not get beyond grade 5 or the elementary examination of one of the major bodies. Such children are not aiming at a professional dance career but derive pleasure, educational benefit and personal enrichment from their dance studies and the attention a good private teacher can give. They form the great majority of children who study dancing. We emphasise the importance of good teaching because our experience suggests that teachers who have themselves been well taught are able to communicate through these classes a very positive

---

* Respective addresses and telephone numbers are:– Council for Dance Education and Training, 5–7 Tavistock Place, London WC1 9SS Tel No 01 388 5770. Scottish Council for Dance, 261 West Princes Street, Glasgow G4 9EE. Tel No 041 331 2931. Dance Council for Wales, Welsh Arts Council, Museum Place, Cardiff. Tel No 0222 394 711 Full details are given at Appendix F.

appreciation of dance which stays with a young person for the rest of his or her life. On the other hand the numerous small studios run by teachers with only a limited training (usually in classical ballet) often do considerable damage to their pupils for the reasons described later in paragraph 247. Bodies conditioned by poor early training (especially in classical ballet) may never recover. It is these limited teachers who tend to rely most on examination syllabi. This is why we return to this problem in chapters 15, 18 and 19.

221 Gifted and talented children Among those who attend the weekly private class will be a relatively few children whose latent dance talent is such that they are potential professional dancers or could make an important contribution in the amateur field. A key issue is that their talent should be identified correctly at the earliest possible stage. Some of them will come from families with a cultural background and in such cases talent is probably spotted if it exists. But talented children born into families with no particular dance or relevant cultural background often depend on the private teacher or someone at school to advise them. It is here we think the system works less well than it should. A well trained private teacher is among those most likely to spot talent and help it forward. The problem lies in the less talented teacher, the teacher who holds on to talent too long for selfish reasons rather than recommend it for audition at a professional school, and the general lack of information about which direction the talented young person might follow. As we shall see the amount of advice available from the private sector to parents, local authorities and young people is very small. The deficiency is made worse by lack of contact between the private teacher and the child's school and between the private sector and local education authorities. More consultation and more and better guidelines are needed to help young talent into vocational training.

222 The unidentified The two groups of young people identified so far at least have had the chance of attending a private studio. From private studios at present come the majority of professional dancers in Britain. It is surely important, therefore, that the dance profession should be certain the nation's reservoir of dance talent is fully identified and provided with adequate opportunities to develop. What about those whose parents cannot afford to send their children to a private teacher, and the many more children, particularly in inner city circumstances, who never know what a private studio might offer them but who might gain immensely in ways described in paragraph 186? For 50 years the private sector in its present form has concentrated on the children of those who can afford to pay studio fees. This has been the livelihood of its members and therefore a necessary priority. Today, one result of this concentration is a virtual exclusion of many children from any chance of training for a professional dance career in classical ballet. The fault, of course, lies not only with the private sector but with local education authorities, although the private sector has been insufficiently concerned.

110

It needs now very much to be concerned. The fall in the child population affects its interest as much as those of the maintained sector, while rising costs make increasingly essential some form of dialogue with local authorities to see how best the expertise the private sector possesses can be placed at the service of the widest possible number of children. We return to this problem in the next chapter.

223 The system and its dancers Finally, (because we devote the next chapter to the fifth problem identified in paragraph 219) how does the system serve the professional dancers it produces? British Actors' Equity, the dancers' trade union, looks after their material needs and there is increasing provision for alternative careers once dancing is finished. It is obvious, too, from the success of British dancers that those who enter the system receive, on the whole, a good professional training, although we hope to show how it can be improved in a number of ways. How far, though, does this training also turn out reasonably educated human beings prepared for all the opportunities of the late twentieth century? How much has each dancer been assisted realistically to make the best of his or her potential? How prepared are the dancers as citizens able to argue the dancer's place in a changing British society? Our experience suggests that dancers are insufficiently prepared for these broader issues. We welcome, therefore, the initiative of dancers who have come together in recent years to form discussion groups of similar organisations, often around particular interests. There is the Association of Dance and Mime Artists, for example, drawing together for mutual self-help a range of dance collectives, dance co-operatives, individual dance artists, teacher-performers, performer-therapists and community groups. There is Dance Umbrella, developed from an idea in the United States, which aims to investigate and develop new dance partly through festivals mainly for small companies; partly through assisting the administrative needs of small companies; partly by providing a forum for discussion and further study. There are dance-in-education groups working with the Standing Conference of Young People's Theatre (SCYPT). There is beginning to be a 'Dance Lobby' and a British presence in international dance organisations. It is important, we think, to record such developments, to encourage dancers to consider their art in the context of society around them, and to note that dance, too, can be part of the very wide movement of social concern involving artists of all kinds across the world.

14 The Local Authority and the Private Sector

224 Purpose of the chapter

In paragraph 219 we identified relations between the State and the private sector as a problem area which needs examination. The problem arises because the private sector provides a specialist training for very young children upwards from which emerge most of today's professional dancers and which, if it received more support from public funds, might discover or assist many more talented children than it does today. Thus the private sector is making educational provision which the maintained sector does not make. Therefore, we argue, the private sector should receive a much larger measure of public support in recognition of this provision than it does at the moment. This chapter develops this argument.

225 Approach to specialist dance education

The pre-requisite of an adequate response to the challenge of providing specialist dance education is acceptance that the familiar arguments about élitism and unfair preferential treatment, which dominate so much of the national education debate, are out of place in this context. The Education Act 1976 specifically recognises dance and music as exceptional cases to which the educational, social and political arguments against specialist selection do not apply. As with music, the number of children gifted, or even talented, in dance is statistically insignificant. Their educational and technical requirements are highly specialised and the amounts of money needed to meet them are miniscule. If something like a specialist dance wing were established in a comprehensive school or sixth form college, as has been done for music, relatively little financial support would be needed compared with the benefits derived. Other options may range from paying for fees at a specialist school or for dance lessons with a local private teacher, to organising a system of peripatetic specialist teachers or setting up special ability classes. No one option is better than another. We believe each local education authority should take the initiative in providing for the special needs of its children and should be flexible in the policy it decides to adopt. In doing so it will be providing no more specialist assistance than is often provided unquestioningly for children gifted in a branch of sport.

226 Education before the age of ten

We outline, therefore, the probable educational path a would-be professional dancer is likely to follow in his or her chosen career. By 'career' we mean a very broad range of dance from subsidised dance theatre to music theatre of many kinds, cinema, television, cabaret and the growing area of community, fringe or 'new' dance. The professional dance world is small in numbers but broad in influence. To become a member of this profession, the future dancer, like all other young people, will enter primary education in a maintained, voluntary or private school and may also begin to study dance at a private studio

112

outside school hours. Such private study is not essential to a future career in dance but is advisable for any child hoping for a career in classical ballet.

227 Choices at age ten

At the age of ten a child aiming at a career in classical ballet has the choice of seeking entry into one of the specialist non-maintained dance schools described in chapter 16 or of continuing in the maintained sector, and taking private lessons, until transfer to a vocational dance school at the age of sixteen. For a career in other forms of dance it is less necessary to consider entering vocational dance school before 16 or 17 but, advisable, for reasons which will be apparent, to study with a private teacher. From the age of 16 to 18 or 19, concentrated training will be necessary in a vocational school, aiming to enter professional life at no later than 19 years. Whatever path is followed, provision in the maintained sector therefore, is, or could be, significant to the result, remembering that a professional career in dancing necessarily requires young people to start serious dance study at least during secondary schooling and probably before.

228 Need for local education authority involvement

The various routes and possibilities for professional training are described in the next two chapters. The important element we emphasise here is the inevitable and inextricable involvement of the local education authority with the private sector if it really wishes to ensure adequate opportunity to all its gifted children, not just those whose parents can pay fees, and if it is to give to dance the measure of support often given more readily to other arts.* At school age the local education authority contribution might take one or more of the forms outlined in paragraph 225. This ought to include some kind of link with, and support for, teachers in the private sector, particularly where an authority accepts an obligation to support opportunity in all forms of dance.

229 Decisions to be made

Local education authorities who accept this obligation (as many do although sometimes in a very limited form) are likely to be faced with important decisions on behalf of students around the ages of 11 and 16 in consultation with parents. Mostly these have to do with the fees, studios, general stage schools, independent dance schools and vocational dance schools described in the next chapters. This is where a local education authority adviser counts and where there ought to be more information and advice available from institutions of the private sector than there is at the moment. There is, for example, the special factor of fee support needed from 16+ instead of from the age of 18, as for many other subjects. Again, does putting children into some kind of special

---

* In drama, for example, the Central School of Speech and Drama receives help from the ILEA. Four other leading drama schools are also helped by their local authority. In music all the principal music colleges, except the London College of Music, receive aid of some kind from public funds. Painting and sculpture have long been supported by the maintained sector.

school reserved for gifted would-be dancers help or hinder the development of their personalities? Many parents of junior age children, in any case, may not wish to have them living away from home. Parents, teachers and dance advisers will have to weigh very carefully all the factors involved before committing a child gifted in dance to one course of study rather than another. It might be useful, even essential, to consider some kind of trial period, say for a year, during which the child and its parents could explore the nature of the commitment they are about to make. There will be some cases where there are overriding practical arguments in favour of sending a child to one of the specialist schools. A local education authority may not be able to provide for its gifted young dancers for several reasons: it may not be able to bring to a dance centre children who are geographically remote; it may not have a dance centre or any equivalent, say, of the ILEA's special ability classes; it may have no appropriate specialist teachers; above all it may have no means of providing for daily dance training, practice and experience. Therefore, we urge such authorities to support their children gifted in dance at the appropriate schools wherever these might be located outside the authority. The financial commitment will be slight as such children are rare.

230 Additional help from larger authorities

Having said this, we feel that there are certain parts of the country, notably larger conurbations, which ought to be able to develop without too much difficulty additional ways of helping specialist dance education, whether by individual grants for study outside their authority or by provision within their own authority. Half the population of Britain lives in or near the eight metropolitan authorities – Greater London, Greater Manchester, Merseyside, South Yorkshire, Strathclyde, Tyne and Wear, the West Midlands and West Yorkshire – while over four-fifths of the population lives in or near towns of over 100,000 people, including large cities like Bristol, Leicester, Nottingham and Southampton. It follows that in many of these places a dance centre, say, or a specialist dance department, attached to a comprehensive school, drawing on the specialist expertise in the area, would certainly have enough pupils to be viable and could be sufficiently near for a daily journey, albeit sometimes a long one. Here again is a situation in which public and private sectors should look to each other for help because such centres ought to be able to recruit the specialist knowledge of teachers in both sectors.

231 Remote areas and the private sector

We acknowledge that such an approach would not be practicable in remote areas though we were interested to see a recommendation in the Cameron Report to the Scottish Education Department.[37] This proposed to set up in a secondary school in Glasgow or Edinburgh a specialist unit with hostel accommodation attached to provide specialised education for gifted young musicians and dancers including those from remoter parts of Scotland. We have noted also the considerable success of the Renfrewshire Schools Dance Project in helping talented young dancers from rural as well as urban areas.

114

232 Private teachers as a resource

We feel there is scope for more flexibility and closer contact between local authorities and experienced local private teachers. The alternatives to paying for a private dance lesson are to ignore the poorer child who is ambitious to dance, which ought to be unthinkable, or pay for the child to attend as a boarder at one of the specialist schools. Seen in this context the subsidy of first rate local private teachers to give free lessons to talented children is both sensible and an economically sound investment. Therefore, we believe that local education authorities should draw up panels of local dance teachers whom they consider suitable, in consultation with the DES, the SED, the Council for Dance Education and Training, the Scottish Council for Dance and the Dance Council for Wales to teach in dance centres and to give private lessons to children sponsored by the local education authority.

233 Needs of specialist dance education

To reinforce our consideration of the provision made for potential young professional dancers by local education authorities, we discussed the argument that specialist dance schools are at variance with much of current educational philosophy. The opponents of such schools believe that the special treatment of a small number of children is élitist and that such schools improverish the general life of the school community by removing gifted children from it. This was an argument encountered similarly by our music colleagues in preparing *Training Musicians.*[2] We respond in the same terms because within the British school system as a whole, however good the general provision of dance education, we have seen already how difficult it is to sustain a high degree of specialist dance training at the necessary level to ensure the full development of the most talented children. Teachers do not always recognise the demands of such talent. Its realisation requires the early development of mental resources and physical proficiency of a sophisticated kind, imposing special requirements for tuition and practice. Teachers who have the ability to achieve this are rare, so the geographical isolation of pupils and the economic use of resources often points to concentration in dance schools specialising in one form of dance or another, depending on the talent of the child. It has been our experience in visiting these schools that the possession of such talent is overwhelmingly important to the children themselves, and they need the stimulus and friendship of others similarly talented, and regular and frequent access to teachers who can understand their gift and who can help them.

234 Arguments for specialist dance education

Therefore, the broad arguments in favour of a specialist dance education in our opinion are: there is close association with similarly talented children who can provide the stimulus of competition and example; mime and dance of various kinds can all be part of the curriculum and not left to the rush of the dinner hour or the exhaustion of after school. The opportunity thus exists for developing real dance quality, as distinct from technical proficiency, through daily practical training, training in theory and wide discussion between teachers and students; there are facilities for further private practice during the day to correct

115

weaknesses or develop particular interests. This is vital for most young dancers, especially those with choreographic potential; opportunities for performance are far more frequent and varied than in non-specialist schools; there is the possibility of master classes by distinguished dancers visiting the school; sufficient elasticity of the timetable exists to meet the essential needs of the individual pupils; provision is often made for boarding which means there can be more time for dance and, above all, practice within the environment of the school; only with classes of roughly comparable ability is it possible to give experience of working as a group.

235 Problems of specialist dance education

Alternatively, parents may ask themselves whether the academic education will be as good as in an ordinary school. What happens if the child fails to make the grade as a dancer? Is there a danger that the education will be too narrow in terms of the development of the child's personality? Conversely, how will the really talented child fare in an ordinary school? Will the distractions of all the activities available in, say, a large comprehensive school sap the child's commitment to dance? Will the child be able to devote enough time to practise and at the same time keep up with the rest of the class when it comes to O- and A-levels? Will the teaching available either privately or at school or at the Saturday dance centre, if it exists, be of a high enough standard for the really gifted child? Clearly, there are no automatically right answers and it is a great mistake to be dogmatic. What may be right for one child will be wrong for another. As with so many things in education, we are convinced that the decision has to be made in the light of what seems right for the particular child in question. This decision ought to involve careful discussion between parents, the local education authority and the specialist private teacher or relevant private institution.

236 Why local education authorities should support the private sector

We hope that this description of the needs of gifted children illustrates the necessity for local education authorities to support the private sector on a scale much larger than at present. There are three main reasons for this. First, children who have been identified as gifted, or potentially gifted, need specialist help likely to be available mainly in the private sector. Second, we drew attention in paragraph 222 to the number of children who receive, as yet, little or no exposure to dance in their schooling, and so no opportunity to reveal dance gifts if they have them. These children are mostly in inner city or remote rural areas. Their loss of opportunity is a potential loss to British dance culture as well as to themselves. Only local education authorities can tackle the problem and, when they do, they will need the combined skills of teachers in the maintained and non-maintained sectors. Finally, it is evident that the private sector possesses particular knowledge and expertise which could be deployed to supplement and augment that which is available in the maintained sector. Therefore, it is reasonable to argue that central and local government should consider ways and means of supporting and using the considerable resources of the private dance sector.

116

237 Positive discrimination

In this connection, if the country's full dance potential is to be realised, we believe it essential to discriminate positively in favour of the under-privileged. This means more free classes or awards for young people at least from the age of 9 or 10 so that those whose parents cannot afford special classes do not miss the opportunity merely through poor circumstances, and those who might benefit from attendance at a special dance school can have their fees paid. Such additional opportunity should be provided generally as a matter of course, but special efforts would need to be made in two ways. First, as we have said, in terms of positive discrimination to search out dance potential among children particularly deprived, such as those in inner cities, the very poor in rural areas, and those in minority ethnic groups, always working closely with the advice of specialist teachers. Second, to impress the parent with the nature of the opportunity provided and their family's responsibility to use it. Regular attendance is vital, involving commitment and, perhaps, sacrifice by the family and the child.

238 Vocational training and other training in dance

The same conclusion suggests itself when considering special support for dance in further, adult and continuing education. We have looked in chapter 11 at these areas of the maintained sector where some authorities recruit help already from the private sector. Such an examination indicates a need to recognise two sorts of division in dance education and training rather than one. There is the division between the maintained and non-maintained sectors which runs through all this report. There is also a division between vocational training for professional dance performance, teaching, notation and so on, and training which leads to other applications of dance, such as social work of various kinds and the whole, immensely important recreational field.

239 The nature of provision

This leads us to consider more broadly the nature of local education authority provision for vocational training for dance and for dance which sometimes needs support from the private sector. We did not mention for example the word 'amateur' when we considered forms of continuing education in chapter 11, nor when we concluded in chapter 9 that one result of the new dance options at tertiary level might be to produce adults interested and knowledgeable enough to continue their dance interest as a leisure activity in amateur form. If they do not do this, indeed, a significant part of the value of their studies will have been lost. If they do, and develop local amateur groups and local opportunity to dance within the framework of continuing education, they are likely to ask the local education authority to draw on some of the specialist skills of local private sector dance teachers, particularly if these skills include performance experience. Thus to provide adequate dance opportunity over the wide field of vocational and pre-vocational training, continuing education and amateur activity is likely to require from the local education authority a willingness to assess and provide from all available local resources, maintained and non-maintained, because 'provision' will need to be something more than paying for classes. To be adequate, we suggest it will need 'to include the quantity, quality and use ... of resources of all kinds, accommodation, equipment, text books, reference books, books for wider general reading, audio-visual and other aids to learning, supporting staff ... teaching resources ... and the appropriateness of the time allocated.' This interpretation of provision by HM Inspectorate in *Aspects of Secondary Education in England* is linked with a philosophy of response which we feel can summarise the relationship we seek between the local education authority and the private sector, assuming the private sector possesses an expertise the local authority needs. It is an exchange in which the local education authority provides what HM Inspectors urge for each school, a provision which 'included the way in which the school saw its obligations to all its pupils, and how it sought to fulfil these obligations through its curriculum in the widest sense and by its organisation of appropriate support and guidance.'[18] The recipe is one we hope will be applied to support those young dancers who need help from the private sector for vocational or other purposes.

15 Private Dance Studios

240 Structure of the private sector

In this and the next two chapters we review the structure of private and vocational training in the non-maintained sector of English, Scottish and Welsh education. By and large the opportunities and problems are the same in all three countries, except that vocational training in Scotland and Wales, as well as the remoter regions of England, requires particular dedication to overcome distances and the lack of large centres of population. It may be helpful to begin by summarising the structure of the private sector. It falls into four parts. First are private dance studios whose situation and future we examine in this chapter. Second are vocational training schools, that is, the general stage schools, independent dance schools, and specialist dance schools we examine in the next chapter. Third, are the tertiary institutions and processes examined in chapter 17. Fourth, are specialist teacher training institutions examined in chapter 18.

241 Definition of private dance studio

By private dance studio, sometimes called local dance school, we mean a studio run by an individual teacher, usually self-employed, often helped by one or more (usually part-time) assistants, to teach dancing in some form to children, non-vocational older students (though some retain older students for vocational purposes), and/or (usually in London) professional dancers and students. The studios or schools usually have about 200 pupils, the pupils probably attending one class a week. The classes range from infants,[73] aged 2½—5 years, to students over 18. Mostly the studios cater for young children, only a very small proportion of whom attend with any vocational purpose. All the studios are private enterprises charging fees for their service.

242 Special research

Special research, summarised at Appendix E, enables us to show the geographical distribution of the institutions discussed in this and the next chapter, and to indicate here some of the characteristics of private studios. We were able to undertake this special research because all the significant studios and schools discussed in this and the next chapter regularly submit candidates for examination to the four major examining bodies of the United Kingdom — the Royal Academy of Dancing (RAD); Imperial Society of Teachers of Dancing (ISTD), including the Cecchetti Society; the International Dance Teachers' Association (IDTA); and the British Ballet Organisation (BBO). Each body maintains records of its examinations and of the studios and schools concerned. Hence it becomes possible to study this important part of the non-maintained sector through an analysis of records in the possession of the major bodies. We were allowed to conduct such an analysis for the years 1973—1976 and are grateful to these bodies for making this possible for the first time in Britain. Intentionally the research omits ballroom, Latin American and sequence dancing. Although very important forms of social and recreational dance, these

119

forms nowadays are generally unrelated to dance in the educational system or to vocational training for the stage or dance teaching. We say 'generally' because we know of schools which organise social dance classes, usually with a visiting teacher, to the great benefit and enjoyment of students. We recognise, too, that proficiency in social dancing is an asset for life.

243 Geographical distribution of studios .

During 1973–1976, 2,888 general stage schools, independent dance schools, specialist dance schools and private dance studios in Britain submitted candidates for the grade or major examinations of the four principal examining bodies. The geographical distribution of these schools and studios is shown on the map at Appendix E. 51% of the 2,888 institutions are concentrated in London, the Home Counties and the South East and South West of England. 30% are concentrated in London and the Home Counties alone where live 23% of Britain's population. Others are concentrated mostly in the areas of big cities, but Scotland and Wales seem very poorly served in all areas. Of the 2,888 institutions less than 100 comprise general stage schools, independent dance schools or specialist dance schools described in the next chapter. We are discussing, therefore, about 2,800 private dance studios mostly run by just one or two teachers. A statistically insignificant number of members of the examining bodies failed to enter candidates during the years in question and the 10.5% overlap or dual membership, which we checked, was smaller than we had expected. Therefore we feel these figures give a fairly accurate picture of the private studios whose teachers are confident enough in their standards to enter candidates for examinations held by one or more of the four principal examining bodies. There is no reason to suppose that any significant change has taken place since 1976.

244 What the studios teach

Over 94% of our 2,800 studios include classical ballet in their curriculum. 57% teach ballet only and a further 35% teach ballet with one or more options such as modern dance, national dance, tap and so on.* Classical ballet, therefore, is overwhelmingly the strongest influence in the non-maintained sector at the present time, although the increasing popularity of the ISTD's modern dance and national syllabi may indicate the change to which we drew attention in paragraph 216. The largest career opportunities nowadays require dancers competent in classical ballet and modern dance, a double need which is bound, in the long run, to influence what is taught in private studios.

245 Who the studios teach

In sum, the courses offered by a private teacher usually concentrate upon the age range 5–11 or 12 and are based on classical ballet. Many offer classes at the two ends of this range for infants and for students aged 16 or more. Very few — less than 1% in our researches — submit candidates for the higher level of professional examinations such as the

* The option of teaching contemporary dance, as taught, say, at the London School of Contemporary Dance is omitted because such teachers tend not to enter students for examinations and/or teach in the community situations.

major examinations of the RAD and its equivalent in the other examining bodies. In the youngest classes there may be some boys but many of these drop out after the age of 6 or 7. Since almost all teachers enter children for the grade examinations of the major bodies, discussed in greater detail in chapter 19, we can calculate that the number of children served by the four major examining bodies of the private sector is about 270,000, or 2.9% of the total child population. Most of these children attend once a week and boys probably represent only 5% of the total.

246 The 'grey' areas of private teaching

In analysing these figures and comparing them with what some of us know in detail about particular areas of the country, and what is known of the work of smaller examining bodies, it is clear that there remain a considerable number of private studios which lie outside our research. Some of these studios are of good quality by any standards. Some, particularly in London, cater for the professional dancer rather than for children and grade examinations. These are considered in chapter 17. Some, however, claiming to teach classical ballet, jazz, tap, stage dance and so on, lack standards to an extent which we think may endanger their students in ways indicated in the next paragraph. The problem, of course, exists in the maintained sector, too, but in the private sector, where dance studies may be more intense, it can be that much more damaging to the child. Teachers in these 'grey' areas in both sectors imperil by unacceptable standards the children they teach and the livelihood and reputation of the rest of the dance teaching profession. The size of the area in the private sector is hard to quantify but we believe it to be sufficiently significant to make it a matter of urgency to introduce some kind of licensing system which can establish and maintain nationally agreed criteria for all private dance teachers, ultimately related also to dance teaching in the maintained sector.

247 Need for a licence system

At present no one requires a dance teacher to register with any statutory or professional body. Yet it is compulsory to register with a local authority if one wishes to open, say, a job agency. No one requires a dance teacher to register with the DES because dance is not regarded as a form of academic education. Yet dance teachers are guiding and forming young bodies which can be damaged permanently by inadequate teaching. Less obvious, but no less serious, is the danger to children's personal development as a result of intense competition and exhibitionism, and the effect of poor taste and low standards on their developing aesthetic judgement. There is no system which tests every private dance teacher's experience, knowledge of physiology or anatomy, psychology and child development, professional background, understanding of steps and music, or the suitability of premises used for dancing. A licensing system is needed. Like the accreditation of schools recommended in paragraph 248, we know such a system will take time to introduce and may be a painful process. But both measures are necessary and will benefit the profession.

121

248 Establishing a licence system

A licence system can take several forms and base itself on a number of models, like the Scottish Register of Teachers to which we have referred already. The aim is to create a national and local register through which dance teachers can be licensed to teach in the way doctors, solicitors and other professions license their members to sustain standards and regulate entry. In the first instance the register might base itself on procedures introduced at the time when unqualified teachers in the maintained sector were required to become qualified. By these procedures all future teachers needed to pass the proper qualifying examination while existing 'unqualified' teachers with, say, ten years teaching experience and a good teaching record, were accepted for the register alongside teachers with a recognised qualification. We believe that the establishment of such a register and licence system should become an urgent priority for the National Councils, recently established in England and Scotland, and in Wales. For this reason it is important that these councils for dance education and training are so constituted as to give confidence that their accreditation committees will be able to discharge their great responsibility in a competent manner. An equal balance of specialists in various forms of dance is needed, together with educationists who are experienced in methods of assessment.

249 Low status of private dance teaching

The need for a licence system draws attention in turn to the disregarded status of the private studio dance teacher. But a licence system will not elevate this status unless other factors too are considered. We think the most important of these factors all contribute to the present low status of private dance teaching. They are: the social isolation of the private teacher; lack of professional status; poor local authority liaison; inadequate information to parents; prevalence of the apprentice system of training; low salaries and fees; poor premises; failure to recruit boys. Briefly, we examine each of these factors.

250 Isolation of private dance teachers

The world of the private dance teacher is bounded usually by her (the vast majority are women) studio and students, other teachers in the local group of the examining body to which she belongs, and her own family. She has few professional contacts with other dance teachers, such as dance teachers in the maintained sector; few links with the local government structure around her in spite of its daily influence upon her life; few interests outside her dancing. Of course this generalisation has many exceptions but we believe it not unfair. As much as anything it is a result of too narrow a training, particularly if she belongs to the older generation trained through the apprentice method described in paragraph 256. Younger teachers tend to have a wider view but young or old, on the whole, tend to be excessively suspicious about the activities of dance teachers in their own area outside their own group (even sometimes within it!) and extremely ignorant about the workings of local government and how it might help them. Such suspicion and ignorance work constantly to their disadvantage and mean there is no representative voice to speak for dance teachers at local level.

251 Over-
coming isolation To overcome this isolation requires conscious effort within an already overburdened schedule. It means contact with relevant local government departments, especially the new leisure departments often organising dance events, more contact with local schools and regular liaison with fellow teachers. Because all this takes time a number of teachers' groups have suggested to us the need to form Councils of Dance Teachers within each local education authority area, bringing together private dance teachers of every persuasion with those teaching dance in the maintained sector. We welcome very much this idea because we think it particularly important that teachers of dancing in the private sector should know more about the training and philosophy of teachers of dancing in the maintained sector and vice versa. Such Councils also could discuss matters of common interest such as provision for gifted children, representations to the authority over the allocation of resources within the area, and so on. Other teachers' groups have remarked that since so few private teachers are informed about the issues raised, for example, in the terms of reference for this Dance Study, or about local authority and economic matters, it is the duty of their professional bodies to organise regular workshops on such subjects. They criticise their professional bodies for too narrow a concentration on examination syllabi to the exclusion of wider professional needs. This is a point to which we return in chapter 19.

252 Lead by
professional
bodies While there might be historical justification for criticising the parochialism of professional bodies in the private sector, it is not entirely fair today. To begin with, the professional bodies have taken a lead in establishing national representative councils in each country. Next, two leading bodies, the RAD and ISTD have made strong efforts to enlarge their professional interests and to co-ordinate examination requirements and procedures. Finally, all the professional teaching bodies of the private sector do already, of course, organise local groups of their members usually for practical purposes to do with teaching the techniques in which they specialise. It seems to us, therefore, that the broadening of local contacts might best be encouraged by extending these initiatives through discussion. The discussion would need to embrace the Council for Dance Education and Training in England, the Scottish Council for Dance and the Dance Council for Wales, all developing connections in their respective countries with professional dance bodies, local education authorities and teachers themselves in each area. The result might be local dance councils of the kind already suggested or the establishment of local branches of each national council. Whatever the method the need for local collaboration between the maintained and non-maintained sectors and all dance teachers to end a damaging isolation is as clear as the fact that only these interests themselves can take the most suitable actions.

253 Raising
professional
standards The isolation of private dance teachers from most of the community around them reflects also their lack of professional status. The need to elevate professional status, assisted by some system of licensing for

123

dance teachers, has been a major concern in every area we have visited. Meeting these two needs, however, depends upon strengthening the newly established national professional bodies. Only when the dance teaching profession in the private sector possesses a single professional body organised nationally and locally, able to license dance teachers, accredit schools, sustain agreed national examination and teaching standards and fix agreed fees to avoid undercutting, will the individual teacher be more protected economically and the profession itself achieve the national status which is its due, whence comes the power to speak with a national voice to central and local government. We welcome unreservedly, therefore, the establishment of the Council for Dance Education and Training in England (CDET), Scottish Council for Dance (SCD) and the Dance Council for Wales (DCW), all under the impulse of this study.

254 Strengthening liaison with other bodies

A national register and licence system supported by a national professional body would strengthen immeasurably the position of private dance teachers in their communities, particularly their relations with other bodies. Relations with local authorities have been discussed already in chapter 14. A similar close liaison is needed with RAAs. Examples of collaboration already exist. Best known is the Royal Academy of Dancing Scholarship Centre funded by the Yorkshire Arts Association. This is a development of a scholarship scheme which has existed almost since the Academy was founded. Its aim is to discover and promote young talent in classical ballet through special classes by visiting teachers arranged within the region. It illustrates one way in which a RAA can encourage good teaching and good teachers as well as young talent. Other ways include the collaboration of private dance teachers and their students in the educational residences of visiting professional companies funded by RAAs, and collaboration between teachers and association officers who have been given responsibility for dance. These initiatives, however, are still comparatively rare so that, as with local authorities, the two sides need to see in each other a resource to be developed. In particular it is important in due course that RAAs should appoint officers with principal responsibility for dance, as in the Greater London Arts Association, rather than treating dance always as a secondary subject.

255 Better guidance for parents

As with local authorities and RAAs, so with parents: liaison is needed. Inadequate guidance to parents is a grave problem, coupled with the lack of agreed scales of fees for each area referred to in paragraph 260 below. Hence parents turn to the cheapest, but not necessarily the best, teacher; or judge teachers on their ability to produce quick results in examination and medal tests, regardless of the quality of these tests. Solutions to these problems lie again with the existing professional and national bodies. In this connection we believe it important that the central reference and information service, mentioned in chapter 11 should serve teachers as well as local authorities, parents and students. Teachers are a natural source of information in their areas. Many

124

teachers, therefore, feel a need for guidance and information about vocational requirements and possibilities to pass on to students and parents. Such a broad information service would need to be accompanied by the production of appropriate literature and an educational campaign to warn parents of the dangers of inadequately trained instructors.

256 Apprentice system of training   A factor which compounds the isolation of private teachers, and may limit their professional ability, is the prevalence of the apprentice system of training dance teachers.* This usually means that a teacher develops one or two of her keenest students to become assistants over a number of years, with perhaps the benefit of coaching from one or more outside experts. If the assistants remain in the business they might 'inherit' a teacher's practice when she retires, or move away to open their own studios. In any event, the training received is of the narrowest, confined to a range of technique appropriate to young pupils. It was to overcome the limitations of this method that the major examining bodies established training colleges to prepare teachers for the private sector and to reduce the number of apprentice-trained teachers. We believe it important that the private sector, like the maintained sector, should require all new teachers to have passed one of the appropriate training courses, and that this should be a part of any licensing system which might be introduced. We return to this issue in chapter 18.

257 Low salaries   Linked, of course, with training and career prospects, and affecting every other aspect of a teacher's work, is the problem of salaries and fees. We think it undeniable that the remuneration of private teachers is so unacceptably low it should be the immediate concern of all relevant national bodies. Inseparable from it are the costs of running a private local studio/school and the fee levels which can be charged realistically for classes. 'None of us could afford to teach without some kind of financial support from husbands, private income or a part-time job,' wrote one group of teachers in evidence to us. 'One school has changed hands three times in the last few years. The first time two teachers, having lost their husbands, were forced to find a job with a living wage. The same school has lost pianists for the same reason.' If it was not for the institution of marriage, private dance teaching today would be greatly diminished. All over Britain private teachers are subsidising students by working for salaries which are too low because they feel parents cannot pay more.

---

*   Our attention has been drawn to a use of the term 'apprentice' to mean a student who wishes to be a teacher and who serves a certain amount of time, even a year or so, assisting a local teacher before moving on to a teacher training course at an established college. This, of course, is not the apprentice system we criticise here since it is preliminary to a proper professional training.

A first step towards some national agreement on dance teachers' salaries and class fees in the private sector was taken in 1977 by four of the main professional organisations concerned – the BBO, the ISTD which has initiated several attempts to publish information and issue recommendations on salaries, the LSCD and the RAD. They have recommended jointly that a young teacher of 21 with intermediate executant standard and two years' teaching experience should receive £2,100 a year in a full-time post or £2 an hour part-time. 'Younger, less experienced teachers would receive appreciably less. Teachers with higher qualifications and longer experience should receive considerably more.' Some schools already pay above these rates but a very wide segment of schools and private studios at once declared the recommended rates too high. Consequently the recommendation was never generally implemented even though the rates are some way below the rate for a maintained school teacher of comparable experience, or the current Equity minimum of £78 a week for a young dancer. Class fees, it was maintained, cannot be increased at the present time without risk of losing children altogether. Therefore, some witnesses argued, it would be better to develop regional agreements appropriate to the economic level of each region. While we recognise that the development of regional agreements might result marginally in raising the general level of remuneration for private dance teachers as a whole, it would also attract the best teaching talent to richer areas able to afford better salaries. Thus the disparity between rich and poor would be increased unfairly penalising children in the poorer areas. We think, therefore, an agreed national level is essential if the private dance teacher is to remain in business.

Private teachers have represented to us that 'many schools are facing a battle for survival for two main reasons: rising costs, and the growth of dance in state education. In rural areas this (running a school) involves hiring a hall in four or five different towns and villages at many varying rents. Public transport is either non-existent or too time consuming, therefore a car is a necessity. Pianists, if available, require transport. In many cases as much time is spent on travelling as in teaching. Classes are often very small and therefore uneconomic. Even in these conditions there may be two, or even three, teachers covering the same area, sometimes even using the same hall on different days.' We think this is a truthful portrait of the problems of the private teacher in rural areas. Some of the problems belong also to teachers in urban areas. The evidence of rising costs, for example, threatening the existence of private teachers throughout Britain is incontrovertible. But the problem needs to be faced principally by teachers and their organisations themselves. Services need to be rationalised; co-operation needs to replace competition; a united front needs to be presented in dialogue with local education authorities; above all, to build upon rather than reduce the growth of dance in the maintained sector. Increasingly the maintained sector is able to satisfy the needs of children who might otherwise attend a local dance school once a week. These children, however, are the bread and butter of the local dance school. Without them the private teacher cannot survive. There is a genuine problem here which can be resolved only by dialogue with local education authorities who should accept that private dance teachers are a resource upon which they should draw in the interests of the children they serve.

260 The problem of fees   To meet rising costs and pay for better teacher remuneration some increase in class fees in unavoidable.* An increase is important particularly if the private sector of dance teaching is to be enriched by recruits retired from the dancing profession, many of whom will have families to sustain. The ISTD, which regularly issues advice on fees, suggested in July 1979 that 'the norm should be £8–£10 a term with leading schools in expensive areas commanding £12–£14. We were recently asked to advise on the salary for an experienced and well qualified teacher of ballet/modern and – calculating the hours per week over the year at the very moderate rate of £2 an hour – produced £3,750 a year which is not a high salary nowadays. But how many assistants, or indeed principals of small schools achieve this income?'[68] First, the low remuneration of private dance teachers threatens recruitment and standards in the profession. 'New members' remarks the ISTD, 'will not enter the profession until a proper and professional basis of remuneration is established.' Second, the conflict between income and outgoings on salaries, rent, heat, light, and pianists is so acute that it can be resolved only by concerted action from the whole private sector of dance teaching. There are some areas, like Manchester and the South East, where the number of private dance teachers is increasing and dance in the maintained sector also receives strong support suggesting a correlation worth testing elsewhere. In general, though, it is difficult to be optimistic about long term prospects for studio teachers, however valuable their service, unless the maintained sector contributes in some way to sustain the best of these services, and the private sector introduces a licence system through which minimum fees, salaries and standards can be enforced, and, equally important, 'introduces sanctions to reduce the undercutting which is rife.'[68]

261 Premises   Central to the problem of costs is the problem of premises. Falling school rolls have closed a number of schools which now can provide admirable spaces of the kind we have in mind. The difficulty of finding suitable premises for teaching movement and dance, lecture–demonstrations and examinations increases as city centres are pulled down for redevelopment. Consequently this problem is a major concern of bodies like the Physical Education Association and the Movement and Dance Division of the Central Council for Physical Recreation as well as dance organisations. In rural areas the problem has always been acute. In urban areas the purpose-designed office blocks, now replacing the

---

*   One well-known teacher running two studios in Wales told us she felt the maximum she could charge for children was 50p a lesson, but this was not enough to cover studio rents, heating, lighting, petrol and pianists. She got nothing.

multi-purpose buildings which represented a city's commercial and domestic past, rarely contain appropriate floor spaces for conversion to full- or part-time use for movement and dance purposes. This issue demands comprehensive action by all the dance and movement organisations concerned. For a start, local surveys (like one undertaken by the Greater London Arts Association for the outer-London area) could be carried out by RAAs, or by local headquarters of dance and movement teachers' organisations, to establish where potential studio spaces exist. But a piecemeal approach, dependent on local finance and time, is not likely to amount to what is required for the country as a whole. Ideally, a policy is needed to include teaching/performance spaces in re-development plans* or, temporarily, an assessment should be made of what is available year by year. This can come about only through pressure by national and local organisations.

262 Today's studios

The premises which teachers use today and the number of pupils they are able to teach show no consistent pattern across the country. The better known studios probably own their premises, or at least possess them on a long lease, and may have two or three hundred children on their books, with a staff of several teachers. In this event the studios will be equipped with barres of suitable height round the walls. There is likely to be a piano reasonably tuned and/or a tape- or record-player, toilets, proper heating, a changing room, and even a small office for administration and, above all, a suitable floor. Such studios are a minority. Most teachers hire a hall from a church or some other institution for the hours they need it on anything from one to six days a week. At other times the hall will be available for other functions. This probably means a hard, unsuitable floor, no barres, often no piano and almost invariably inadequate maintenance, cleanliness, heating, toilets and changing facilities as well as classes which are unavoidably too large. Thus classes are conducted in premises which are unsuitable in most respects.

263 Local authority spaces

Many private teachers feel their problems would be eased if allowed to hire school spaces at reasonable rates during out-of-school hours. The unwillingness of local education authorities to allow this is widely resented, although the problem is not easy to solve. We have pointed out the general lack of communication between studio teacher and local education authority for which the teacher is at least as much to blame as the authority. There is also a lack of communication with head teachers. Nearly always head teachers prefer to approve hiring their spaces to someone they know. This means private dance teachers should make personal contact with local head teachers, particularly where their pupils are members of the school in question. Reasons for

---

*   This should include early contact with Planning Officers, emphasising that floors should not be laid on concrete if they are to be used for dance or other forms of movement. See note 30 and Appendix G.

unwillingness to release school spaces are variable, ranging from outright refusal on the part of heads and caretakers, even if the authority itself agrees, to the application of a fairly common rule that school (public) buildings must not be used for purposes of personal gain.* For example, out of a postal survey of 20 outer London boroughs undertaken on our behalf on this subject, 15 replied. Of these, seven applied the rule against personal gain (the financial reward of the teacher), but the other eight seemed to have no overall policy and so would refer applications for committee approval. Most said they would support voluntary dance groups and societies, many also would pay the tutor. Very often the criteria for use is to 'any organisation within the Borough whose aims are educational or whose objects are closely associated with the teaching given in schools'. Hence there are opportunities for dance schools. The Leicestershire authority allows the use of school premises by an approved teacher subject to examination of the profit-making aspect. It is also possible that polytechnics, schools of education and universities might be willing to co-operate in this way, especially if their own students can benefit through special classes. The Sports Council has conducted a number of studies and experiments in different areas on this subject so should also be consulted locally. Principally, however, there should be immediate negotiations between national dance organisations and Local Authority Associations on measures to make available for dance use suitable spaces in local authority areas, perhaps using where necessary the special moveable floor described at appendix G.

264 Recruitment of boys

The last of the factors we think affects the professional status of the private dance teacher is the failure to recruit boys to dancing in numbers which can match the girls. This is a problem discussed already in the maintained sector and much of what we noted there applies here. The introduction of a modern theatre dance syllabus for boys by the ISTD, however, seems to be having a success from which others might learn. At present this has been developed from grade 1 to pre-elementary level but it will continue soon to the advanced syllabus. The response from teachers not only in Britain, but throughout the world, has been encouraging, but particularly encouraging has been the response from boys. The number joining classes and taking the grade examinations grows daily, whereas in the past the number was minimal. The boys' work is exciting and athletic in approach while maintaining the same qualities of flexibility and rhythmic development contained in the basic syllabi for girls.

---

* In our experience the term 'gain' is frequently a misnomer. A dance teacher may certainly make a profit from the transaction, so the rule may apply. Often, though, he or she breaks even in providing what might be termed a community service. The answer, as much as anything, lies in proper liaison and explanation on both sides.

265 Conclusion Private dance teachers, then, presently provide a service costed far below its true value, often at considerable personal sacrifice. Usually they teach classical ballet, modern dance, national dance, jazz or tap and prepare their pupils for the grade and (sometimes) major examinations of the examining body of their choice, as well as entering pupils for local and national dance festivals. In time she or he may become an examiner of one of these examining bodies and/or a festival adjudicator. Although rarely having the opportunity to teach children showing signs of potential beyond the age of 10 or 11, they have, nevertheless, a reputation for generosity in passing on talented pupils to vocational training, and of doing their best for their pupils within their limitations of individual ability, training and experience. Although a reasonable living must be a consideration, and is a growing problem, this is not the main objective in most cases. For years, in fact, such teachers and their sacrifices have been the basis of the private sector and the foundation of the dance profession. Although today their position is threatened, we believe private teachers will remain essential for many years to come in the pattern of dance education and training in Britain. If their contribution is to continue effectively, however, a wide range of improvements is needed. These are listed in our recommendations.

16 Vocational Training for Theatre Dance

266 A new situation

Before moving to a more detailed consideration of the categories of vocational school discussed in this chapter we feel we should clarify our warning in paragraph 14 of a crisis threatening the system described here and in the next two chapters. Since the beginning of the academic year 1979/80, and whilst we were considering the final drafts of this report, evidence began to accumulate that more talented students than in the past are failing to receive grants from their local education authorities to study dance, whether to become professional dancers or teachers of dancing. The schools, colleges and other institutions we have consulted all believe that unless there is a change in Government policy this situation will get worse in 1980/81 and beyond. It is impossible to judge exactly what will happen, but we believe all these institutions, which depend on discretionary grants, have good cause for alarm. This is why we have made urgent recommendations that the talented, rather than the monied, should be supported in vocational training and that the leading private schools and colleges of the British vocational training system are able to survive with undiminished standards.

267 Basis of classification

We should clarify also our attitude to the various kinds of dance covered by the categories of school we discuss and our reasons for the classification we offer. We make no assumption that any one style, such as classical ballet, is more important than, say, modern dance, jazz dance, ethnic dance or forms of popular dance. We acknowledge the contribution and importance of popular dance culture and have urged already that the teaching of dance in the maintained sector should take more account of this culture in the education of young people. The same arguments apply to the non-maintained sector. Within the broad context of all dance in Britain, however, the professional dancer makes a particular contribution through the creation, recreation and re-interpretation of roles in established and new choreographic works. This might take place in a large subsidised theatre like the Royal Opera House, in a regional dance company, in commercial music theatre or in films or television. To prepare for this contribution a special training is required. Within this training particular schools, or groups of schools, tend to point students in particular directions. These emphases form the basis of our classification.

268 Classification

Some distinction is needed, we think, between schools whose graduates pass primarily into the commercial dance theatre, cabaret, television and the cinema and those whose graduates pass primarily into the subsidised sector of classical and modern dance companies. There is no exclusivity in either case. Since most of the first group combine general education with a general stage training in acting, singing and dance, we call these schools general stage schools. The second group of schools combine general education with an emphasis on dance even when other

131

theatrical skills are taught. Here further subdivision is needed. The majority are independent dance schools, and colleges, independent because they are unconnected with any particular dance company, and independent in the accepted educational sense. The Royal Ballet School, however, and the London School of Contemporary Dance have a special link respectively with the Royal Ballet and London Contemporary Dance Theatre. Hence we call these two schools special dance schools, treat them separately from other independent dance schools, and welcome the possibility of a third such school to support The Scottish Ballet in Scotland, discussed at greater length in paragraphs 288–291 below. This classification is arbitrary but necessary.

269 Structure of the chapter

The non-maintained sector of dance training has developed over half a century without plan or co-ordination. The result is a confusion of often excellent institutions which Government and others have found difficult to help individually. Only now is the whole sector beginning to work together. Out of this mixture we identify a pattern which seems to us logical even if the dividing lines of our classification are often blurred. In the paragraphs which follow we describe in turn general stage schools; independent dance schools; special dance schools; and the educational plans of The Scottish Ballet. Next we identify and comment upon particular problems revealed by our examination.

270 General stage schools

General stage schools are private, fee-paying institutions which offer a training as singers, dancers and actors to many of the young artists who enter a range of employment from commercial music theatre to community theatre. In the sense that they do not specialise in dance more than other theatrical skills, they are borderline to our inquiry. Some of their graduates, however, aim to enter a subsidised classical or modern dance company. In this event they will need to complete their training at one of the other independent or special schools. The training they receive at general stage schools, therefore, has significance here, and still more so if they seek or find employment as professional dancers in commercial theatre.

271 Requirements of commercial dance theatre

To succeed in today's commercial dance theatre, a candidate should have had a full ballet training, be familiar with a modern dance technique and probably also tap, and have a natural flair for today's popular dancing as well as having singing and acting ability. To acquire such a range of skills puts the general stage school and student under considerable pressure. So far as dance is concerned, producers and choreographers have complained to us that many schools train the bodies of their students but fail to equip them adequately to meet the demands the commercial theatre now makes. 'They have physical technique and a dancer's vocabulary, but very little "dance" ', runs the complaint, 'a dancer should be trained to be able to "attempt" any form of dance. Obviously pointe work may not be the forte of all, nor tap, nor even jazz, but all dancers should have some knowledge. Examination certificates and letters of recommendation do not make dancers, nor prove anything.' We believe this implied criticism is justified. Although a few of these schools sustain with ease a national reputation and general stage schools as a group play an important, even unique, role in vocational training for the commercial dance theatre. We have found their standards to be erratic, often revealing a considerable gap between what is taught and what is actually needed by commercial dance theatre as it has developed since the 1960s.

272 Need for more theatrical experience

There is, for example, a lack of proper professional preparation. At auditions one can see a marked difference between the majority of young dancers arriving straight from a general stage school and those who have had some professional experience, however little. Those from school rarely know what is required at auditions in dress, manner, appearance, standards or style. The conclusion must be that their teachers also do not know, probably because very few general stage schools, even in London, have the services of teachers who have been performers and are able to give their pupils something to *dance* in class instead of sequences of steps interpreting nothing. Hence 'school' graduates all too often lack adaptability in different styles of dance. They are able to interpret what a choreographer gives them only in the style in which they have been taught. They are not trained to grasp differences and appreciate nuances of various choreographic expressions. Thus they are not prepared properly for a professional life in which adaptability is a major requirement. Especially is this so in television, where choreographers and dancers usually need to work very fast, often adopting several different approaches and/or moods within the same show.

273 Need for a broader approach

The lack of a professional approach which we have found in the teaching of so many general stage schools, and their narrow view of vocational training, is reflected also in frequently inadequate material conditions within which that training takes place, and a general lack of richness in syllabi. Students are rarely encouraged, or have the time, to read, listen to or reflect upon the wider background of theatre and general culture within which the profession exists. This, we believe, is not the most appropriate way to train theatre artists, particularly when the professional child invariably must enter full-time training at school-leaving age and so can have had no more advanced studies. Enrichment should mean the proper integration of dance with general education rather than separating these elements into two compartments as so often is the case. From all points of view, therefore, it is incumbent on general stage schools to review the balance of their courses, to seek to produce graduates more richly prepared for the growing demands of professional life and the wider opportunities now before their students. Such criticisms do not deny the very real dedication and hard work undertaken by staff and students at general stage schools, especially those which have built a solid reputation on the basis of a curriculum offering full stage training. We believe, therefore, that improvement is a matter primarily for the private sector itself, and in particular for the Council for Dance Education and Training in England and its equivalents in Scotland and Wales. Standards might improve if these bodies can prepare lists of accredited schools and if local education authorities restrict their grants to these schools.

274 Independent dance schools

Graduates from independent dance schools aim at careers in subsidised classical or modern dance companies, the commercial dance theatre and, sometimes, the dramatic theatre. They are of two kinds. Some are fee-paying boarding or day institutions which children enter by audition between the ages of 10 or 11 (sometimes younger) and 14. Others accept children by audition at the age of 16 (sometimes a little older) exclusively for vocational training. As a category, therefore, they cover a wide variation of age range and curricula. Constantly, members of our study returned from visits impressed by the general life of such schools. But the most noticeable difference between these independent dance schools and general stage schools is the quality of dance education and the facilities available. At present, therefore, these schools form an important element of a system of vocational dance training in Britain which is entirely unsupported by the State. Some of their students will transfer in due course to the Royal Ballet Upper School or the London School of Contemporary Dance or to one of the other vocational theatre courses now available in drama and/or dance. Others who obtain the necessary GCE qualifications and have reached a set standard of dance may elect to remain, or will enter (if it is a post-16 institution) for a course preparing them for a professional career on stage or to move on to one of the established dance teacher courses.

275 Regional role of independent dance schools

We suggest that some of these schools are valuable potential regional centres to which could be sent young dancers of promise on grants from surrounding authorities: centres where specialist courses could be arranged, and sources of expert advice and opinion when assessments for grants and so on are required by local authorities. There seems general agreement among the schools that an important part of their future lies in being used, and funded, in this way. Such a development would help, too, to mitigate four of their major problems. The first is their almost exclusive female composition. The second is their comparatively narrow social base. The third is the difficulty of recruiting dance staff who are proficient in their subjects but also have the broad cultural perspective necessary to see the school as a whole and relate academic and vocational work. The fourth problem is their finance. Local authority support at the moment, (ie grant aid for students) ranges between 25% and 50% and seems likely to fall rather than increase.

276 Need for relationship with maintained sector

Only some closer relationship with the maintained sector can alter this decline. Most of the schools accept this situation even though a proportion of parents are unwilling to discuss changes which would alter in any way the schools' independent status. The choice, however, is clear — either elimination sometime in the future as the maintained sector develops its own dance teaching and expertise in the field of these

134

schools, or collaboration now to establish a partnership between the maintained and private sectors to benefit everyone concerned. How the partnership will be initiated and developed is a matter for the partners and will vary from region to region. We consider, nevertheless, that independent schools could make so valuable a contribution to the region around them that discussions to establish them as regional centres should be initiated at once with the authorities concerned.

277 Special dance schools: Royal Ballet links with maintained sector

We turn now to special schools, first the Royal Ballet School. It is divided into two sections, an Upper School at Barons Court, West London, and a Lower School at White Lodge in Richmond Park, Richmond. Entry to the Lower School is at the age of 11, or in relatively few cases, 12; entry to the Upper School is usually 16, though foreign students may, exceptionally, enter up to 19. It is important to note a third section of the school, that of the Junior Associates, aged 8—10, whose classes, twice a week, take place in the Upper School and, as from Autumn 1979, at Sadler's Wells Theatre. Membership of the Junior Associates classes brings no automatic acceptance by the Lower School at the age of 11, but it is a useful preparation. The particular significance of the Junior Associates is that since 1977 a scheme has been developed, in co-operation with local education authorities of Greater London and the ILEA, to recruit them from the maintained sector and not only, as previously, from the private dance schools. At dance sessions, organised by the local authorities' advisers among the schools, teachers from the Royal Ballet School attend and make a series of selections, culminating, for a few children, in the offer of a place in the Junior Associate classes. So far this scheme has operated only in London, where in 1978—79 (the scheme's first full school year) some 3,500 children were seen. Of these 12 were offered Junior Associate places. Arrangements are now being studied for extending the scheme outside London — probably, in the first instance, to Wales. The significance of the Royal Ballet School's 'LEA Scheme', as it is generally known, is that it represents a first attempt by the School to look for talent among the mass of school children instead of receiving candidates only from the private schools of dance. The number of children recruited under the scheme, relative to the large number seen at the dance sessions in the boroughs, is bound to be small. The scheme, nevertheless, represents an important new policy.

278 Royal Ballet Lower School

Only the Lower School for children aged 11—16 years receives any fee assistance from the DES. In this, unlike the Upper School, it is comparable with the Menuhin School of Music which receives fee assistance up to the age of 18. Thus the Lower School is unique among vocational dance schools in the United Kingdom. Yet the support provided since 1973 is not total. Direct assistance with school fees from the DES requires also a parental contribution based on income. In addition parents pay for uniform, optional extras such as music lessons (important to a dancer) and shoes. This last creates a particular financial outlay for girls since each pair of shoes now costs between £5—£6 and lasts 2—3

135

weeks, illustrating a further anomaly in grant aid for dance students. Not only is assistance restricted to, and partial in, the Lower School, but there is no equivalent of the allowance for materials which is provided, for example, in grants to art students. Moreover, a successful student in the Lower School could be prevented, as already pointed out, from graduating to the Upper School by the refusal of the local authority to provide the necessary discretionary grant. Up to now ways and means to help talented students have always been found in the absence of a sufficient grant. But within the present system of discretionary grants, having regard to present financial restrictions, there remains the very real possibility that the Upper School might have to reject a talented candidate because there is, as yet, no State support for the Upper School.

279 Entrance to the Lower School

The Lower School accommodates about 116 boarders and 5 day pupils. Applicants are invited to attend a preliminary audition at the age of 10; admission to the School is at the age of 11. There are a few places for 12 and 13 year olds. Preliminary auditions are held in London weekly throughout the year, also once a year in Manchester and Bristol. It is clear that there are many more candidates from the London area or near it than from further away. This implies that Londoners or near-Londoners have the greater opportunities for being auditioned. But it does not follow that, in present circumstances, the number of audition centres in the regions or the frequency of the regional auditions should be increased. The School used to hold auditions in other regional centres but eventually limited itself to the present two (Manchester and Bristol) because of the very poor response and inadequate conditions elsewhere. If Londoners, then, have the greater opportunities for admission to the School the reason would seem to be that there are more good teachers in the vicinity. One qualification should be made: the Junior Associate classes in the Upper School (twice a week for 8–10 year olds) are, manifestly, available only to those children who live in or about London. In this very young age group, therefore, geography may be said to favour the candidates for the Royal Ballet School who live in or near London. Nearly all the candidates have, until now, come from teachers in the private sector, that is from families who are paying for private tuition. From this it might seem to be at least arguable that candidature for the School was limited to the relatively well-off. But, in fact, the candidates are from too wide a variety of 'financial levels' for any such generalisation to be safely made. What is certain is that before the LEA Scheme, outlined in Para 277, began to operate, the pupils of the Lower School, chosen as they were almost exclusively from among children taught in private dancing schools, were being taken from a very small section of the child population of Britain. The operation of the LEA Scheme, seeking out talent, as it does, among the 8–10 year olds who are not getting private dance lessons, has begun to change this. But not until the scheme has spread nationwide, and until local authorities make it possible for all children

136

in their areas to have the opportunity for classical ballet training will the Royal Ballet School be able really to develop a system which assesses all possible talent in the country from preliminary to final audition. In this event the average number of 25 girls and boys at present taken each year for the first form might well stay the same, but the standard would rise because the School's area of recruitment would be very greatly enlarged.

280 Options at the Lower School

Entrants to the Lower School are accepted only on one year's trial in the first instance. The curriculum is that of a grammar school offering a range of subjects which prepare pupils for GCE, CSE, and, potentially, for tertiary education outside dancing if this should prove to be necessary. Successful students remain at White Lodge for a period of five years, at the conclusion of which they take their GCE and/or CSE examinations. But of course there is opportunity to discuss the limitations of a career in ballet. This may be for one of several reasons: an unforeseen physical change (this the most usual), temperamental unsuitability or a loss of interest. During the fourth year students are advised whether or not they will be offered a place at the Upper School. This would provide training for another two or three years, or up to the point at which they can audition for a company. Those who are accepted have no assurance that they will enter the Royal Ballet, since that decision is made only by the director and ballet masters of the Royal Ballet itself.

281 Entrance to the Upper School

Applicants to the Upper School who have not been through the Lower School may apply to be seen at preliminary auditions held throughout the year in London and in certain regional centres. The age limit for entry is from 16 years to 17 years 3 months for British applicants. Foreign students are considered, within reason, up to an age limit of 19 years. Candidates should preferably have attained at least an elementary standard of training in one of the accepted methods, though there is no rule about this. Final auditions are held in April of the year in which candidates wish to enter and, before acceptance, they have to undergo an orthopaedic examination. The usual intake for the Upper School is, roughly, 50 girls and 10–16 boys, not including those graduating from the Lower School. There is, therefore, substantial opportunity for dancers trained at general stage and independent dance schools, or with private teachers, always bearing in mind the limitations described in paragraph 267. Pupils are offered two years in the first instance, with an option on the School side not to renew after the first year. This is because, at the age then reached, there are possible faults which it is impossible to eradicate, or the physical development, especially of girls, has changed rapidly.

282 Options at the Upper School

Towards the end of training some students are selected for the School's graduate classes by the director of the Royal Ballet and his assistants, although this, of itself, is no guarantee of acceptance by the Royal Ballet as members of the Company. Students in the graduate classes of

137

the Upper School may be used in the corps de ballet of the Royal Ballet as 'extras' at Covent Garden, thus assisting the ballet master and teachers to assess their possibilities as future members of the Company. The number of students in the graduate classes varies from year to year, according to the talent in the school at the time of selection. Students are advised about auditions to be held elsewhere in Britain and are helped to apply for auditions to companies abroad. Although the recruitment of British dancers for companies on the European continent becomes increasingly difficult, it is notable that many students from the Royal Ballet School continue to achieve European employment, particularly in West Germany, but also in Switzerland, Belgium, Holland and, occasionally, France.

283 Finance and fees

Both Upper and Lower Schools are financed from fees, but on different bases. The Lower School, being 'fee assisted' from the DES has a measure of security lacking in the Upper School. In the Upper School students may be private fee-paying, or (as is much more usual for British students) assisted by discretionary awards from local education authorities. We return to the problem of mandatory and discretionary awards in paragraphs 293 and 294. Certain scholarships are offered also by the main ballet teaching organisations, such as the RAD, the Cecchetti Society and the BBO. These, in each case, are offered yearly to one girl or boy, the candidates being submitted by the organisation concerned. Thereafter, the final selection is by competition, the judges being the director of balletic studies and staff of the Royal Ballet Upper School. Overseas students are offered one year at first, and, in some cases, can be given a second year or even a third.

284 Special dance schools: London School of Contemporary Dance

The London School of Contemporary Dance was established in 1966 as a private fee-paying institution and five years later was recognised by the DES. It offers two courses. The main three-year professional course offers a liberal arts education built round a daily class in classical ballet and in contemporary dance technique (usually Graham-based), both taught by teachers who have themselves been professional dancers. This is likely soon to become a four-year course which will be beneficial especially to students with no previous intensive dance training. Choreographic classes and regular performances are considered particularly important in the training as is the tutorial system introduced in 1978. There is also a one-year course adaptable to the special needs and interests of older students and graduates whose work can be based upon the training offered for students wishing to become professional contemporary dancers. The result has been to create in little more than a decade a specifically British style of contemporary dance whose characteristics were acclaimed by American critics and dancers when the London Contemporary Dance Theatre made its debut in the United States in the summer of 1978.

285 Entrance requirements and career options

Selection is by audition and interview. A few places are open to students with exceptional creative or physical potential and to mature 16-year olds who have completed their schooling, but otherwise five O-levels are required and the minimum age is 17 at the time of entry in September. Auditions start in the previous December, and almost all British applicants come from the maintained sector. Its potential area of recruitment, therefore, is much broader than that of the Royal Ballet School. The ratio of male to female applications is also much higher than for classical ballet. Certificates are awarded to full-time students upon successful completion of the three-year course. Details of employment obtained by former students are given in paragraph 352. In sum, career options lead to professional performance or choreography, further study of a post-graduate nature, or teaching.

286 Finance and fees

Financially, the London School of Contemporary Dance has the same needs as the Royal Ballet Upper School, but those needs are relatively more pressing. Its premises in central London, including present rebuilding and enlargement, have been financed entirely from private sources, often at great sacrifice, from fees and from capital grants of £100,000 and £50,000 from the Arts Council's Housing the Arts Fund and from the Greater London Council respectively. At present it has a fund-raising campaign to complement resources which are inadequate to the task of building physically a national school of contemporary dance. A further restriction is the fact that only discretionary awards are available to students. This makes the risk ever-present that real talent might not go forward for training for lack of financial assistance. More common is the inadequate nature of some of the local authority awards. The School's small scholarship system is over-stretched. All in all, therefore, the financing of this important institution is problematic.

287 Importance of the London School of Contemporary Dance

Besides full-time training, the School offers a broad series of courses for all ages and at all levels of proficiency. 300 attend regular evening and weekend classes, and some 350 adults take the summer and other vacation courses. We are agreed that the establishment of the London School of Contemporary Dance with widely recognised and respected professional standards is one of the most important developments in British dance education since the war. Nevertheless, the School has lacked adequate accommodation and staff numbers to achieve all its objectives. Largely, this is due to an inadequate financial structure. The School is similar to the Royal Ballet Upper School in the standards at which it aims and quality of professional training. Thus it needs similar support from central and local government to give it security. We return to this need in paragraph 296 below and in our recommendations.

288 The Scottish Ballet's Vocational Dance Education Scheme

A working party established by The Scottish Ballet to examine vocational dance education in Scotland presented its report* in April 1979. It concluded that the capital and running costs needed to establish a Scottish Ballet School on the lines of the Royal Ballet School made the creation of such a school out of the question at the present time. Instead, a vocational dance education scheme has been evolved within the maintained education structure to make provision for adequate dance training within the daily timetable of ordinary education. We summarise here the background and details of this scheme because it is the second development of its kind to link a professional dance company with provision in the maintained sector for vocational purposes. The first, chronologically, is the Rambert Academy described in chapter 11.

289 Need for the Scheme

The Scottish Ballet's Vocational Dance Education Scheme arises not only from the need of The Scottish Ballet but also from other considerations in Scotland. There is, first of all, a need to provide vocational training opportunities within Scotland itself and within the context of Scottish traditions, outlook and educational custom. Such training would hope not only to provide dancers for The Scottish Ballet, but for other companies including possibly a Scottish modern dance company which will develop one day. The commercial sector of dance theatre as well as television continually require better, more broadly trained, dancers. There are community needs and the application of dance to particular social needs which require the preparation of professional specialists. Lastly, as we have emphasised many times in this report, it is no longer sufficient today to train a professional dancer only in classical and modern techniques. He or she requires a knowledge of character, period and national dance styles, dance history, dance notation, anatomy, physiology, music and art. To do this properly requires resources far beyond the possibilities of the private teacher of dance.

290 Background to the Scheme

In the decade since its formation in 1969 out of the former Western Theatre Ballet, The Scottish Ballet evolved a successful scheme of scholarship classes for children recommended by private teachers of dance. Many present members of the company have passed through this scheme as well as dancers now employed elsewhere. Since 1976 the Scottish Committee of British Actors' Equity Association has allowed two students to train and perform with the company for up to 12 months. In 1975 the Cameron Report to the SED[37] considered the 'general and specialised education of gifted young musicians and dancers' in Scotland and recommended that specialist provision should be made within the maintained sector, associated with a comprehensive school of moderate size with preferably an existing strong bias towards

---

* A private report to the Board of The Scottish Ballet. We have been privileged to see it and to use it here.

the arts and with staff and pupils sympathetic towards the new development. Publication of the report coincided with educational economies so that the recommendations were never implemented.

291 Basis of the Scheme in the maintained sector

Clearly, however, a climate of thought exists in Scotland which has begun to look to the maintained sector for help in the vocational training of dancers. This was emphasised when both the Strathclyde and Lothian education authorities indicated to The Scottish Ballet their interest in the establishment of vocational dance training to help young people from their regions. This interest became the basis of the company's present Vocational Dance Education Scheme. It envisages three levels — primary, secondary and senior — covering an age span from 8 years to 17/18 years. It requires strong links with private teachers and with teachers of physical education in the maintained sector. It projects facilities in Glasgow and Edinburgh provided by Scottish Ballet for the primary age of 8—11; facilities in association with an existing secondary school provided in each region by Strathclyde and Lothian; and facilities for the senior section located at the company's headquarters in Glasgow. Accordingly after school classes were initiated in the autumn of 1979 for two primary and two secondary groups of young people in the Strathclyde Region. The Strathclyde Regional Council meets half the fee for each primary pupil, provided they attend a Strathclyde Region school. The Region also pays session fees for the dance staff and pianists involved in providing classes for the secondary groups. The Lothian Region has provided a sum of £5,000 in the year 1979/80 to provide a pilot scheme and to undertake discussions with their physical education advisers, drama advisers and careers officers to assess how best to proceed. Plans are well advanced for classes for the pilot scheme. Other possibilities of similar facilities are being investigated in the north. Scottish Ballet is also discussing with Strathclyde in-service courses for physical education teachers in identifying gifted children.

292 Continuing importance of private theatre schools

This Scottish initiative adds an extra dimension to any consideration of resources available to develop vocational training for theatre dance at the present time. It underlines the significance of the Rambert Academy* in London, formed in 1979 as a partnership with the maintained sector to provide, among other aims, dancers for Ballet Rambert trained in the Rambert style. This tendency of major professional companies to develop their own vocational schools should not be allowed to diminish the importance of the work of established theatre schools and colleges in the private sector. They have a record over many years of providing well-trained dancers for professional companies and of unselfishly passing talent on to special schools. We are as concerned that this work continues to flourish and be safeguarded. Indeed, it is

---

* Not to be confused with the Rambert School of Ballet which has had no link with Ballet Rambert for some years, but still prepares dancers for a professional career.

essential that a variety of theatre schools should flourish alongside the special schools to cater for the variety of dance gifts young people possess. Again and again we have been impressed by the variety and by the way a dance gift may do better in one school rather than another.

293 Need for mandatory grants

The recurrent problem affecting all vocational dance education and training in Britain is the uncertainty of discretionary grants. We believe that the 2½% increase in estimated expenditure on discretionary awards within the 1978/79 Rate Support Grant settlement may have been a helpful influence on some local authorities in this respect. Nevertheless we are deeply concerned by the reaction of other authorities in present circumstances to cut all, or most, discretionary grants. We have evidence of this already affecting to a considerable degree the London School of Contemporary Dance and the Laban Centre to mention two leading institutions of this kind. This threatens the whole structure of vocational training in dance. We do not believe that special pleading is a way forward in such a situation. Rather we think the time has come for a radical re-consideration of the whole discretionary system, not only because of inconsistencies many of which we outline in the next paragraph but also on an issue of principle. This is, that no talented child, wherever he or she is domiciled in Britain, should be prevented from attending a school which has accepted that talent because a local authority refuses to pay the fees. The logical response to this principle is that mandatory grants should be awarded for vocational training in dance on the same basis as grants to the majority of other students for other subjects, and that the Government should reconsider its present limits in the size of mandatory grants as being unrealistic in terms of actual fees at vocational schools.* If this is accepted it follows further that grants should be made mandatory also for vocational training in drama[1] and music[2] as recommended in Gulbenkian Foundation reports on these subjects.

294 Inconsistencies in discretionary grants

We make this recommendation the more urgently because of inconsistencies in the present discretionary grant system. It is, to begin with, complex in operation and inconsistent towards dance students. It is complex because it operates four levels of decision: grants pre-16, 16–18, post-18, or no grant at all. Decisions often seem arbitrary, rejecting talent regardless of increasingly expert advice from directors and local education authority officers. Within these limitations pre-16 awards and post-18 grants seem relatively clear cut, although we have argued for more understanding of the needs of young dancers pre-16.

---

*   Grants for non-maintained institutions will almost always need to be higher than for maintained institutions because fees have to cover *all* costs including items like maintenance of buildings. Such items in maintained institutions can be covered from other sources. The true cost in maintained institutions can be seen more clearly in the amounts charged to overseas students.

Awards in the 16–18 range are the problem. Whereas drama students do not need to start vocational training before 18, it is essential that dancers should be able to start at 16. Some authorities do not acknowledge this need or reject it on grounds of cost. Yet the proposition is less expensive than it sounds because dancers are through their training and into jobs by the time they are 19 and so do not need public support after 19 as other students do. A 16–18 award, however, should not be allowed to detract from an 18+ grant if the student dancer wishes to proceed to further study, such as teacher training. Besides this complexity, which can work to the disadvantage of dance students, there are a number of anomalies. It is anomalous that there should be considerable divergencies in discretionary grant-giving criteria and practice between one local authority and another; that discretionary grants can be given at amounts lower than comparable mandatory grants and sometimes so small as to be ridiculous; and that allowances for materials should be included in grants to art students but not to dance students who have comparable needs equally essential. For all these reasons we recommend a complete review of the discretionary grant system and its replacement by a mandatory system as a matter of urgency, with mandatory grants meeting the genuine costs of vocational training.

295 Need for capital grants   The next important consideration is the co-ordination, use and development of the dance training institutions which have grown up over the years. It does not make sense that all this achievement should have no more public support than is provided through discretionary grants, and sometimes not even that. What form of public support, however, will so benefit institutions, students and staff that the result is in the interests of the country as a whole? All schools, plainly, need the security which comes from capital and recurrent finance on a regular basis. If a measure of security derives from mandatory grants in recurrent expenditure the corollary in capital grants is assistance with building and development costs. These need to be divided as fairly as possible between authorities at different levels: national support for the Royal Ballet School, London School of Contemporary Dance and the educational plans of The Scottish Ballet; regional support for potential regional centres; and local support for particular local schools of quality. The aim should be the development of centres of quality at various levels. The case for institutions at national level seems clear, each having a separate and special contribution to make. Those at regional level might take as example the Royal Northern College of Music, sustained by a number of authorities. Those at local level need to be assisted according to local need and existing provision.

296 Anomalies in present practice   The case for public support is strengthened by anomalies in present practice. The Royal Ballet Lower School, for example, is fee assisted but not the Upper School. Yet an exactly comparable institution, the

143

Menuhin School of Music, is fee assisted for all students up to the age of 18. The Royal Ballet Upper School should surely, therefore, at least be fee assisted. If it is fee assisted it follows that the London School of Contemporary Dance, having comparable standards and objectives, should have the same degree of support from public funds, including capital grants, as is given to the Royal Ballet School. It is an anomaly that such institutions of national importance, contributing so much to tourist and other national revenue, should need to devote time and energy away from their professional tasks in order to raise private money for capital needs of building and development when these buildings have acquired national value and significance.

17 Tertiary and Continuing Education and Training

297 Nature of tertiary education and training

Tertiary education and training in the private sector are of two kinds: the academic study of dance, and the preparation of teachers through institutions such as the Laban Centre for Movement and Dance and the London College of Dance and Drama. The work of the Laban Centre is discussed in this chapter because its wide range makes it a link institution between the degree level courses of the maintained sector and the vocational training courses of the private sector. The work of the London College of Dance and Drama and other teacher training institutions is discussed in the next chapter. There is also a limited amount of continuing education organised by the major examining bodies which, we suggest, could be expanded. Thus tertiary training has to do with the education and training of professional dancers beyond secondary level and after their retirement from professional dancing. This is an area rarely considered in depth so that our examination raises important questions of policy and practice. Does or should the education of the professional dancer stop at secondary level? At the moment his or her general *education* mostly finishes at 16 or 17 as full-time vocational training takes over. Professional *training*, however, continues through whatever company the young dancer joins at about the age of 18 or 19. For some time leading members of the dancing profession, and many dancers themselves, have questioned this lack of balance and the noticeable narrowness to which it seems to lead in most professional dancers' intellectual interests and resources. In this chapter, therefore, we seek first to argue the need for better educated dancers through some continuing educational provision as a part of professional life. Second, to record developments which already show the beginning of new opportunities at tertiary level for the professional dancer. Third, to suggest other developments.

298 Laban Centre

We turn first to tertiary education in the private sector. The principal institution is the Laban Centre*. This has diversified its work in recent years to be able to offer new courses very different from the teacher training on which it once concentrated. What makes the Centre unique is its link with the London University, its Trustee. It is sited on the campus of University of London, Goldsmiths' College. Its beginnings as the Art of Movement Studio in Manchester in 1943 are described in Appendix B. Subsequently it moved to Addlestone in Surrey, then to Goldsmiths' College. Six years ago the Centre launched a three-year

---

* The Laban Centre should not be confused with Goldsmiths' College dance department which operates on the same campus, concentrating on combined degree courses as part of the maintained sector. The Centre is part of the private sector and devotes more than half of its work to professional dance training of various kinds.

145

full-time dance theatre vocational training course for dancers and choreographers and two years later received approval from the CNAA for the first BA Honours Degree course in dance available in Britain. Thus its distinguishing feature today is a wide variety of courses, including theoretical and practical studies in technique, movement analysis, choreography, dance notation, dance performance and production, history, criticism, aesthetics and philosophy. Some of these are in an exploratory stage related to specific studies. The Centre is now able to offer also MPhil and PhD studies in dance, and is planning a full-time one year MA for submission to CNAA. Technical training is not confined to any one style but there is a continuing and general reference to the principles of Laban.

299 Entrance requirements and career options

The Centre pursues this many sided approach through one-, three-, or four-year courses. These range from its honours degree course and theatre certificate to a three- or four-year training course for intending teachers of dance. It offers also a one-year course leading to the University of London Diploma in Education with special reference to movement and dance, a number of one-year advanced courses including one in choreography and one in Labanotation, and a similar variety of part-time and short courses. All candidates for full-time courses, over 90% of whom come from the maintained sector, should be aged 17 or over, are assessed by interview and by audition, and must have 2 GCE A-Level and 3 GCE O-Level passes if entering the degree courses. The Centre aims to produce graduates who will stay in the field of dance which best reflects their abilities. Therefore they may move into practical areas of dance theatre as performers, notators, administrators or some kind of dance animator, teaching, post-graduate study, criticism or some other literary or theoretical field.

300 Finance and fees

In September 1979 the full-time student population of the Laban Centre numbered 150. All these students are fee-paying, mostly on discretionary grants from local education authorities, with the balance, mostly students from abroad, paying privately. The Centre, therefore, is as subject as other private dance institutions to the uncertainties of the discretionary grant system, never knowing whether authorities will support an applicant. Student grants represent the Centre's principal income to which should be added income from its short courses and its classes for adults and children from the local community in South-East London, although the latter are provided very cheaply as a community service. In sum, the income covers running costs on a rather uncertain basis, but leaves nothing for capital costs and development, all of which have to come from funds raised privately.

301 Significance of the Laban Centre

The size and organisation of the Laban Centre, its link with Goldsmiths' College and its location in the deprived, multi-racial inner city area of Lewisham, provide an opportunity to make two additional contributions to dance education, both much in need of attention. One is in the

146

field of theoretical dance studies; the other is the application of professional dance to purposes other than the established theatre, especially community situations, with all the new career possibilities implicit in this development. We think, therefore, that the special place of the Laban Centre in British dance education should be acknowledged by a dialogue between national, local and university authorities to give the Centre the recognition and mandatory grants it needs to develop a national role. We appreciate that the Centre is not a maintained institution and so, technically, is not eligible for mandatory grants. But it is surely an anomaly which needs correction that students at the Laban Centre cannot receive mandatory grants for degree courses approved by the CNAA when students in the maintained sector receive mandatory grants for almost exactly comparable courses.* We return to this point in our recommendations.

302 Expanding a continuing education service It may be that the pressure of falling rolls and reductions in the teaching force will compel other private training institutions described in the next chapter to follow the Laban Centre example and diversify their courses. In any case we hope all tertiary institutions in the private sector will expand or diversify into the particularly important area of continuing education which is often neglected. We have shown for example how the Laban Centre and London School of Contemporary Dance offer a growing programme of evening classes and weekend courses. Major examining bodies like the RAD and ISTD operate similar programmes sporadically. We feel there are possibilities of expanding this element of the private sector at a time of standstill or contraction in the maintained sector. We think there is a likelihood of public response which could add usefully to the private sector's income and that the private sector should seek to collaborate with university extra-mural departments and local education authorities in this extension of its service to students and the general public.

303 Expanding ethnic dance We should like to see also development of ethnic dance in the private sector. Ideally there should be a structure of private studios, schools and further education facilities as for other forms of dance. A start has been made through the establishment of an Academy of Indian Dance

---

*   Two extracts from Hansard illustrate confusion, even in ministerial circles, over the fact that there are some degree students who do not receive mandatory grants:
'Dip HE and degree courses attract mandatory awards, so the problem is really that of the student without A-levels who wishes to take a degree equivalent course.' Shirley Williams, 10th February 1978.
'Mandatory awards are available for full-time and sandwich courses leading to a first degree, Dip HE, HND or the higher diplomas of the Technician or Business Education Council, and for designated courses of initial teacher training.' Gordon Oakes, 20th March 1978.
Thus under present regulations, it is the nature of the establishment and not the level of the course which determines the type of grant.

in London, in April 1979, and with the work of Aklowa. The Academy of Indian Dance aims to provide high standards of teaching and performance in Britain and to strengthen cultural ties through its work. It conducts regular classes in two classical Indian styles, holds introductory workshops and gives lecture-demonstrations, recitals and so on. Aklowa is a centre of Ghanaian music and dance. It conducts workshops and courses, sustains a company which tours, and introduces people of all ages to Ghanaian culture. Other organisations in England, Scotland and Wales pursue similar objectives on behalf of Chinese, Cypriot and other cultures.

304 Continuing education of professional dancers
We turn to the specific problem of the education and training of professional dancers at tertiary level. We suggest there are three simple, but convincing, reasons why dancers should be well-educated. First, as with all people, a good general education which includes a cultural background embracing art, music, literature, history, psychology, sociology and science, will help them as developing personalities and will enrich their lives permanently. Second, such an education will help the transition from professional dancer to some new career once dancing comes to an end. Third, a good education is essential if they are to become first class artists, not just technicians able to dance steps. Whatever high standard of professional skill is acquired during vocational training this needs to be complemented by the enriched personality and intellect, which comes from a balanced education, if professional dancers are to be able to meet the constantly growing demands of today's dance theatre. Good dancers need a good education as well as good training, and this education should not stop during professional life.

305 Need to broaden vocational training
The basis of this education needs to be laid at secondary level with opportunities to continue at tertiary level during professional life. One way to strengthen this basis at secondary level, as well as provide more time for practical dance study, would be to add an extra year to the present two or three years of vocational training. Another way is through schemes like the Scottish Arts Council's music and dance awards and the Welsh Arts Council's dance awards. These are bursaries to performing artists who put forward a plan to extend their knowledge and experience. Yet another way is through a dance degree course as part of vocational training such as is common in the United States and is beginning in the United Kingdom. A fourth is to provide special foundation courses as at the Rambert Academy and Laban Centre. There are advantages and disadvantages in all these methods but we have been impressed by the widespread recognition among teachers and students to whom we have talked of the need to broaden the intellectual and artistic content of present vocational courses. It is a need which those responsible for vocational training should consider very seriously for the reasons set out in paragraph 297 above.

306 New opportunities at tertiary level

A broadening of vocational training becomes more urgent because of the emergence in recent years of a range of opportunities at tertiary level for professional dancers. In March 1974, when the Gulbenkian Action Conference was convened from which came this study among other initiatives, it was not possible for a professional dancer to contemplate the new opportunities at tertiary level which now exist. There are courses now — at the Institute of Choreology, for example, and RAD — where a professional dancing career is a necessary qualification. It begins to be possible to study for a degree, certificate or other qualification during vocational training which will be valuable later in the transition from dance to another career. The Dancers' Resettlement Fund, then beginning, now actively assists further training and continuing education. There are widening opportunities in a variety of institutions for the application of dance and dance notation to industry, medicine, education and social welfare. New honours degrees involving dance have begun to initiate new relationships between the professional dance theatre and academic institutions. There are possibilities in the International Dance Course for Professional Choreographers and Composers for a national choreographic institution for the advanced study and encouragement of choreography and related musical composition.

307 Master classes

Broadly speaking this tertiary provision divides into three groups. There is that which advances the dancer's professional career on stage, such as master classes and choreographic opportunities; that which prepares an alternative career once the stage career is over; and that which helps the dancer's personal development during a stage career to enrich his or her whole life. Dancers develop their stage careers, of course, through classes and performance, the coaching by their teachers and producers and through working with new choreographers, especially those of international reputation. Direct help to a dancer, however, is through the provision of special classes by visiting master teachers. All companies arrange such classes from time to time by teachers who either come from abroad or have a particular reputation in Britain. The alternative is for such teachers to establish their own studio, say in London as did Enrico Cecchetti and others. This form of special tertiary education for professional dancers is now threatened by rising rents and prices but we urge that it should be preserved as far as possible. It is hard to believe, for example, that British ballet could have reached its present eminence without the help of such teachers in its early days.

308 Master teachers

The master teacher we have in mind will certainly have been a professional dancer and will probably have had a distinguished dancing career. He or she will also have the ability to communicate this experience to other professional dancers in ways which are creative and influential. The tradition of teachers of this kind establishing themselves in London from other parts of Britain and abroad goes back many centuries and is described in Appendix C. It gains extra significance today because of the increase in the number of Britain's professional dance companies and the knowledge such teachers can communicate to dancers in these companies through private teaching. Teachers of this kind usually offer open classes and private lessons. The open classes are at working dancer level, occasionally, open also to advanced students. They are paid for from dancers' salaries and the part-time earnings of students. The teachers give one or two classes a day with more demand for private lessons than time or studio space can allow.

309 Problems of the master teacher

A feature of this type of teacher is generosity towards dancers whose work merits attention so that many dancers are helped through temporary financial difficulties by being allowed to take classes on credit. Because of this degree of personal involvement and the day-to-day basis on which working dancers attend classes, not to speak of seasonal variations in numbers attending, it is often difficult for master teachers to cover their living expenses. Hence this type of private teacher is among those most threatened by inflation. Yet their loss would be very serious to professional dancers at all levels and out of all proportion to the actual number of teachers involved. Therefore, because of their value, some system of assistance is required. They need studios and security, a need compounded now by the loss of most of the studio space formerly available in London for private teaching. Consequently we should like to see the possibility of dance teachers' centres or co-operatives encouraged by cheap loan facilities from the local authority, not only in London but in other major conurbations. In this event, where teaching is offered not only at 'master' level but out of performing, or equivalent, experience, the quality of teaching (now ranging in Central London from very good to poor) would need to be protected by some appropriate application of the licence system already suggested.

310 Background to choreographic opportunity

The other regular form of help to dancers during a stage career is the provision of choreographic opportunity. This is a complex provision, nowadays often starting during vocational training. Upon it, and the development of the choreographers it makes possible, depends the future of performance dance in Britain. But choreographers need dancers, music, rehearsal space and, ultimately, an audience in order to develop their talent— an expensive need for companies with limited means. Consequently, organisations of the professional dance world have sought to create opportunities in which choreographic talent can reveal or develop itself at minimum risk and cost. The beginning of these opportunities has been described in paragraph 218.

311 Need for an advanced choreographic study centre

Today, provision to develop professional choreographic talent in Britain is financed precariously, to say the least, but will be sustained, enriched and understood the more dance and dance creation become accepted as a regular part of education in the maintained sector. If the financial assistance we have suggested is implemented for the Royal Ballet Upper School and the London School of Contemporary Dance, there is no doubt the choreographic departments of these two national schools will continue to grow, helping to nurture and launch talent. One of the

150

strengths, too, of the Laban Centre's work is that choreography/composition lies at the centre of every course, thus strengthening future provision. But there is as yet no centre for advanced choreographic development and experiment, such as the International Dance Course for Professional Choreographers and Composers could become. This is now held annually at the University of Surrey, Guildford, to provide, in effect, post-graduate choreographic opportunity. It is now supported by the European Economic Community. We believe such a centre should provide opportunity not only to choreographers aiming to work in professional dance companies, whether at Covent Garden or in community centres, but should also organise advanced choreographic and dance composition study for dance teachers in the maintained and private sectors, thus strengthening the creative element in their work. Such study could be organised as in-service training. We urge, therefore, discussions between the International Dance Course for Professional Choreographers and Composers and the DES to develop such choreographic in-service experience, and between the Course and Arts Council of Great Britain to provide a regular subsidy for its administration, the balance of costs to be found through bursaries for the beneficiaries.

312 Dancers as teachers

We have discussed tertiary education for dancers, and dancers becoming master teachers, and how some dancers have potential as choreographers. In the next paragraph we outline other possible careers for former dancers. But historically the most obvious alternative to dancing, already regularly used, is to teach dance although not necessarily as a master teacher. It is because not all dancers make good teachers that we refer to the growing number of alternatives. Many dancers do make good teachers of dancing, however, and it is important that this potential be used in both sectors. We draw attention, therefore, to the next chapter which reviews teacher training in the private sector, including the preparation of former dancers. We emphasise the need for discussion with the education profession since what former dancers might give as teachers in the maintained sector can be used to the benefit of dance education without, of course, imperilling the employment of existing teachers.

313 Dance as a career for life

Two new factors assist the resettlement of professional dancers after performing is finished. The first is a change of public attitude; the second the establishment of a resettlement organisation. The two are linked. The Dancers' Resettlement Fund reports that many employers today are showing a marked change of attitude towards those who have had the discipline of a dance career. There is greater willingness to recognise that this discipline has a value in itself which can be related to other ways of living and working and which, therefore, is worth absorbing, redirecting or retraining for new purposes. Surprisingly, the dance profession has been slow to draw this conclusion for itself. Its needs have grown for directors and administrators as well as choreographers and teachers. Ideally these should be drawn from its own ranks. Unfortunately, professional dancers today are mostly ill-prepared by their

151

education to exploit these new opportunities. It is true that they possess the unique qualification of professional performing experience, which can be assisted by additional academic training. This is a compelling reason why the dance profession has begun to move towards tertiary education and tertiary education has begun to move towards the dance profession. We conclude, therefore, that the idea of dance as a short term career is out-of-date. It needs to be seen as a career for life, part of which may be spent in the theatre and part of which will apply dance knowledge in some other form, perhaps after a period of resettlement training.

314 Dancers'
Resettlement
Fund

We have referred above to 'resettlement' and the Dancers' Resettlement Fund. The existence of such a fund is fundamental to much of what has now become possible for dancers in one aspect of the tertiary level, that is, further education or vocational training once a dancing career comes to an end. The Fund came into being in 1973 and was one of the principal recommendations of the Arts Council of Great Britain's Opera and Ballet Report, 1966—1969. Details of the way it operates are given at Appendix H but it should be noted that one of the strongest arguments for its creation was the experience of the Royal Ballet's Benevolent Fund in dealing with the two periods of insecurity in the lives of many dancers: at the end of their dancing career and at normal pension age. Experience showed that the need at the end of a dancing career is for retraining and vocational guidance rather than the relief of poverty as such. To date more than a hundred dancers have been assisted, including helping dancers who needed to obtain O- and A-levels as part of the entry requirements to professional courses. The Resettlement Fund, therefore, represents a remarkable achievement by the dancing profession and its advisers to protect the interests of its members, and a significant success by its first officer, Margaret Lawford. What is more remarkable, however, is the absence of provision by the State for contingencies of this kind which affect other short-life professions as well as dancers. This is true, equally, of dance teachers who often have no pension scheme at the end of their careers and no provident scheme operating within their profession. We suggest that this need be investigated, including the possibility of dance teachers joining a dancers' pension fund.

315 More
about educating
dancers

We said above that further education or vocational training for a second career was ' one kind of tertiary level' for dancers. We think it should be emphasised that professional experience in dance companies of whatever kind represents another tertiary level, especially when the company is subsidised and the dancer has a reasonable chance of permanent employment. The young dancer joining such a company has completed the equivalent of a secondary education. His or her professional training will be completed through company experience. This usually means daily work which starts at 9 or 10 in the morning and finishes 12 or 13 hours later. Sundays are often occupied by travel. Is it reasonable to suggest that somewhere in all this pressured existence, time should be found for the broader development of a young dancer's intellectual and artistic qualities? We think it is. We return, therefore, to the argument about educated dancers with which we opened this chapter.

316 Paid educational leave

A number of us have experienced the pressure of a dancer's life and have been responsible for directing dance companies. We know that company routines and attitudes are founded on tradition and response to the pressures of performance. They will be difficult to change. We are convinced, however, that the interests of the dance profession and its audiences, no less than the artists themselves, will be served best if dancers who so wish (particularly those coming to the end of performing careers) can take advantage of release schemes, sandwich courses at tertiary level and so on, such as the idea pioneered by the Scottish Arts Council's Awards Scheme. We know a dancer's need to continue daily training under any circumstances and we know that company cast lists always need every available dancer. Therefore it may be necessary to allow companies a small percentage of dancers surplus to establishment, to permit some form of paid educational leave. Such an idea means we are talking of a future less restricted by finance than now. But we think it should be the norm, rather than the exception, for dance companies to make provision to advance particular abilities in their dancers, having some regard to the long term future, just as commercial business companies today release particular members of staff for special training or for day or other kinds of release schemes supported by Government funds.

317 Education within dance companies

Within dance companies, especially major companies, we think that the larger interests of the dance profession, the companies themselves and the dancers, require more regular provision (with consequent re-thinking of schedules, priorities and hallowed methods of administration) for dancers to acquire artistic and intellectual experience outside normal routine. Occasionally this happens through the engagement of a distinguished visting teacher or musician. We are arguing, therefore, to extend and broaden this practice. We know, for example, the stimulus dancers of Ballet Rambert and London Contemporary Dance Theatre gain through flexible company policies which allow them from time to time to take advantage of outside opportunities in small groups as well as individually. Well known too, is the stimulus derived from company choreographic workshops giving dancers the chance of original creation, or new interpretation. Such workshops also illustrate the need for co-ordination with outside institutions — such as the International Dance Course for Professional Choreographers and Composers — so that the event is not an isolated instance but can be seen as something related to the profession as a whole and gaining in value as a result. In short, while recognising all the problems which dance companies face today, we urge them to accept the responsibility which must be theirs for the broader education of their dancers as artists and members of society.

153

18 Private Teacher Training

318 Varied nature of private sector teacher training

Teachers in private dance studios and vocational schools are trained in a wide variety of ways as the briefest glance through *The Dancing Times* will show. There is no co-ordinated system leading to generally accepted qualifications such as can be found in the maintained sector. There are four different methods of private sector teacher training and we examine them in this chapter. They are: the apprentice; the dance or stage school; retraining professional dancers; specialist training colleges. Here, and in the associated problems of the future, one finds expressed in different ways, with particular force and conflict of views, the philosophical difference referred to in paragraph 207. This has lain beneath the surface in all our discussions of dance teacher training for this study. The conflict is about the balance in training between the achievement of high technical/performance competence and the acquisition of academic, pedagogic and other learning. Will not the time spent on learning hinder the achievement of a high performance level? In other words, what kind of dance teacher should this training produce for what kind of purpose?

319 Apprentice training

We have referred already to the apprentice method of teacher training in paragraph 256. It remains more prevalent in private dance studios than we suspected when we began this study. Yet it is not really a method. The quality of the training varies from studio to studio according to the quality of the teacher in charge. In some cases — training with a master teacher, for example — it can be very good. But usually the training provided is of the narrowest, concentrating almost entirely on the teaching of a technique for the examinations of one or other examining body in the private sector. There is no syllabus other than the examination syllabus, no acquisition of a range of supporting knowledge; no pedagogic training or training in child development; few outside contacts; no final qualification; no recognised scale of fees or salary for assisting the studio owner in what is too often no more than cheap labour teaching. If a licence system for dance teachers is introduced we hope it will lead to the quick elimination of apprenticeships of this nature.

320 Stage school training

A better, but sometimes similar, method of training is provided through a 2–3 year course at one of a number of private dance or general stage schools offering teacher training. There is no co-ordination or consultation between these schools so the only elements in common are likely to be the professional executant examination the student may be required to pass during training in the syllabus of one or other of the professional examining bodies. At the end of the course the school occasionally sets its own examination and issues its own certificate. This is no guarantee of standard because there is no check at the moment on the standards which young teachers carry with them from these schools into the vocational sector. It is rare, too, that they will acquire other than a limited range of supporting knowledge and pedagogic training. By and large we do not think that courses of this kind at present provide the breadth and depth of training we believe to be necessary for dance teaching. A few, however, possess the potential for conversion to BEd degree courses under the guidance of the CNAA or a university. We think that courses which can achieve this status should do so and/or that they should take steps to co-ordinate their methods, standards and final awards with those of the specialist training colleges listed in paragraph 323, so that some agreed level of excellence emerges. This could be part of the review of courses and exchange of experience recommended in paragraphs 332 and 333. We think that institutions which cannot achieve these standards should cease to train teachers.

321 Retraining professional dancers

The longest established source of dance teachers comes from the practice of retired professional dancers opening a private studio on savings from a stage career. Retired dancers who wish to teach have three options. They can become a teacher in a professional company in Britain or abroad; join an existing vocational dance school or private studio; or, as we have said, open their own private studio. We discussed in the last chapter the contribution of retired dancers to the teaching of professional dancers through classes which supplement other classes or provide some special quality which flows from the experience and eminence of the teacher. Such teachers are rare. Most retired dancers who open studios or turn to general dance teaching will teach children or young people up to age 16. Here their initial problem is likely to be a lack of adequate pedagogic experience and training. On the other hand, former professional dancers can bring into the studio and classroom a rich stage experience, including details of the choreography and music of many ballets in which they have danced. The aim, therefore, should be to help stage experience to enrich the work of the private studio, as it does already the training of professional dancers.

322 Professional Dancers' Teaching Course

With this intention the RAD established its first Professional Dancers' Teaching Course in 1974 as we were beginning to plan this dance study. It was supported by the Dancers' Resettlement Fund (described in paragraph 314 above), the Gulbenkian Foundation and the Government's Training Opportunities Scheme (TOPS). Today the course lasts for one year having been lengthened gradually from its original six months. Numbers on any one course are limited to 15 students having regard to present employment difficulties. Selection is made in June and the course starts each year in September. It is restricted to professional dancers, aiming only at the moment to prepare them to teach the Academy's syllabi in private studios and similar institutions in Britain and abroad. Successful as this course may be in preparing former dancers to teach the Academy's syllabi in private studios, we feel that the wider range of opportunities in, say, the fields of youth service, community arts, and the expanding area of leisure and recreation require a broader preparation. This implies an approach to teaching

155

which is not limited to a particular syllabus. It would need to include some introduction to comparative methods; more guidance in understanding the types of work suitable at different stages in a child's development; and considerable attention to the importance of creative work.

323 Specialist training colleges

The other significant sources of dance teacher training for the non-maintained sector is provided by four private training colleges. All four have a national, rather than local, relevance providing the possibility of some central co-ordination of national standards in this sector, albeit through a number of different national bodies. These colleges are maintained by the societies or institutions of the private sector which have grown up over the years and are described in chapters 16 and 17 and Appendix C. At present all are London based although one will soon move from London. In order of foundation they are: the London College of Dance and Drama, (the college of the ISTD) which will move in 1980 from London to Bedford; the college of the Royal Academy of Dancing; the Laban Centre for Movement and Dance; the Teachers' Training Course of the Royal Ballet School.

324 Changed situation of the colleges

Until recently all these training courses had links with colleges of education through which they were able to make arrangements for suitable students to achieve the Certificate of Education and thus become qualified teachers in the maintained sector. In each case the links were slightly different and are described in the paragraphs below. What is common to all, however, is that the cut-back of teacher training places in the maintained sector combined with the replacement of the Certificate of Education with a Bachelor of Education qualification for teachers and the general re-organisation of non-university maintained higher education, have combined seriously to restrict these arrangements. Additionally, the development of public sector teaching into a graduate profession faces the private sector with a further dilemma. Will not this translation increase the status and salary gaps between teachers in the maintained and non-maintained sectors, making it even more difficult for teachers in the private sector to work in the public sector? Should the private sector therefore seek to develop its own degree courses for teacher training? The major institutions of the private sector have approached these problems in different ways.

325 London College of Dance and Drama

The London College is the oldest of the private institutions, its origins described in Appendix C. The College has always sustained close links with the maintained sector and was the first private institution to bridge the gap between the two sectors. It does this through two parallel courses. Course A is a four-year course where students become registered with a College of Education* for their second and third years at London College before moving on to the College of Education, thus

---

* At first the College was Dartford College. Presently it became East Sussex College of Higher Education. Now it is Brighton Polytechnic.

receiving mandatory grants for teachers destined for the maintained sector. Course B is a three-year course from which successful graduates can obtain a diploma to teach in the private sector. In the summer of 1978 10 students graduated from Course A and 20 from Course B. The College has no problem, of course, in continuing the preparation of teachers for the private sector through Course B. It has been concerned, however, to secure the academic future of course A as teaching becomes a graduate profession. The association with Bedford College of Higher Education in 1980 will not only assure the future of the A Course but provide large resources of staff and facilities and allow the development of a dance component within a BEd degree course in Human Movement Studies, including a second subject so that students can obtain posts in the maintained sector.

326 College of the Royal Academy of Dancing

The origins of the Teacher Training Course of the Royal Academy of Dancing are described in Appendix C. Today the Course has become the College of the Royal Academy of Dancing with a function to train teachers of classical dance on the basis of the RAD syllabi. 23 students graduated at the end of the summer term 1979 and thus received the College's diploma. The syllabus concentrates upon the teaching of classical ballet. Almost all successful graduates become teachers in the private sector. We comment below on the problems of developing a syllabus of this kind into an equivalent of degree level studies.

327 The Laban Centre for Movement and Dance

The work of the Laban Centre and its link with the University of London have been discussed extensively already in chapter 17. The Centre has a long association with the maintained sector so that today intending teachers of dance at the Centre can follow one of two routes to a degree. The first is the Bachelor of Education route. An average of 22 students a year have completed this course over the last four years, all trained to teach in maintained secondary schools. The second route to a degree with teaching qualification is the Bachelor or Arts Honours route. The Centre's BA Honours course in dance does not, like the BEd, include a teaching qualification. Nevertheless it is providing a popular route to teaching since the option of career choice need not be decided until the end of the third year when intending teachers can proceed to study for a post-graduate teacher training diploma.

328 Teacher training at the Royal Ballet School

The Teachers' Training Course of the Royal Ballet School was started in 1963 and its first graduation took place in 1966. It is a three-year course designed to equip students who have a vocation for teaching with the important principles needed for such a career, principally in private dance studios. At one time it had an arrangement for students to move to a college of education after completing the three-year course to achieve the Certificate of Education, but this arrangement no longer obtains. Today, between 30 and 34 students attend the course at one time, including usually two or three overseas students. At the end of each year there is an assessment and sifting out so that, for the final year, there are usually about eight students who can normally be expected to complete the course successfully and receive the School's

Diploma for the Teaching of Ballet. After leaving the School some graduates move on to acquire stage experience before becoming teachers; others join the staff of professional dance schools in Britain, or go abroad to teach or form their own schools or teach locally. The evidence seems to be that the standards of the Diploma's recipients is generally regarded as high although the worth of a diploma, as an award, must now be under review as teaching becomes more and more an all-graduate profession. There is no doubt, however, that for some years to come diplomas from the major institutions, qualifying teachers for the private sector will be valued and needed not only in Britain, but over-seas.

329 Degree problem for classical teacher training

Thus two of the four institutions have moved towards degree studies, validated by the CNAA, as a means of adapting to the new teacher training requirements. The problem of resources for these studies has been solved by an association with larger institutions in the maintained sector, Bedford College of Higher Education on the one hand and Gold-smiths' College on the other. The remaining two institutions have important reservations about following a similar course. These are centred mainly on their commitment to classical ballet and the implications of the commitment, as they see it. They argue that the study of classical ballet requires a more rigorous physical discipline than many other dance forms and that the achievement of appropriate executant standards creates a problem, (in the words of the chairman of the RAD) of reconciling, 'the academic requirements of a degree level course with high standards of dance teaching.'*

330 Options for classical teacher training

We recognise that the problem thus posed is a real one and note that on this account the Royal Ballet School is not seriously considering at the moment any exploration of the degree field. It hardly has need to do so because the market in the private sector for its relatively few graduates each year is likely to remain buoyant. For the RAD things are different. For one thing it has many more potential teachers under training. For another, although under its charter one of its principal purposes is to improve the standard of classical dance teaching in the private sector, it is bound to have some students with the inclination and aptitude to teach in the public sector. One hopes, indeed, that this may be so increasingly. For them the RAD must provide a means of entry into the public sector even though this is not a line for all. The need is recognised by the RAD although so far a solution has not been found. We think, therefore, that the RAD and any other like-minded institution, should take steps as a matter of urgency, either individually or by collective arrangement, to offer their students the possibility of working for a degree. This would be primarily a means of gaining entry to the maintained sector but also of securing better recognition for dance teachers within the private sector. We think that unless such

---

*   Letter commenting on a draft of our report, 25 September 1979.

institutions can take this step now, they may be jeopardising their own future since the time may come when the private sector will require degree qualification for its own dance teachers.

331 Resources and finance We do not think that resources are likely to be a principal difficulty in advancing along these lines. It is recognised — certainly at the RAD — that any attempt to institute a degree level course would need to be in conjunction with other like-minded institutions of the private sector, or with tertiary institutions in the public sector, or with both. A principal difficulty is likely to be the problem of reconciling academic standards with executant requirements. The next difficulty is one of finance. Private teacher training colleges have to be content, no less than everyone else with the caprices and vagaries of the discretionary grant system. Their situation confirms the need for a complete review of the discretionary grant system to eliminate the anomalies listed in chapter 16. The same applies to capital grants for building and development.

332 Need for a review of present teaching courses To strengthen the case for the colleges, in such an event, we suggest a need for the private sector to conduct its own review of present private teaching courses of all kinds in order to broaden their scope, where possible, and monitor standards. Our own studies have revealed, for example, that 'theory' on many courses consists only of an analysis of movements and steps, and the knowledge of how to correct faults. Often, too, the approach to teaching is limited to a particular syllabus with little discussion of comparative methods. There is a general need for more creative work and the application of a more carefully considered pedagogical component. Lack of these elements, we think, is mainly responsible for the limited attitudes commonly found amongst dance teachers and so merits a review to correct the problem.

333 Need to exchange experience Whatever the future development of the institutions we have considered, we think there is a strong case for them, and any other private teacher training course of similar level, to exchange experience both within the private sector and between the private sector and the maintained sector. How, for example, to develop the broader artistic and intellectual studies required at degree level? We have no doubt that the private institutions concerned will consult and urge them to do so at regular intervals. We have urged already the need for regular consultations between tertiary institutions in the maintained sector which offer courses with dance as an option. Such consultations might provide a suitable forum for consideration of ideas put forward in this report for the development of teacher training courses in the private as well as the maintained sector. We hope that both sectors, in any case, will recognise the value of a forum where experience can be exchanged on a regular basis to benefit teachers and students of dance throughout Britain.

334 Importance of the private teacher We think it follows from what we have said in this and preceding chapters that the private sector of dancing has a special contribution to make to dance education and training in Britain. This contribution derives from the private teacher's special knowledge of a particular form or style of dancing. In the first place, therefore, the private sector becomes a means whereby, for example, a particular tradition of the classical school of ballet can be kept alive and grow in Britain. Cecchetti's teaching is an example. Or forms of modern dance can be introduced as they have been through the Contemporary Dance Trust, thus invigorating the whole British dance scene. In the second place, the private teacher becomes a specialist resource, particularly at local authority level where he or she, if invited, can enrich dance education by contributing specialist knowledge. It follows, then, that there will be a continuing need for this contribution in the foreseeable future, but on two conditions: that central and local authorities, and private dance teachers themselves, understand the nature of the contribution private dance teachers can make; and that the training of private dance teachers is re-organised to prepare for the opportunities and responsibilities of the 1980s.

19 Assessment and Examinations

335 Content of the chapter

This chapter is about assessments and examinations in the private sector. It is important to make clear the distinction. Through assessments teachers note the periodic progress of their pupils in light of their own objectives. Through formal examinations, like must be compared with like. Paradoxically, work in the theatre does not depend upon success in examinations because the only realistic test for a theatre career is the test of performance. Even the highest awards, like a solo seal or gold medal, do not guarantee theatrical success although the training makes an essential contribution. Nevertheless examinations and other forms of assessment are important, not only for the posts which require them, but also in preparation for a performing career. For parents, students and teachers they are a way of measuring progress and, often, of sustaining interest. Hence there is a link, albeit sometimes tenuous, between assessment and employment. Therefore we consider the system of assessment and examinations in this chapter before turning to the problem of employment in chapter 20.

336 Validity of assessment

Any stage audition of dancers is an assessment. In this sense the vocational sector has experience of dance assessments over many centuries. They are based on appropriate observation and experienced discrimination related to what is known of a dancer's potential. In a more formal sense, the vocational sector has conducted dance examinations in Britain, based on specific syllabi, for approaching half a century. Its experience agrees, therefore, with conclusions in the maintained sector that dance, like any other subject, contains within itself its own mode of assessment, canons of judgement and validating criteria. Thus we do not need to re-argue here the criteria for assessment and examination. At the same time, within the present climate of inquiry into all aspects of assessment in education, we question much of the current system of assessment in the vocational sector and the number, variety and standard of its dance examinations. We begin, therefore, by outlining the system of grade and major examinations which the examining bodies of the vocational sector have developed over the years.

337 Grade examinations

Generally speaking, grade examinations in classical ballet are for children from, say, age 6 to 15 or 16, although in January 1979 the RAD introduced also a senior grade for young people up to 17 years of age. During the academic year 1978/79, the last year for which figures are available, nearly 106,000 children entered for these examinations of the RAD, an increase of 3.3% on the previous year. A comparable breakdown of figures for the RAD, ISTD and BBO is not possible because records are kept in a different form but the nature and organisation of the examinations is much the same. The ISTD's Modern Theatre Dance Branch, for example, has six syllabi from primary in various grades to pre-elementary. Thus, judging from the income details in paragraph

161

339 below, the number of entries to children's grade examinations throughout the private sector lies between 150,000 and 200,000 a year. All these grade examinations aim in part to measure and test physical skills in a particular form of dance but are mainly a dialogue between examiner and student seeking to establish the student's theoretical and intellectual grasp of a syllabus with no specific vocational purpose.

338 Major examinations

Major examinations follow the grade examinations at pre-elementary, elementary, intermediate and advanced levels. About 8,800 young people entered for the RAD's major examinations in 1978/79. Often these examinations imply a vocational interest, usually teaching, since such examinations are not necessary to a professional dancer. The RAD also offers a dance education syllabus at three levels in both classical ballet and character dancing. Beyond this, and additionally, the major examining bodies conduct various advanced solo examinations, tests and awards for candidates of special ability, including choreographic ability. Such is the examination pattern in the private and vocational sector. It seems logical until it is seen to be conducted not only by the four principal examining bodies we have named, but by 11 other examining bodies as well, some with remits only in particular regions. We return to this problem in paragraph 342 below.

339 Income of examining bodies

As in the maintained sector, this examination system produces the greater part of the gross receipts of all the 15 examining bodies which exist principally from examination income. The RAD records an income of £485,381 from this source during 1977/78. This includes overseas examinations and amounts to 56.2% of total income for the year. For the same financial year (though the accounting years are not always the same) the IDTA recorded an income of £391,888 from all examinations and medal tests (90.06% of total income) and the ISTD showed an examination income of £276,290, including the Society's share from overseas examinations. This was 74.33% of total income. If we exclude the ISTD's ballroom examination fees (for better direct comparison with the RAD) its Theatre Faculty examination income totals £212,759. The greater part of the income of the IDTA comes from ballroom and recreational dancing rather than theatre dance. Thus the joint examination income of these three bodies alone totals £1,153,559 in the 1977/78 financial year. If one adds the income of the other smaller examining bodies the total probably exceeds £2,000,000.

340 Need to control examining bodies

There is a strong case, therefore, for some control of examining bodies to reduce their number and co-ordinate better their syllabi fees and examination standards. One way to do this could be a licensing or registration system for examining bodies, such as we have recommended already for teachers. The system might be supervised by a central examination authority which would be a voluntary body and would need some form of endorsement from the DES and SED. The Authority would relate to examining bodies much as the Independent

162

Broadcasting Authority relates to independent television companies. The examining bodies would retain their independence and examination incomes, and continue to provide the services they now provide subject to co-ordination and monitoring of standards by the Authority. The sanction would be loss of the licence to examine. The benefit would be the evolution of a national examination system for the private sector without losing the strengths and choice of the present variety. The way towards this objective might be through an extension of the consultative procedures described in paragraph 346 below.

341 Too many examinations

The need for reduction in the number and variety of private examining bodies comes clear from even the simplest review of the number and variety of examinations on offer. To take just two of the major organisations, the ISTD and the RAD. The ISTD is organised in ten branches divided into a theatre faculty and a ballroom faculty. The theatre faculty comprises two kinds of classical ballet — Cecchetti method and the ISTD syllabus — and branches in Greek dance, historical dance, modern theatre dance (including tap), national dance and Scottish dance. The ballroom faculty comprises ballroom, Latin American and sequence dance. Almost all these branches organise their own four or five grade examinations and/or medal tests for children and adults. After the grade examinations follow three or four major examinations of the kind already mentioned. The RAD conducts much the same system except that it concentrates on classical ballet. Both conduct examinations overseas from which they derive an important part of their income. The two organisations, therefore, are comparable in seeking to offer a complete structure of examinations throughout the age range of candidates. Many of the other examining bodies try to do the same. At a conservative estimate we calculate that the non-maintained dance sector offers at least 500 examinations of varying content and standard to children aged 6 to 18 throughout the United Kingdom. No wonder that parents, local authorities and others find this mass of examinations in the non-maintained dance sector confusing!

342 Need to limit dance examinations

The lack of national system in practice demeans the profession and, in all probability, the national standard of achievement. A teacher or parent who feels one set of examinations unduly demanding simply moves to another examining body which is less demanding. This may be why both the Royal Ballet School and London School of Contemporary Dance report a number of candidates from private schools so badly trained they have to be rejected even though they have passed examinations. Examinations by themselves, therefore, do not sustain standards, particularly where there is no agreed national control of standards.* Indeed, the present situation of dance examinations in the non-maintained sector actually reflects five weaknesses to which a consulta-

---

* This view is supported by the Society of Education Officers in a paper commenting upon the consultative document, *Devolution: The English Dimensions*. They 'consider that in what is essentially a national service, substantial variations in standards would be unacceptable.'

tive committee of the Board of Education drew attention as far back as 1911 when it was asked to review public examinations at secondary level: there are too many examinations; there is little co-ordination between them; the necessary preparation for examinations unduly influences the curriculum; the pupil aims to absorb information and dance technique rather than form judgements leading to performance which is a personal interpretation; the teacher has to teach according to the dictates of the examination. It is the teacher, therefore, rather than the pupil who selects the material, and frequently it is limited to what is to be examined.

343 Need for a fresh approach

There is, then, a compelling moral and rational case to reduce the number of dance examinations as well as the number of examining bodies. At the same time we acknowledge the problem which has brought about the present system. So insistent is the demand for examinations that a dance teacher imperils her pupils and her status and income if she does not prove herself competent by examination success. We think, therefore, that more encouragement should be given to teachers interested in teaching children dance unrelated to examination syllabi.* Such a change would require an open debate in the private sector to discuss a fresh approach to teaching the classical technique. The need for a fresh approach has been represented strongly to us for four reasons. First, there should be an approach which is *not* aimed at examination syllabi. Second, in teaching children the approach should take account of the suitability of the work at particular stages of a child's development. Third, a fresh approach is needed to take account of the fact that many more people are studying dance today, and for a greater variety of reasons. Some are starting at a later age and therefore need special corrective exercises. Classical teachers should be able to contribute to this movement because the classical technique is recognised as particularly valuable to the training of dancers of all kinds. Lastly, there should be an essential requirement at every age level for teaching with more imagination and understanding than is generally the case at present.

344 Restrictive influence of examination

If even only part of these arguments for a fresh approach are conceded, it follows there are few teachers at the moment with experience broad enough to cope with the needs and the many new problems posed by the new situation in which the private sector finds itself. Undoubtedly an important restrictive influence is the need to concentrate on examinations rather than an alternative, broader method of assessment. Concentration on the teaching of specific syllabi may not only kill creativity in students but also in teachers! This conclusion applies with particular force to the running of championships in classical ballet, modern dance and tap dance, senior and junior, all of which we deplore. To award trophies for achievement in a class is one thing, but championships are

---

*   This view is supported by two recent contributions from HM Inspectorate: *Aspects of Secondary Education in England*, and *A View of the Curriculum*, both already quoted. See notes 30 and 53.

nonsense because any genuine champion in, say, classical ballet would be in a professional company. Therefore, since all the leading training schools ignore such events and championship winners are rarely professional dancers, the championships are meaningless. They are also frequently very superficial in assessment, being no more than the performance of a short dance. As such they demean standards and the profession.

345 Pressure for change from individual teachers

How are the changes we propose to be brought about? They seem to strike, after all, at the existence of all examining bodies. Yet there is a climate of opinion in the non-maintained sector which supports our views and which has been presented to us in evidence. To begin with we have the example of the Natural Movement Branch of the ISTD which has concluded that 'its work is drawing to a close as a Branch of the Society . . . No further examinations will be held after 1979.'[69] Next, individual teachers have indicated growing resistance to the economic pressures which influence dance schools to concentrate too much on examinations and festival work. Parental influence plays a part in this because parents frequently demand some proof of achievement from the dance classes for which they are paying. If children are not entered for examinations they are often withdrawn from the school. If they fail they are also withdrawn even though rising examination standards now make it very difficult for students to hope to pass an examination on one class a week. To counter this potential loss of students many teachers told us they give free extra classes to achieve the required examination standard, or, as we observed above, change to the examinations of a different organisation where standards are less rigorous.* Hence the climate of opinion among private teachers begins to argue the merits of an alternative comprising two elements. First, a single, nationally applicable and reputable examination syllabus for which not all students would necessarily enter, which would demonstrate to local education authorities, parents and others the requirement for a standard of teaching which constantly improves, which would also therefore be a safeguard against physical damage to young children, and which could not be undercut, as now, by some other examination of lower standard. Second, the exploration of alternative forms of assessment which can satisfy parents, students and local authorities and would meet many of the arguments for the fresh approach advanced in this chapter.

346 Moves to rationalise the present system

In line with this new climate of opinion, leading examining bodies are consulting about the confusion of dance examinations in the non-maintained sector. In 1976 a project was launched by two of the examining bodies in classical ballet to evaluate the major syllabi used by each to establish at what stage each system of training demands strength, mobility, speed and brilliance; what dance vocabulary is expected at each stage and how the vocabulary is to be used; and the

---

* Evidence through the Imperial Society of Teachers of Dancing.

weighting of each syllabus in the various sections. Since 1977 the three major syllabi of the RAD, the Cecchetti Society and the Classical Ballet Branch of the ISTD have been demonstrated and discussed in turn. As a result the three ballet organisations are satisfied that, making allowances for different approaches and methods of training, comparable demands in technique are made at each stage. In view of this there seems every chance of establishing a joint examining board as an essential pre-requisite towards rationalising dance examinations in this area. We warmly welcome these important developments because we are convinced that rationalisation of its present examination system is a matter for the dancing profession itself. At the same time we urge the profession to extend the steps already taken so that in liaison with the maintained sector, a simpler nationally applicable system of dance examinations will offer appropriate alternatives for developments in the interests of students, teachers and the dancing profession. Consultations should include, we think, the exploration of alternative forms of assessment suggested above.

347 Assessment and examinations These developments, we believe, endorse our view of the significance of well-conducted assessments and examinations to parents, students, teachers, local education authorities and employers as a means to measure progress. For school staff as a whole teachers' assessments provide the chance of insight into the ability of individual students and so can be of value in career guidance should a student not prove suitable to a performance career. In the matter of examinations the credibility of dance examinations requires that there should be as few as possible, conducted always in a form appropriate to each particular occasion. Given this approach, we think that dance examinations will weigh increasingly with the growing number of employers* who accept that dance training has relevance for careers other than just dance careers. Strengthening of the quality of dance examinations will also, of course, raise standards for those seeking outlets in careers which require dance or movement training in one form or another. In sum, therefore, we think that examinations should seek to cater for the interests of everyone engaged in dance and that examination structures should make this possible through the modifications and restrictions suggested above. We think it a matter of principle, however, that this should be without prejudice to those who wish to pursue dance with some other form of assessment, or no assessment, and that provision should be made accordingly.

---

* Evidence of the Dancers' Resettlement Fund on the attitude of employers to those who have received vocational training in dance.

20 Employment in Performance Dance

348 Are too many children being encouraged?

One question central to our inquiry is whether too many students are being trained in the vocational sector, particularly in the established vocational training institutions in London, bearing in mind the employment available. At younger age levels, before arrival at the major institutions, we have indicated our concern that too many children are encouraged to consider dance as a professional career only to find, when they audition for an established institution, that they are not acceptable for reasons which could have been foreseen much earlier. We have two observations. First, those few who are accepted should not then be prevented from developing their ability for lack of a discretionary grant. Second, those not accepted might not be in such a situation so comparatively late in their education if there existed the better information and liaison between all concerned which we recommend in chapter 13. Only the really gifted should be encouraged to hope for a career as performers. At the same time it follows there should be more encouragement and provision for amateur dance performance as suggested in paragraph 239.

349 Theatre employment available

Although dance employment now is greatly increased over, say, 30 years ago it is still a small sector of theatrical employment generally. We calculate that existing theatre dance jobs amount to no more than 1,150 at most. Of these 300 are in subsidised theatre (almost half of them in the Royal Ballet), and 700 are in commercial theatre in London and the regions (including cabaret on Equity contract) at 'premium periods'* such as summer shows and winter pantomimes. To these theatre opportunities must be added film and television openings which sometimes duplicate theatrical work by using the same dancers. For this reason screen openings are unlikely to add more than another 100 jobs, if that. Then there is the growing area of performance dance in the community, educational and social field. At present employment is erratic but perhaps offers as much as 50 jobs, not all full-time or year round. This makes a total of 1,150 jobs in all in the United Kingdom. Admittedly, turnover is high, particularly among women, but we doubt if the effect of this increases jobs by more than 10%, meaning that there are something like 30 new dance jobs a year in subsidised British theatre, 70 in commercial theatre and 5 or 10 in the community and educational field where turnover is highest of all. Additionally, the reputation of British dance training means that there are many openings abroad.

---

* This is a term used by Equity's Commercial Theatre Department. We are grateful to the respective departments of British Actors' Equity for their informed views which supplemented and confirmed our own research.

350 Supplying the subsidised theatre: Royal Ballet School

However, dance statistics are to do with real people, so it is advisable to look at what actually happens. Over the two academic years 1978/79 an average of 41 students a year graduated from the Royal Ballet School. In 1978, 45 students completed their courses in the Royal Ballet School. 42 went direct to jobs as dancers in major companies in Britain, or, more particularly, on the European continent. 11 of the 42 went to the two companies of the Royal Ballet, including 2 into Ballet for All, during its closing months; these 2 were subsequently employed by other companies. In 1979 there was an exceptionally large number of graduates (14) from the School Teachers' Training Course. All found posts, 4 as dancers, 10 as teachers. Among the rest of the graduates from the School in 1979 34 got jobs as dancers. 12 of these went into the Royal Ballet and the Sadler's Wells Royal Ballet, one going nominally as a member of the corps de ballet but in fact as a choreographer.

351 Supplying the subsidised theatre: London School of Contemporary Dance

Over the four academic years 1975–1979 an average of 19.5 students a year graduated from the London School of Contemporary Dance. Of these, 7 entered London Contemporary Dance Theatre, 2 entered Ballet Rambert, and 15 went to smaller British companies such as EMMA, Extemporary, Junction, MAAS Movers and Moving Being, 5 joined European or Israeli companies, 3 entered established American companies, 6 found work in the commercial theatre and 10 are in 'regular fringe' groups, whilst 10 others obtained contracts partly as performers, partly as choreographers and/or teachers abroad. 12 graduates entered full-time teaching posts in various institutions of the private sector, 2 took employment as body conditioning specialists and a further group went to the USA for advanced study or to teach. Such figures illustrate the significance of the growth of contemporary dance in Britain during the last ten years. In the late 1960s there were no openings. Today contemporary dance accounts for about 25% of job opportunities. The figures also show the dominant position of the Royal Ballet School and the London School of Contemporary Dance in the subsidised theatre.

352 Other schools and commercial theatre

A small number of graduates from the Royal Ballet School and London School of Contemporary Dance pass into commercial theatre, films and television. Other vocational training institutions, including independent dance schools and general stage schools, send varying proportions of their graduates into the subsidised theatre, including community theatre, as well as commercial theatre and into non-performance posts which require a dance training. Of the 35 students passing out of the Dance Theatre Course at the Laban Centre during 1976–1979, 11 are now in professional companies of various kinds, 8 are in community work or teaching in small private studios, one is studying advanced notation in New York and 2 are undertaking advanced training in theatre design and costume design. A similar story of placing comes from the major independent schools and the leading stage schools except, of course, that a proportion of their talent is creamed off to specialist schools or leading teacher training centres before the question of employment arises at the school where most of their training has taken place. None has reported serious employment problems.

353 Need for correlation between schools and jobs

Conclusions are clear. First, in the improved employment situation compared with even ten years ago, there is a good chance for talented graduates to enter the dancing profession in Britain or abroad, always remembering, of course, that entry into the theatrical profession is controlled by British Actors' Equity.* Second, the evidence suggests a concentration of opportunity in London and abroad, but with every sign of growing opportunity in the regions. There is a need therefore for the Arts Council of Great Britain and RAAs to encourage more regional openings as well as dance-in-education, dance in community arts and other new applications of dance. Third, some correlation will be needed sooner or later between the numbers emerging from vocational schools and the number of job opportunities. At the moment a correlation may be achieved, in effect, through the work of the accreditation committee of the Council for Dance Education and Training. This will limit the number of vocational schools recommended to local authorities for discretionary grant purposes. Combined with a licence system for teachers it is hoped that the result may be a reduction in the number of sub-standard schools, and hence of poorly trained dancers competing for jobs. At the present time, however, dancers emerging from reputable vocational dance schools do not seem threatened with an overcrowded profession to the same extent as actors because there is still much unexplored potential demand. There is, however, a continuing need for effective links between vocational schools and tertiary education so that dance graduates can continue into degree or other courses if theatre openings are not available or their career inclinations turn in different directions.

354 Need for better statistics

Our final conclusion is a need for more detailed statistics to be kept over this whole field by the Department of Employment and the DES, coupled with a more detailed study of the economic situation of performing artists than is available at the moment. It has been even more difficult to obtain statistics about the employment/unemployment of professional dancers and dance teachers than it was about the unemployment of professional actors.[1] Theatrical performers tend all to be placed in the same category by the Department of Employment even

---

* Figures of openings in subsidised theatre have been checked and confirmed with Mr G B L Wilson, adviser at the Royal Ballet School and specialist in dance job opportunities. He estimated that in mid-1977, based on the experience of previous years, the total number of new openings a year for classically trained dancers in UK and Europe was about 65. British trained dancers took many of these, but since then, European opportunities have become fewer because of the development of schools such as the Stuttgart School and because of the economic situation. Even so, it is rare at the moment for talented graduates from British vocational dance schools to remain unemployed for long.

though the needs and opportunities of actors, singers and dancers are very different. The Government's Central Statistical Office also has been unable to help.

355 Life style of professional dancers

The matter is complicated further by the pride and life style of professional dancers. Those in subsidised companies are usually on annual contract, renewable year by year. This provides a measure of stability and security although injury or sickness can end a career almost overnight. For those in commercial theatre, even in London's West End, employment is more spasmodic with a practice of finding part-time employment between jobs to leave time to attend and pay for daily classes. In commercial theatre outside central London, seasonal employment, relatively low pay and regular part-time work in another field are the rule. Hence those who register as unemployed tend to be a minority of those who are 'resting' and may also include a number who have opted out and are moving into a different career. Indeed, our talks with young dancers suggest that the area of most concern to them is not professional performer unemployment so much as failure to obtain initial performer employment. Unemployment, too, is much more a problem for women dancers than it is for men who are always in short supply. For all these reasons we have concluded that our comparison of demand and supply is likely to be a more accurate guide to the nature of employment and unemployment in the dancing profession than any other guide available at the moment. Our comparison, too, has emphasised the dancer's unique need for daily training during unemployment. It is essential to re-employment as a dancer, and, therefore, we think it should form part of unemployment benefit — a matter for British Actors' Equity perhaps.

356 Teaching opportunities

The same pattern — and the same lack of statistics — can be observed in teacher employment in the private sector. Graduates from the major vocational training centres appear to have little difficulty in finding jobs. Figures available over five academic years 1974–1979 show that all these institutions placed all their graduates who qualified, totalling around 90 graduates a year, although not all the teaching posts to which they went in the private sector were full-time and salaried. Some were undertaken on a self-employed, freelance basis combined with marriage. In addition a small number of graduates from these institutions entered professional dance companies as dancers in Britain or abroad. The difficulty in this area of employment lies in three factors which are a result of conditions already described. They are: the variable salary structure leading to low pay, particularly outside London; the variable standards of training outside the principal institutions; and the lack of a really progressive career structure in the private sector of teaching. Excellent potential teachers graduate every year from the major institutions often to enter dead-end jobs in private studios from which it is hard to move. It is a tragic waste of good people: these graduates are unable to progress further for lack of adequate career opportunities.

Recommendations
A national plan for the 1980s

We present below our principal recommendations beginning with those requiring immediate action. We have assembled these recommendations under various heads to form a coherent national plan which we believe can be fulfilled during the 1980s, notwithstanding present restraints.

We are encouraged in this belief by the growth of interest in dance, charted in our report, and by its relevance to areas of imagination, creativity, self-awareness and personal experience which now occupy a central place in curriculum debate and in the concern of very many educationalists. Dance is not a peripheral activity, but one of those significant subjects essential to training the imagination. Training the imagination, we argue, is one of the most important functions of education today, as important for Britain's industrial, commercial and scientific future as to the quality of individual lives, the enrichment of leisure and the preparation of minds and bodies to contribute their best to society. We think it no accident that the nature of the curriculum has grown to be a matter of intense public concern and involvement during the last five years. This concern has been ours throughout our study and is, therefore, the background to our plan for dance education and training during the 1980s.

We know that a plan of this nature will not be fulfilled quickly, even if we lived in a time of prosperity and boundless resources. Many consultations will be needed, with much goodwill and give and take on all sides, as well as some funds. There are, for example, expenditure implications in a number of our recommendations to local education authorities. This does not necessarily imply additional expenditure, but it does imply a different use of existing resources. The Department of Education and Science, in particular, has underlined to us the new economic climate within which our recommendations will need to be considered. For this reason we do not suggest (as some have urged we should) the introduction of more specialist courses and staff into all or most schools. Rather we are seeking to give dance a fair place in the overall curriculum as it exists now because, as we show in our report, dance has a strong contribution to make to personal, social, physical and aesthetic development within the curriculum at all levels.

In the private sector the response to our plan needs to be a little different. First, this sector is more at risk as a consequence of economic cutback even than the maintained sector. Therefore our recommendations begin by drawing attention to the need to protect the leading institutions of vocational dance training without which British dance theatre cannot maintain its present level at home and abroad. Second, paradoxically, the private sector has much more freedom of action for self-help than the maintained sector. There is a great deal which can be done by the private sector itself to realise our recommendations. We hope it will exercise this freedom.

Generally speaking, greater recognition for dance in both sectors, and the contribution which each can make to British life today, depends upon a more sympathetic and co-operative attitude, which will lead in turn to more dance in maintained schools at all levels. This implies more facilities. We are confident that local education authorities which respond sympathetically to our recommendations will use ingenuity to meet these needs. Minor Works Projects, for example, might be used for adaptations which will embrace a range of 'subjects', and Furniture and Equipment might take into account the opportunities presented by the mobile dance floor described in Appendix G. Where there is conviction about the value of dance we believe that local education authorities and others will do their best to provide the means which lie within their power. 'It would be a pity,' remarked Her Majesty's Inspectors, 'to assume that there is nothing which can be done until and unless additional resources appear.'[18] This is why we have concentrated so much in our report on demonstrating the relevance and importance of dance at every level of education, from which follows the need to give it a fairer share of the resources available.

Taking these considerations into account, we believe that what we propose is a constructive way forward for dance education and training during the next decade, that it is realisable even at the present time, and that the fulfilment of some of our recommendations is now very urgent if dance education and training are to be able to make their proper contribution to national life and to the personal development of all our young people. These key recommendations are marked with an asterisk,* and those requiring immediate action with a double asterisk.** We think the plan as a whole could be achieved by the end of the 1980s. This means starting now.

Policy Objectives

Five priorities seem to us to emerge from our study:–

A Every young person should have some experience of dance during primary and secondary years of schooling, and an opportunity to choose to extend their studies in this field at VIth form level and in tertiary and continuing education;

B The provision of such opportunities should be based on the acceptance of dance as an art equal in status with other arts in the curriculum;

C All young people with outstanding talent should have the opportunity of vocational training in dance. The criteria for such opportunity should rest on the basis of talent, *not* on the ability to pay fees for private tuition;

D The leading vocational institutions, which are now facing grave financial problems and upon which vocational training in dance depends, must be preserved;

E Opportunities should be developed for all people in the community to continue their interest and involvement in dance after the end of formal education.

For immediate action during 1980/81

**1   Since the financial basis of the private vocational sector of dance training has long been so insecure as to threaten its standards, and since the service it gives is unique and unprovided for in the maintained sector, we urge upon central and local government:–

a) recognition of the anomalies inherent in the application of the present discretionary grants system. This threatens the country not only with the loss of talented artists and dance teachers, but loss of schools built up over the years and loss of the talent needed to sustain a theatre art which helps to contribute substantially each year to British cultural life, British overseas reputation and British tourist earnings;

b) recognition, therefore, of the justice of the case for mandatory grants to vocational students of the performing arts as a matter of equity. Such recognition

172

would provide comparability for dance students with students of other subjects in universities and the maintained sector of higher education;

c) recognition of the need to sustain the training of dance teachers in the private sector.

**2   Bearing in mind these considerations we recommend:—

a) that until such time as the economic situation allows the introduction of mandatory grants, there should be an immediate and thorough review of the present discretionary grant system aiming to improve and rationalise it by establishing agreed criteria to be applied equally by all authorities, removing anomalies between one authority and another, and thus preventing irreparable damage to the present vocational training system;

b) that local education authorities recognise the special situation of vocational dance students, properly assessed in the manner recommended in paragraph 56 (h) below, particularly in their consideration of discretionary awards for students under 18;

c) that discussions should be initiated between relevant national, local and university authorities to give the Laban Centre the status and recognition it needs to develop its special role in private tertiary education combined with vocational training. To fulfil this role there is a particular need to remove the anomaly whereby its students cannot receive mandatory grants for an honours degree course in dance properly validated by the CNAA;

d) similar action should be taken, particularly in respect of discretionary grants, to safeguard the College of the Royal Academy of Dancing, the London College of Dance and Drama and the Teacher Training Course of the Royal Ballet School as being the principal teacher training institutions of the private sector;

e) local education authorities should review their present support for private dance teaching institutions in light of accreditation recommendations from the Council for Dance Education and Training and Scottish Council for Dance under the procedure recommended in paragraph 56 (b) below.

**3   a) The unique position and direct comparability of the Royal Ballet Upper School and London School of Contemporary Dance should be recognised as being the only schools directly linked with major professional dance companies. Therefore, both schools should be supported equally so that neither need refuse places to talented British students who have satisfied their entry requirements;

b) For purposes of this recommendation the Royal Ballet School should be regarded as one school with the same system of support for vocational training in both the Upper and Lower Schools;

c) Consideration should be given to ways in which support for the Royal Ballet School, the London School of Contemporary Dance and Laban Centre for Movement and Dance can include capital grants for buildings and development.

**4   To protect dance at the present time in the maintained and university sectors of education, we recommend:—

a) application of the principle that subject areas such as the arts — and dance in particular — at present underfunded by most local educational authorities, do not suffer relatively greater cuts than other subjects;

b) local education authorities and head teachers should take special steps to safeguard good dance work in primary and secondary schools as part of their measures to safeguard standards generally;

c) special steps should be taken in a similar way in tertiary education to safeguard centres of dance research and post-graduate dance study, such as the work at Leeds University, and centres of dance training with potential for research such as Dunfermline College of Physical Education;

d) as part of the general research recommendation in 6 below, further research should be initiated as soon as possible to assess evidence of the contribution which dance makes within the educational experience of children and to establish what would be considered a 'fair place' for dance in the overall curriculum.

I Action across both sectors for the 1980s
Action at National Level

*5   Ethnic Dance. The Commission for Racial Equality, the local authorities, Regional Arts Associations and leading institutions of the private sector should consult to encourage the study and practice of ethnic dance, particularly supporting the Minority Arts Advisory Service as the principal private organisation providing guidance and liaison for the cultural organisations of the ethnic minorities.

*6   Research. More research is needed urgently across the whole field of dance education and training, particularly in the context of a general need to explore and develop expressive subjects and all forms of communication available to children. We recommend, therefore, that institutions with research capacity, such as universities, polytechnics and colleges, and organisations with funds or research influence, should consult with the education authorities at each level, research councils and other relevant bodies in both sectors, to devote part of their capacity, funding and influence to commission research and special studies about dance in all its aspects.

7   Statistics. Noting the deplorable lack of statistics in the field of dance we recommend that records should be maintained regularly concerning, in particular, employment for professional dancers and dance teachers in both sectors; the relationship between training and work; and the economic situation of professional dancers and dance teachers in both sectors.

8   Archives. Dance institutions in both sectors should recognise the importance of dance archives for education and training purposes, and their own responsibility for safeguarding the material under their control. A conference should be called as soon as possible to concert and discuss the preservation and use of dance archives in Britain, and appropriate appeals to funding bodies.

Action in Broadcasting

9   The significance of dance needs to be recognised more fully in broadcasting particularly through co-ordinated dance policy within the BBC, IBA and television and sound companies. Accordingly, the BBC, IBA and television companies should reconsider their approach to dance, treating it as an art, discipline

and subject in its own right, deserving its own time slots, its own producers with dance experience and its own production department, (even if this should require a small unit initially) rather than permit dance to continue as part of music or popular entertainment.

10   The special role of television broadcasting in dance education should be recognised by educational television bodies, including the Open University. Consultations should be initiated with dance companies, dance teaching organisations and other organisations to produce television programmes related to each level, even within the present constraints.

11   A new form of contract should be explored by broadcasting authorities, the relevant unions and associations with copyright or contractual interests to allow for educational purposes the use of dance and other material in general output programmes and/or in sound and television archives, as recommended by the Advisory Council for Adult and Continuing Education.

12   To encourage the development of broadcasting as a key element in continuing dance education, liaison groups should be formed between broadcasters and dance teachers from both sectors at regional level to stimulate a) local radio and television education programmes about dance; and b) the use of other educational and general output programmes, publications and dance activities for informal education purposes.

Action by Teachers of Dance in Both Sectors

13   Greater efforts should be made by teachers of dance in the maintained and non-maintained sectors to interest the trade union movement in the educational, cultural and social value of dance.

14   There is need to strengthen the links between organisations which assist the promotion of dance education in both sectors and sports, and recreational organisations which involve dance.

15   More initiatives need to be taken by teachers of dance to use media of every kind for education and information purposes. This includes liaison with local radio, press and television; use of video to record and show good work where performance is not possible; use of printshops, local community communications and resource centres, and so on.

Action in Music and Related Arts

16   Colleges of music should make available to all students (future performers, teachers, composers and conductors) courses on dance/movement, Dalcroze Eurythmics, choreographic principles, and so on, and should encourage interest in dance performances. Courses could be extra-mural, where an appropriate dance resource is nearby.

17   Dance teachers in both sectors should encourage students to listen to and enjoy music as an essential part of the general education of young dancers, and through studying an instrument to learn the basic rudiments of music.

18   Dance teacher training courses should include a basic music training which emphasises the relationship of music to dance/teacher to musician, high standards of instruments and of musical performance.

19   In the interests of the development of dance, as well as the art of mime with which dance is closely connected, a measure of priority should be given to overcome the current neglect of mime by assisting mime and mime training wherever possible in both sectors.

20   We emphasise the importance of relating dance to other arts because the arts enrich each other. Knowledge of them is essential to any balanced conception of dance as an art form, cultural force and significant educational resource.

II The Maintained Sector — action for the 1980s

Action by Local Education Authorities
Dissemination of Knowledge and Expertise

*21   A strengthening of the dance advisory service should be effected so that every authority has an adviser familiar with or aware of a wide range of dance education and training.

*22   Fuller use, at realistic salary levels, should be made of private teachers able to offer particular dance expertise.

23   There should be a greater use of advisory teachers to supplement the work of the non-specialist teacher, especially for the upper ages in the junior age range.

24   More provision is needed to disseminate information and details of successful dance work in schools.

25   Dance specialists and dance advisory teachers within an authority should be encouraged to pass on their skills to non-specialist teachers in primary schools as a principal means of raising the quality of dance teaching.

26   The principle should be accepted that provision for dance is needed at every level of continuing education, full-time and part-time.

Setting Standards

*27   To encourage higher standards by demonstrating good examples, local education authorities should assist schools and colleges to promote more visits from professional dance companies, individual professional dancers, and visits to dance events outside the school.

28   Local education authorities should encourage Days of Dance and other less formal sharing situations as well as performances by the County, Regional or Area School of Dance, or arts centres, in order to demonstrate standards of achievement and the range of possible dance activities.

Special Provision

29   Special provision should be made for the handicapped through:—
a) the recognition that both physically and mentally handicapped children can often be helped through dance and so have thereby a special claim on local dance teaching resources;

b) consultation with the Department of Education and Science, Schools Council, National Foundation for Educational Research, foundations for the disabled and so on about special needs in this field;

c) provision to help handicapped children at primary and secondary level through close liaison between local education authorities and specially selected private teachers of dancing.

30   Special provision should also be made for gifted or talented children, ('gifted' defined as those with professional performance potential and 'talented' signifying others showing unusual proficiency) through:—

a) consultation with the Department of Education and Science, Schools Council, National Foundation for Educational Research, and specialist bodies about special needs in this field and assistance for teachers in identifying the gifted;

b) provision for special classes and other help for gifted and talented children at primary and secondary level through close liaison between local education authorities and specially selected private teachers of dancing;

c) the preparation of panels of local dance teachers with appropriate expertise to carry forward a programme of special assistance indicated in (b) above through free private lessons to children sponsored by the LEA, in consultation with either the Council for Dance Education and Training in England, the Scottish Council for Dance, or the Dance Council for Wales;

d) the recognition of the need of gifted and talented children to practise and undertake special study at an age younger than most children who have other talents.

Action in Tertiary and Continuing Education

31   Responsible bodies should engage in discussion to establish continuing consultative links between all departments involved in dance in universities, polytechnics and colleges of higher and further education.

*32   The University Grants Committee should encourage a university initiative to establish a Chair of Dance, or a joint Chair including Dance, at a British university.

33   Responsible bodies in higher and further education should make every effort to arrange performances on campus by professional dancers.

*34   Ethnic dance study, with its potential for fostering racial understanding, should form an especially important part of dance in further and adult education, perhaps developing further the Schools Council's programmes on Developing the Curriculum for a Changing World and Special Needs and Problems of Individual Pupils.

*35   Local authorities should give encouragement to youth dance groups, matching that given to youth orchestras and drama groups, including professional advice and help in production skills.

36   Provision in terms of special courses, facilities and teaching and information aids about dance should be made for youth workers and careers officers.

37   The coopération of the Dance Section of the National Association of Teachers in Further and Higher Education should continue to be sought in matters concerned with dance in higher and further education.

Action in Teacher Training Establishments

*38   More time for practical dance experience needs to be given to teachers preparing to teach dance in primary and secondary education so that,
a) primary teachers acquire greater confidence in practical teaching;
b) secondary teachers acquire mastery of at least one form of dance, including personal competence in performance.

39   Teacher training institutions for candidates intending to offer a specialism in dance, whether at middle or secondary level, should consider requiring some evidence of the candidates' own dance experience as an entry requirement.

*40   A proportion of available funds should be redistributed to provide more induction and in-service schemes for teachers of dance to raise standards at primary and secondary level and to counter the effect of a relatively static teaching force.

41   Parallel with more in-service courses for dance teachers should go regular seminars on dance for head teachers enabling them to support their own resident and visiting dance staff.

*42   Lecturers in dance in polytechnics and colleges of higher education should be required to hold an appropriate additional qualification in dance which may include post-graduate studies and/or professional dance experience.

43   Dance teacher training should be concentrated in institutions which are recognised as national or regional centres having appropriate staff and physical resources.

44   Every effort should be made by teacher training institutions to exchange experience with the dance profession through professional dancers-in-residence, the visits of professional companies, and the involvement of professional dancers wherever possible, especially in choreographic and production work at secondary level.

Action for Dance Spaces and Resources

*45   Because dance needs special spaces authorities and architects should consult with appropriate dance teaching organisations in both sectors and combine to publish appropriate criteria for general guidance.

46   Through redeployment of resources the development of a County, Regional or Area School of Dance should be supported to provide opportunities for dance at a high standard in each local education authority area, and encouragement should be given to already existing arts centres with dance facilities, so that schools' dance activities can be accommodated, thus providing a community as well as an educational focus.

47   Particular attention should be given to dance in deliberations of the Advisory Council for Adult and Continuing Education to compensate for present deficiencies in teaching, spaces and visual aids in these areas of education.

48   Dance centres, being a particularly valuable resource, need systematic development by each authority.

49   The provision of adequate dance spaces and resources should involve the identification and allocation of spare resources and empty spaces on a fair basis, both

for local use, to facilitate the exchange of experience between professional teachers and professional dancers and to provide rehearsal and performance facilities for visiting professional dancers.

Action in Assessment and Examinations

50   We recommend, as ultimately desirable, the development of agreed national criteria for assessing dance at secondary level in the maintained sectors of England, Scotland and Wales with consequential co-ordination of standards, embracing an appropriate variety of options.

*51   In discussing agreed criteria for examination or assessment in dance, we think that the concept of dance as a many faceted subject, presented in our report, should guide assessment practice. Thus, for examinations involving primarily dance performance, we recommend that over 50% of an assessment should be for the practice of dance performance, quality, technique and so on, and that continuous assessment should therefore be accepted as valid for a proportion of the examination. Examinations involving primarily dance history, dance criticism, dance aesthetics, dance anthropology or some other area of dance study should give a similar weighting to their area of emphasis.

*52   We think the application of agreed criteria should be developed at O and A level in the General Certificate of Education, in all Modes in the Certificate of Extended Education and Certificate of Secondary Education (so long as it remains) and in the Scottish Certificate of Education.

*53   There should be regular assistance for teachers and examiners to develop assessment standards and techniques through courses and conferences.

54   Closer contact is recommended between secondary schools and higher education institutions offering dance so that entry standards at tertiary level can be raised.

III The Non-Maintained Sector — action for the 1980s

Action to Develop National Dance Organisations

*55   The private and vocational sector of dance education and training has needed for a long time a national structure with organisations able to speak for it as a whole to government and local government, regulate its affairs and sustain professional standards. We welcome, therefore, the establishment of the Council for Dance Education and Training and the Conference of Dance Schools in England; the Scottish Council for Dance; and the Welsh Dance Association soon to become the Dance Council for Wales. All are private, self-financing organisations with constitutions outlined at Appendix F. We believe, however, that to be fully effective in the many tasks this report recommends for them, they will need to be able to speak with an authority which is seen to derive from three principles, all equally sustained — a representative function covering all sides of the dance teaching profession; a devotion to standards; and an endorsement by central and local government.

     To fulfil these important principles we think that some adjustments may be necessary to the work or constitutions of these organisations as they have evolved during the last two or three years. We note, for example, that dance teachers of the maintained and non-maintained sectors are represented success-fully in the Scottish Council for Dance through elected representation. Accord-ingly we recommend the Council for Dance Education and Training to explore the possibility of a similar broad representation of dance teachers from the maintained and non-maintained sectors in England. Likewise we invite the Dance Council for Wales to develop parallel functions so that it can fulfil purposes similar to those of the English and Scottish Councils. We recommend, as a matter of urgency, that all three organisations seek the endorsement of the Department of Education and Science/Scottish Education Department and the relevant Local Authority Associations for the activities outlined in their con-stitutions at Appendix F and/or recommended below. We think, too, that the Conference of Dance Schools should be strengthened and encouraged in every way to represent the interests of private schools to the Councils above, particu-larly in matters of standards, accreditation, syllabuses, assessments and the exchange of experience.

Action by National Organisations

*56   We recommend that, in consultation with the Department of Education and Science or the Scottish Education Department, and in consultation with relevant local government associations and trade unions concerned, the Scottish Council for Dance and/or the Council for Dance Education and Training, in concert with the Dance Council for Wales, should, in the interests of the profession as a whole:—

a) move to establish a licence system for private dance teachers by agreement with the main examining and teacher training bodies, which system should be recognised and accepted by central and local government, and should provide the means for recommending suitable private dance teachers to local authorities or parents;

b) continue to develop the national accreditation system now being introduced for all private dance teaching institutions. To accomplish this successfully we recommend that criteria should be publicly stated, regularly reviewed and applied through an accreditation committee which includes practising teachers of dance elected by their peers and with such other safeguards as the Councils shall lay down from time to time;

c) negotiate and enforce through the licensing of teachers minimum salary scales and a minimum fee structure for private dance teachers;

d) negotiate with local education authorities and colleges to ensure from them greater co-operation in the use of private teachers in their locality whenever local appointments are made and opportunities occur;

e) negotiate with local education authorities to finance, possibly through mort-gage or other loan arrangements, the establishment of local spaces for private teaching and the greater use of spaces, equipment and other resources presently available under local education authority control;

f) consult with the medical profession and appropriate research centres to develop the measures necessary to prevent or heal injuries and mitigate strains particular to dancers;

g) consult to establish a National Advisory Service to assist local authorities, Regional Arts Associations, parents, teachers, students and others with information about all aspects of vocational dance teaching;

h) consult with local education authorities to develop the service, already established by the Council for Dance Education and Training, whereby students can be assessed for local education authorities in the making of discretionary grants for vocational training in dance.

Action in Teacher Training

*57   Teacher training institutions of the private sector should take steps, as a matter of urgency, either individually or collectively, to offer to their students the possibility of working for a degree, not only as a means of gaining entry to the maintained sector, but to enhance the status of dance teachers within the private sector.

58   Courses seeking to retrain former professional dancers as teachers for the private sector should consult with relevant professional bodies to enlarge the range of retraining to include preparation for the youth service, and work in community arts, ethnic dance, leisure, recreation and so on.

59   Teacher training institutions of the private sector should introduce regular joint consultations on curricula, entry qualifications and standards to co-ordinate their work and strengthen the status of their institutions.

*60   Examining bodies, teacher training institutions and other interested organisations of the private sector should consult to investigate the desirability of a pension scheme for private teachers of dancing similar to the existing scheme for professional dancers.

Action in the Assessment of Standards

*61   Examining bodies with national and international interests should consult to develop as a matter of urgency consultative procedures already initiated to:—

a) co-ordinate examination dates, standards and fees;

b) reduce drastically the number of examinations at every level;

c) establish joint boards where possible;

d) examine and report on the value of a single, nationally applicable dance examination syllabus offering appropriate alternatives for development in the interests of students, teachers and the dancing profession;

e) consider the feasibility of establishing a Central Examination Authority to licence examining bodies and to supervise standards, paid for through a levy on examining bodies.

Action in Tertiary Training

*62   The Arts Council of Great Britain, Scottish Arts Council, Welsh Arts Council, professional dance companies, vocational dance schools, relevant trade unions and other interested bodies should consult to strengthen by every means opportunities for choreographic creation, particularly through:—

a) the development of the International Dance Course for Professional Choreographers and Composers into a centre for advanced choreographic study with Arts Council and other support;

b) flexibility of professional company choreographic workshops in accepting creative work from outside the company:

c) the development of in-service courses at various centres of advanced choreographic study for dance teachers from both sectors to strengthen the creative element of their work;

d) the encouragement of choreographic opportunity within existing vocational dance schools.

63 Those responsible for vocational dance training at secondary level should consider how best to strengthen the intellectual and artistic content of present courses to prepare dancers better for opportunities at tertiary level.

64 Professional Dance Companies should take steps, in consultation with relevant funding bodies, to organise sabbatical periods of paid educational leave for long-serving dancers to enrich their work as artists and/or help them to prepare for an alternative career when their performing life comes to an end.

*65 A National Teaching Resource and Communications Centre for Dance and Related Arts should be established to offer advice about books, slides, films, video and other materials; conduct research; establish a holding of resources for sale; organise lecture tours and provide similar services.

Special Action in Scotland

66 Consideration should be given to the development of a professional contemporary dance company in Scotland.

67 As professional dance in Scotland develops, consideration should be given to stronger representation of dance interests in the central councils of Scottish artistic and education policy making institutions.

IV Action to Follow-up the Report

68 Following publication of our report we think that action along the following lines might be appropriate:—

a) the Council for Dance Education and Training, Scottish Council for Dance and Dance Council for Wales might invite comments from a comprehensive list of organisations within each country about ways to carry out the recommendations of the report;

b) parallel with this activity, and in consultation with the organisations concerned, the Committee of the National Study of Dance Education might reconvene to discuss and animate a series of supporting meetings, briefing sessions and other activities designed to concentrate on particularly significant areas of the report;

c) in light of these discussions action-conferences might be convened in England, Scotland and Wales to determine priorities and to develop plans of action.

69 Consideration should be given to the possibility of publishing a regular *Dance in Education Journal* to act as a forum for all the developments proposed in this report; to promote cooperation between dance teachers in both sectors; to disseminate information about the work of the National Councils, Associations, Authorities and Institutions of Britain concerned with dance; to reproduce the results of significant dance research wherever undertaken; and to report on relevant developments abroad.

Epilogue: The Task Ahead

When we started our study nearly five years ago we saw it as a very necessary task, though few of us imagined then how long it would take to accomplish. We believe that the report which has emerged now provides a basis for progressive action during the 1980s through the plan outlined in our recommendations. The fulfilment of this plan, however, will depend less on overcoming the formidable economic restraints of the present time than on generating and sustaining the will to accomplish the vision it offers. Visions only become reality through hard work and careful planning based on sound information! To this we must now address ourselves, living in a very different world from that of five years ago and from what we once expected for the 1980s.

In reviewing our new task the first thing to note, though, is the unchanged nature of the salient characteristics of our subject. They remain as we assessed them five years ago in one of the first papers to be discussed by our committee. Dance education and training embrace the areas of seeing, creating, performing and thinking about dance in a balance which will vary from time to time and place to place according to circumstances. They are intensely interdisciplinary, linked with many subjects. Their inadequately recorded history remains a rewarding study for researchers, providing many lessons as we ourselves discovered. They comprise a unity within which different philosophies in the maintained and non-maintained sectors need to make their contribution on the basis of wide discussion. Because this discussion embraces conceptions of dance as part of the history of human movement, culture and communication, traditional concepts of the nature of knowledge and the communication of knowledge will be challenged. Dance thus becomes a test case for many new elements in the curriculum. At the same time much research remains to be done on the contribution of dance to the curriculum and education of young people.

We have found throughout our study a wide acknowledgement that changes are needed if dance is to become more effective in both sectors of education. The changes we think necessary are reflected in our recommendations and derive largely from the evidence and information upon which these recommendations are based. They become the new task ahead. We are concerned therefore that the initiation of this task and the momentum of development should not be lost in the present atmosphere of cuts and retrenchment. Our concern arises not only from confidence in our subject but a belief that dance will have increasing significance in the new society being created by technological change. To fulfil this belief what we have begun in our report will need to be continued by those who act upon it. Particularly important to this end, we think, is the continuing evolution of a philosophy of dance education and training which can define clear relationships between dance and the authorities of the world in which it lives, strengthen the case for dance against cuts and retrenchment, and inspire action. The action, of course, belongs to the teachers, students, parents, administrators and organisations concerned with dance. We look for dialogue with them jointly to advance the task ahead.

Conferences and Seminars

1. March 1974 The Gulbenkian Action Conference on Dance Education

Chairman: The Lord Annan OBE

Terms of reference:
to explore and define current problems in professional dance education and dance in education;
on the basis of the above, to advise priorities which might guide the Foundation in a dance education policy;
to determine whether some sort of larger scale, possibly national inquiry is desirable into some or all of the problems raised and, if so, the limits and purpose of such an inquiry.

Programme:
Introduction: Chairman of Conference

First Session: Professional Training
Chairman: Peter Williams

Second Session: Dance in Education
Chairman: John Allen

Third Session: Higher Education and Dance
Chairman: Arnold Haskell

Fourth Session: Summary
Chairman: The Lord Annan

Conference members:
John Allen, Principal, Central School of Speech & Drama; formerly H.M. Inspector with special responsibility for drama.

Lord Annan, Provost, University College London; Director, Royal Opera House; member of Advisory Committee, Gulbenkian Foundation and Chairman, Dance Conference.

Audrey Bambra, Principal, Chelsea College of Physical Education; Vice-Chairman Governing Body London College of Dance and Drama.

Gerard Bagley, Director, The Dance Drama Theatre.

Diana Barker, Vice-Chairman and Examiner, Cecchetti Society & ISTD; Examiner, AEB; Principal, Anthorne; was representative of ISTD on Dance Unity Committee.

Bice Bellairs, Principal, Bellairs School of Acting & Drama Dance Education Ltd, The Bellairs Centre.

Peter Brinson, Director, Calouste Gulbenkian Foundation, UK & Commonwealth Branch.

Mary Clarke, Editor, The Dancing Times; author and critic.

Margaret Dale, Producer, BBC Television. Former Royal Ballet soloist.

Jane Dudley, Director of Graham Studies, London School of Contemporary Dance; formerly Artistic Director, Batsheva Dance Company, Israel; soloist, Martha Graham Company.

Edward Kelland-Espinosa, Chairman, Board of British Ballet Organisation; Chairman, Trustees Espinosa Memorial Fund.

Beryl Grey, Artistic Director, London Festival Ballet; formerly Director General, Arts Educational Trust; principal, Royal Ballet.

Ivor Guest, Chairman, The Royal Academy of Dancing; ballet historian; author.

Robert Harrold, Advisory member Administrative Council, ISTD; Examiner, ISTD; teacher with special experience of working with boys.

Arnold Haskell, Governor, The Royal Ballet, Royal Ballet School, London Festival Ballet; author, lecturer, journalist.

Betty Hassall, Principal, Hammond School Ltd; Examiner RAD; Chairman, N/W Region (Liverpool Centre) RAD.

David Henshaw, Principal Lecturer & Head of Dance and Movement Studies, Trent Park College of Education.

Stuart Hopps, Associate Director, Scottish Theatre Ballet; Founder/choreographer, Moveable Workshop performing group which also conducts Master Classes & Workshops in schools, colleges & universities in Scotland.

Pat Hutchinson, Principal, London School of Contemporary Dance; formerly Vice-Principal, London College of Dance & Drama; Examiner ISTD; member of first committee convened by Robin Howard to introduce Contemporary Dance to London.

Muriel Large, Administrator, Irish Ballet Company.

June Layson, Lecturer MA course — Aesthetic evaluation of human movement and History of Dance in Education, Department of Physical Education, University of Leeds; guest lecturer and examiner at various universities, colleges & conferences in UK and overseas.

Beryl Manthorp, Principal, Guildhall School of Dancing, Norwich; Chairman, East Anglian Region RAD.

Norman Morrice, Artistic Director & Choreographer (formerly soloist) Ballet Rambert; responsible for introducing Modern Dance training to Ballet Rambert.

Marion North, Head of Movement & Dance Dept, University of London Goldsmiths' College; Director & Principal, Art of Movement Centre.

Phrosso Pfister, Principal, London College of Dance & Drama; examiner ISTD; visiting teacher of ballet to Francis Holland Schools for 25 years.

Belinda Quirey, Chairman, Historical Dance Branch ISTD; author, historian, choreographer and teacher.

Mary Skeaping, Choreographer and ballet historian; formerly Ballet Mistress of Sadler's Wells Ballet and Director, Royal Swedish Ballet.

Professor John Vaizey (Economics), Brunel University; member Advisory Committee and Chairman, Statistical Enquiry into education and the arts, Gulbenkian Foundation; member Nat. Council on Educational Technology; member Nat. Adv. Council on training and supply of teachers. Author of many works on economics and technology of education.

Peter Williams, Editor, *Dance & Dancers;* Chairman, Ballet Sub-Committee, Arts Council. Author and critic.

Jane Winearls, Lecturer (in charge of dance courses) Dept of Physical Education, University of Birmingham; formerly worked as teacher, producer, choreographer with Sigurd Leeder, Kurt Jooss, Molly Lake and Travis Kemp. Author, journalist.

Michael Wood, Director, The Royal Ballet School.

Observers
June Batten Arey, Consultant, Rockefeller Centre, New York, USA.

Keith Bain, Chairman, Dance Panel, Australia Council for the Arts.

Jane Nicholas, Assistant Director: Dance, Arts Council of Great Britain.

Professor Grant Strate, Professor of Dance, York University, Toronto, Canada.

Reconvention: the Conference was reconvened in June 1974 to consider the problems of establishing a representative body for the dance education world, able to speak for the profession to government, local authorities and other national and international bodies.

2. January 1975 Special Meeting of the Dance Study Committee to discuss dance in primary and secondary education with physical education advisers of local education authorities who had submitted evidence to the Study.

Local Education Authorities represented:

London
Miss McLaren, Inner London Education Authority

Miss Jenner, Borough of Barking

Miss Makin, Borough of Redbridge

Metropolitan Districts
Mr John Learmouth, Calderdale (West Yorkshire)

Miss B Neville, Salford (Greater Manchester)

Counties
Miss V A Lewis, Devon County Council

Miss P Dann, Norfolk County Council

Mrs J Eades, Cheshire County Council

Mr M T Gilmour, Leicestershire County Council

The following local education authorities submitted evidence or have since offered other advice but were unable to send representatives:

London Borough of Barnet; Metropolitan Districts of Coventry, Manchester, Merseyside and West Midlands; Counties of Bedfordshire, Buckinghamshire, Cornwall, Essex, Kent and Oxfordshire; Scottish Regional Councils with their Education Divisions – Borders, Dumfries & Galloway, Fife, Grampian, Strathclyde and Tayside. Plus other authorities represented at other conferences in this appendix

3. October 1976 Special Meeting to discuss Discretionary Grants

Terms of reference:
In view of the severe cuts predicted in the area of discretionary grants to discuss: a) what action could be taken to help institutions in danger from cutback or elimination of discretionary awards: b) what form of advice to local and central government and public opinion could best highlight the urgency of the threat to the performing arts and achieve an informed and balanced attitude in the present economic climate.

Membership:
Peter Brinson, Director, Calouste Gulbenkian Foundation, (Chairman).

John Allen, Principal, The Central School of Speech and Drama.

Ray Austin, Assistant Director of Education, Coventry Metropolitan District Council.

Norman Barr, First Deputy Secretary for Education, Cornwall County Council.

Andrew Fairbairn, Director of Education, Leicestershire County Council.

John Field, Director, The Royal Academy of Dancing.

Robin Howard, Director General, Contemporary Dance Trust.

Peter Pearson, General Secretary, The Imperial Society of Teachers of Dancing.

James Porter, Principal, Bulmershe College of Higher Education.

John Tomlinson, Director of Education, Cheshire County Council.

Michael Wood, Director, The Royal Ballet School.

4. 16 July 1976 Welsh Conference on Dance in Education

The conference held in Cardiff was convened by the Welsh Arts Council in association with the Calouste Gulbenkian Foundation, to discuss the terms of reference of the Gulbenkian Dance Study.

Chairman: Peter Brinson

Conference members:

Geoffrey Axworthy, Artistic Director, Sherman Theatre.

Jo Barnes, Theatre Manager, Theatr Gwynedd.

Christine Butler, Bishop Gore Comprehensive School, Swansea.

Paul Chandler, Administrator, Chapter Arts Centre.

J E Christians, Swansea and District Ballet Club.

S N Crosby, PE Adviser, Clwyd County Council.

C J Cook, Heathfield House High School, Cardiff.

G E Cuthbert, Mynyddbach Comprehensive School for Girls, Swansea.

Marylin Davies, Education Department, Mid Glamorgan County Council.

Bill Dufton, Director, Southern Arts Association.

Nigel Emery, South East Wales Arts Association.

Clem Gorman, Moving Being, Chapter Arts Centre.

John Greatorex, Director, Theatr Powys.

Christine Gregory, Llanover Hall Arts Centre.

Sheila Griffiths, Dance and Physical Education, Polytechnic of Wales.

Anne Haines, Peripatetic Dance Teacher, Gwynedd.

Timothy Hext, Welsh College of Music and Drama, Cardiff.

Janet James, Bryn Hafren Comprehensive School, Barry.

Gillian Jeffreys

Glenda John, Education Department, Mid Glamorgan County Council.

P G Joignant, Technical Officer, Sports Council for Wales.

Gail Jones

M A Jones, Teacher/Adviser for PE, Clwyd County Council.

Molly Kenny

Gale Law

Dek Leverton

Pam Mahoney, Llwyncrwn Primary School, Pontypridd.

Dorothy Millar

Eira Moore

Geoff Moore, Moving Being, Chapter Arts Centre.

Penny Nicholas, HMI.

O Parrish, PE Teacher, Clwyd County Council.

Dilys Price, City of Cardiff College of Education.

John Prior

Pamela Rees, PE Adviser, West Glamorgan County Council.

Neil Scorgie, Theatre Manager, Congress Theatre, Cwmbran.

Clare Thomas

M Thomas, National Trainer, Keep-Fit Association of Wales.

Sheila Thomas, Physical Education Adviser, Dyfed County Council.

Roger Tomlinson, Arts Administrator, Theatr Clwyd, Mold.

Iolo Walters, Administrative Assistant, Welsh Joint Education Committee.

Heather Webb, City of Cardiff College of Education.

Wendy White, Dance and Physical Education, Polytechnic of Wales.

Ken Williams, Manager, Aberystwyth Arts Centre.

Margaret Williams, Dance and Physical Education, Polytechnic of Wales.

M A Williams, Ty Gwyn Special School, Cardiff.

Nia Wyn Williams, Drama Department, Y Coleg Normal, Bangor.

Rhona Willoughby, National Trainer, Keep-Fit Association of Wales.

5. 26th October 1976 Southern Arts Conference on Dance in Education

The conference convened by the Southern Arts Association in Winchester in association with the Calouste Gulbenkian Foundation, was attended by 60 representatives of education authorities, dance companies and individual workers in education, physical education, therapy, drama, dance teaching, dance administration and professional dance drawn broadly from the area served by Southern Arts to discuss the terms of reference of the Gulbenkian Dance Study.

Conference members:

R Allen
S Ashtiany
Gideon Avrahami
B Balfour-Smith
F Belfield
Bice Bellairs
Miss Braithwaite
Peter Brinson
M J Budd
M Chapman
A M Charles-Auckland
J Chittenden
A M Covell
B Danelli
Miss Donoghue
J Drake
Eileen Eagle
B Espinosa
J Fear
M Fitzell
Ruth Glick
Miss Greenaway
Felicity Gray
M Harvey
J K Holbrook
J M Howe
V Hunter
M Johnson
R Kayley
J Keirs
Athalie Knowles
J Langridge
Gale Law
B W Lewis

S Main
P Marples
W Martin
Joan Maxwell-Hudson
S Morley
N Murilova
E Nelson
V Newsome
N Norton
Sandy Parkinson
Miss Parmenter
J M Perry
Mrs Pocock
M Poole
Geoff Powell
P Raynbird
G Rawlins
Miss Reynolds
E Salt
S Shelton
V E Shimmin
C Smith
J Sparkes
V Stirmey
S Street
A Turner
M Turner
J Weir
A Wilkinson
V Wilkinson
J Willcocks
G B Wilson
L M Wilson

14

6. April 1977 Scottish Conference held at Dunfermline College of Physical Education Edinburgh

Terms of reference:
to examine the situation of dance in education and higher education, training for professional dance and teacher training in Scotland, in relation to the National Study and to Scottish priorities.

Programme:
First Session: National Study
Priorities for Scotland

Chairman, Miss M Abbott, Principal, Dunfermline College of Physical Education.

Second Session: Dance in Schools

Chairman, Mr B Wright, Director, Scottish School of Physical Education, Jordanhill College

Third Session: Dance in Higher Education and Further Education

Chairman, Mr B Wright

Fourth Session: Training of Teachers

Chairman, Mr S Dunbar, Director, Scottish Arts Council

Fifth Session: Forum and Summary, Mr P Brinson, Director, Calouste Gulbenkian Foundation (British & Commonwealth Branch)

Conference members:
Miss M P Abbott, Principal, Dunfermline College of Physical Education, Edinburgh

Miss M D'Ambosia, President, Modern Dance Society, Edinburgh University

Miss M H Anderson, Principal Lecturer in PE, Craigie College of Education, Ayr

Mr R Anderson, Administrator, The Scottish Ballet

Mr C Bisset, Head of Dept. Dunfermline College, Scottish Physical Education Association

Mr P Brinson, Director, Gulbenkian Foundation (UK & Commonwealth Branch); Chairman, National Study of Dance Education & Training

Mrs H Bryce, Teacher of Dance, Renfrewshire

Mr R Carlisle, Head of PE Dept., Aberdeen College of Education

Miss J Carnie, Secretary, Edinburgh Schools Dance Association

Mr P R Cooke, School of Scottish Studies, Edinburgh University

Mr A Dunbar, Director, The Scottish Arts Council

Miss U Flett, Dance Critic — *Scotsman*

Miss M M Gibson, Secretary, Royal Scottish Country Dance Association

Mr D Goldstein, Dunfermline College

Mrs J Henderson, Dunfermline College

Miss K Lee, Dunfermline College

Mrs D Livings, Vice-Chairman, Scottish Women's Keep Fit Association

Mr J Livingstone, Scottish Central Committee on Physical Education

Miss Janet Livingstone, Scottish Universities Physical Education Association

Miss J H Mathews, Lecturer in P.E. (Dance), Scottish School of Physical Education, Jordanhill College of Education, Glasgow

Miss J Mathieson, Conference of Lecturers in Physical Education, Jordanhill College

Mrs J Maxwell-Hudson, Organising Secretary, National Study of Dance Education, Gulbenkian Foundation

Mr P Moore, Theatre School of Dance and Drama, Edinburgh

Miss W Morrison, HMI, Scottish Education Department

Mr W Mowat Thomson, Director, Theatre School of Dance and Drama, Edinburgh

Mrs N Muir, Advisory Committee on Physical Education, The Educational Institute of Scotland

Miss E Murdoch, Head of Department, Dunfermline College

Miss C Orr, Scottish Official Board of Highland Dancing

Mr R Palmer, Director, Theatre Workshop, Edinburgh

Miss M M Reid, Principal Lecturer in PE, Hamilton College of Education, Lanarkshire

Mr J Russell, Scottish Association of Advisers on Physical Education

Miss Ann B Smith, Secretary, Conference of Lecturers in Physical Education, Hamilton College

Miss Agnes B Smith, Scottish Sports Council

Mr J Spurgeon, Principal, Academy of Ballet, Edinburgh

Mr N Tennant, Department of Philosophy, Edinburgh University

Miss E M W Thomson, HMI, Scottish Education Department

Miss J Tucker, Principal, Academy of Ballet, Edinburgh; Chairman Scottish Region, Royal Academy of Dancing

Miss M Urquhart, Director of Recreation and Leisure, Fife Region Education Department

Miss P Woodeson, Head of Department of Dance/Art, Dunfermline College

Mr B Wright, Director, Scottish School of Physical Education, Jordanhill College

Students from Scottish School of Physical Education and additional staff members and students from Dunfermline College.

A working Party was convened in June 1977 by Miss M Abbott, Principal, Dunfermline College, to discuss the establishment of an Action Committee for Dance Education to carry forward issues raised at the Conference.

7. 3rd May 1977 Seminar on Dance in the Curriculum

Terms of reference: to exchange experience of the contribution of dance to a school curriculum and thus to evolve a case for dance in state education with curricula examples.

Programme:
First Session: The purpose and practice of dance in schools. What are the pre-requisites? Organisation within school — Time-tabling — Nature of dance work — Attitude to examinations — Attitude of parents

Second Session: Advantages derived from dance. Physical — Psychological — Social — Aesthetic — Verbal — Academic

Third Session: Involvement of boys and male teachers of dance. Recruitment and career guidance — Continuity

Fourth Session: Forum

Seminar Members:
M Monkhouse, A Day, Atherton County Infants' School, Cheshire.

Neil Anderton, Headmaster. Mrs. Hargreaves. Heysham High School, Morecambe, Lancashire.

E A Goodman, Headmaster. High School of Art, Manchester.

C W Gardiner, Headmaster. John Auty. Intake High School, Leeds, Yorkshire.

Susan Morris — Ex Manchester High School of Art. c/o London School of Contemporary Dance.

Sister Wilfrid, Headmistress. D Stevens. Saint Joseph's College, West Yorkshire.

M Clarke, Headteacher. V Lewis. Sutton Comprehensive School, Ellesmere Port, Wirral.

Grace Eldridge, Headmistress. (Unable to be present but written evidence submitted) New Parks Secondary School, Leicester.

W K Pringle, Headmistress. M A Inniss. The Friern School, Dulwich, London.

D B Thrower, Headmaster. Mr Bunce. Mr Finlayson (Senior Adviser, County Education Department). The Misbourne School, Great Missenden, Buckinghamshire.

Beryl Loveridge, Headteacher. Jo Butterworth. Starcross School, London.

Miss Kelly, Deputy Headmistress. Miss Carter. Sydenham School, London.

D J E Gould, Headmistress. Hilary Ball. Tower Hamlets School, London.

Appendix B

Outline history of dance education in the maintained sector

1 Need for historical research The history of dance education and training in Britain — indeed of movement education generally — is largely unexplored. Thus it offers challenge and opportunity to qualified scholars, but a problem to us. It is no part of our task to fill gaps in historical research, but some outline of developments, particularly since the late 19th century, is essential to understand today's situation. Attempting this outline demonstrated to us how much needs to be done in this field.

2 Pre-19th century Englishmen excelled in galliards at the courts of Henry VIII and Elizabeth I. Dancing, too, was an important element of the Stuart masque whose brilliance attracted European attention. For all this a dance education was necessary, including a study of manners and courtesies. The dancing masters who taught so wide a range of movements, and often arranged the dances, were important figures in the education of the day. They were retained by all Renaissance courts, the nobility and the newly founded schools of the time. Vocational training for dance and dance in education therefore have a long history within and outside Britain. Advanced Renaissance minds like Erasmus, Francis Bacon, Roger Ascham, John Colet (founder of St. Paul's), William Camden of Westminster (who taught Ben Jonson), and Sir Thomas Elyot, author of *The Governor*, 'the first book on the subject of education written and printed in the English language',[70] all regarded dance as an important and regular element in the education of young people. The confirmation of the political and economic changes of the mid-17th century, through the revolution of 1688, confirmed also the spread of this educational inheritance to the newly monied and the newly gentle. Its value was argued by John Locke in *An Essay concerning Understanding*. Robert Owen extended the principle in the early nineteenth century by including dance in the curriculum of the model school he established for the children of workers at his New Lanark Mills. Up to this time dance teachers enjoyed a status since lost until our own day. In particular a brilliant circle of writers and dancers in early 18th century London, led by Steele and Addison among the writers, and Pemberton, John Weaver and Kellom Tomlinson among the dancers, have left us an important, though much neglected, English literature on the nature of dance and education, the application of anatomical knowledge to dancing, and the characteristics of the English as dancers.[71]

3 19th century, the debt to Sweden The development of dance in British public education looks back to the introduction of the physical education ideas of Ling from 1878 onwards.* By then, in the atmosphere of the time, dance was confined almost entirely to girls' schools. There it was taught 'to cultivate the true perception of gracefulness, to stimulate the aesthetic faculties and impart perfect control of muscles.'[72] Ling's ideas, conveyed principally through the Swedish physical educationalist Martina Bergman Osterberg, initiated a change in attitude towards movement education and led to the establishment of special training institutions. The Bergman Osterberg Physical Training College, for example, opened first in 1880 in a large house in Hampstead, London, with a curriculum which included the waltz and national dancing. Most of the national dance was Swedish because its founder was Swedish. Indeed the debt our dance in education movement owes to Sweden has been too little acknowledged so we are glad to offer some amends here. In 1885 the Bergman Osterberg College transferred to Dartford, Kent, where fifty years later it became the Dartford College of Education. Today it has passed through another transformation, having been merged with the Thames Polytechnic in the re-organisation of teacher training.

4 Pioneer colleges: Anstey and Bedford Madame Osterberg's College was soon not the only one. 'In 1896 Miss Rhoda Anstey, a pupil of Madame Osterberg, took her first steps towards establishing a Physical Training College when she acquired the Leasowes, a rambling country house at Halesowen, near Birmingham, which was formerly the home of the poet Shenstone.'[73] At first the bias of Miss Anstey's new college was towards her health clinic, but two years later the training side was extended and the title page of the prospectus proclaimed the new emphasis: Anstey College for Physical Training and Hygiene for Women Teachers (Ling's Swedish System). Presently, thanks to the work of the Vice-Principal, Ida Bridgman, the College also began to establish a notable reputation in dance. The third college to pioneer dance in education at the turn of the century was Bedford, later to introduce, through Joan Goodrich, the central European tradition of dance in education as we know it today. (See paragraph 10 below.) All three colleges experimented with kinaesthetics and eurhythmics, and all, as the history of Anstey College shows, were closely connected with the movement for feminine emancipation. Development followed similar lines in Scotland, many of the official English documents having their Scottish parallel.

5 The 1909 Syllabus of Physical Training Without doubt, then, the sources which have contributed to dance in the public sector of British education are as rich in their origins as the sources contributing to dance in the private sector. The eurhythmics of Émile Jaques-Dalcroze, for example, were introduced about 1912, a year which connects Dalcroze with Diaghilev and Nijinski who visited the Dalcroze School at Hellerau during a season at Dresden. By that time dance had gained limited official recognition already in the curriculum of English and Welsh state schools through the Board of Education's 1909 *Syllabus of Physical Training.*[74] This syllabus associated dance with physical education and thus began a process over seventy years which has developed dance in the British school curriculum to a point beyond that of many other countries. The dance recommended in 1909 was English folk dance, in which interest had been revived by Cecil Sharp. Presently there were added to English folk dance and the Swedish folk dance of Martina Bergman Osterberg the dances of Scotland, Wales, Ireland and other European countries.

6 The 1919 and 1933 syllabi By the 1930s the first three independent women's Colleges of Physical Education had been joined by four more – I M Marsh in Liverpool, Nonnington near Canterbury, Chelsea College in London and Lady Mabel College at Wentworth Woodhouse, now part of Sheffield City Polytechnic. Just as the work of the original pioneer colleges helped to create the climate which led to the recognition of dance in the 1909 syllabus, so the work of these newer colleges contributed to the 1919, 1933 and 1937 syllabi. The four syllabi argue the values of dance in slightly different terms probably reflecting the arguments of their day.[74] They agree, however, on the value of folk dance and its increased use. Also introduced into schools were character and national

---

*   It is not suggested, of course, that Ling had a close connection with dance. Rather, the introduction of his ideas and system of gymnastics created a new climate in which movement and dance education could begin to be developed.

dancing and some court dances for which a training was given based largely on technique modified from classical ballet. Influential as these syllabi were, however, they aimed to guide the class teacher at primary level for whom Physical Training (P.T.) was one among some dozen subjects studied at training college. For teaching more advanced levels women physical education specialists needed further help. Dance for them was an important part of the curriculum occupying at least four hours a week during their training. This distinction still gives rise to confusion about the definition of 'dance' and 'dance teacher' in schools. We shall return to it.

7 Other influences, Isadora Duncan During the period of development we have just outlined, ideas were emerging elsewhere which changed in time the whole approach to dance education in British state schools. Isadora Duncan (1877–1927) 'whilst not destroying the classical ballet, nevertheless instigated an alternative form of dance which differed in almost every respect from previously accepted notions of dance as an art form.'[72] She freed dance from what she considered to be the limitations of classical ballet and this freedom included the practice of dancing in unrestricted clothing and barefoot work. Others broke from tradition in Britain. Of these the three who probably had the greatest influence on the dance taught in British schools were Ruby Ginner, Madge Atkinson and Margaret Morris. All three were inspired by the arts and ideals of ancient Greece and most of their technique and style of movement was based on the forms of dance and movement illustrated on ancient Greek pottery, painting and sculpture. All three belong essentially to the private sector whose history is outlined in Appendix C. They are included here, however, because of their influence on the public sector.

8 Ruby Ginner Ruby Ginner established her own school of Revived Greek Dance in 1914, and propagated her views through the Greek Dance Association which she founded at Stratford-upon-Avon in 1923. She taught children as well as students and held examinations with the Royal Academy of Dancing. Subsequently, in 1961, her Greek Dance Association became a branch of the Imperial Society of Teachers of Dancing. The foundation of her work was a technique which she herself evolved and which was based on four natural positions of the feet and twenty-one fundamental arm designs. To this was added work with balls and 'nature rhythms', an expression very much of her period. Examples of nature rhythms, in her words, are 'the joyfulness of the opening bud,' 'the anger of lightning', 'the ecstasy of the dawn'.[75] It seems that these nature rhythms were concerned with the interpretation of emotions. Music, too, was important as a source of inspiration for the interpretation of various kinds of dance which she called lyrical, athletic, pyrrhic and bacchic – and she stressed how essential it was that the dancer should be loyal to the composer. For participants in the Revived Greek Dance, Ruby Ginner claimed that 'good movement brought both physical and mental health, the perfect co-ordination of the physical and psychic being achieving moral worth and beauty and the sanctity of the human body.'[75] In 1963 she summarised the evolution of her work: 'My method, though originally inspired by and based on the arts and ideals of Ancient Greece, was transformed by my personal interpretation into a modern idiom . . . I have added many movements of my own creation other than those inspired by the Greek arts and evolved a technical basis which will produce the special qualities needed for this type of dancing.'[76] Although interpretation is still important in the Revived Greek Dance, the 1963 publication stresses much more the physical aims, 'the development of movement control, correct posture, endurance, a sense of rhythm and grace which lead to good health, strength, vitality and enjoyment of living.' This dance was probably most widespread in schools and colleges in the 1930s and is rarely taught today other than in the private sector of education. It is significant though, that many teachers responsible for the spread of modern dance in the 1940s and 1950s had themselves been taught this type of dance at school and college. It is reasonable to suppose, therefore, that the Revived Greek Dance still exerts an indirect influence upon dance in British education.

9 Madge Atkinson In the same period of the 1920s and 1930s Madge Atkinson was developing at her school in Manchester 'The Dance based on Natural Movement.'[77] She was fascinated by the possibility of interpreting natural things through dance movement. All aspects of nature were a source of inspiration and many of these ideas were reflected in the music she chose for her compositions. Great emphasis was laid on musical knowledge, seeking to create a method which would combine a sensitive appreciation of music

194

and movement. A technique was evolved which was based on 'three positions or angles in which the torso and limbs are held, the upright, the forward and the backward position',[77] and all movements had their root in one of these positions. Madge Atkinson achieved recognition in education when schools under the Manchester Authority began to include 'Natural Dance' in their curricula. In 1936 her school was transferred to London, but already in 1930 her outstanding student, Anita Heyworth, had been invited to teach at Dartford Physical Training College (formerly Bergman Osterberg) where she continued until 1944. In that year, Grace Cone founded, with Anita Heyworth,[78] a new college of dance and drama. It opened in Maidenhead, then moved to London in 1954 to become the London College of Dance and Drama with Anita Heyworth as Principal. In 1967 an association with Dartford College of Education was formed which made it possible for students to gain qualified teacher status through a specially established course and to continue study for a BEd degree. Thus two strands of a long tradition were brought together. The subsequent history of the London College of Dance and Drama is described in chapter 18.

10 Margaret Morris Margaret Morris, perhaps the most influential of these British pioneers, was inspired also by Greek ideals. She used Greek positions, evolved from images on Ancient Greek vases, as the basis for her technique, elaborating the images in many ways to suit her purpose. Above all she was concerned to create a living dance form, not to reconstruct a dead one. She saw dance as being fully integrated with other art forms but particularly with music, rather than using music for interpretation or accompaniment. The Margaret Morris School was opened in London in 1910 and for the next thirty years her work flourished. She started a Margaret Morris Club which was to become a centre for free discussion and for the presentation of original creative work. Her first Summer School was held in 1917 and has continued almost annually ever since. To begin with her school's main aim was to train dancers for the theatre but she noticed that the training also brought to the students a general improvement in health and appearance. It was this which led to her interest in the health and remedial possibilities of movement. Whilst still running her school she took training in massage and remedial gymnastics and in 1930 passed the Chartered Society of Massage and Medical Gymnastics (now Chartered Society of Physiotherapy) examination with distinction. Remedial work added a new dimension to Margaret Morris' teaching. She had always stressed the importance of good posture and correct breathing and was able now to bring a knowledge of anatomy and physiology to her work. Her interest in the theatre remained but the remedial work became at least as important. She and her teachers conducted movement classes for the physically and mentally handicapped and for geriatrics and gave exercise therapy for patients recovering from illness in hospital. 'Margaret Morris Movement' she wrote in a comparatively recent publication 'combines medical and aesthetic values throughout. Other methods may achieve more in either one or other but no other movement synthesises these two seemingly different objectives.'[79] She opened schools in Glasgow, Aberdeen and Manchester, as well as in Paris and Cannes, and in 1938 the Basic Physical Training Association started a school at Loughborough College. All these, with the exception of Glasgow, were forced to close with the outbreak of the Second World War. The training, however, continues today in part-time classes and in summer schools and through regular examinations. Students are required to study not only the method of Margaret Morris Movement and its teaching,[80] which includes improvisation and choreography, but also related subjects such as anatomy and physiology. Four grades of teaching certificate and diplomas have been established together with further courses to increase knowledge of movement and dance. More recently the Margaret Morris Movement, Medau Society and other bodies have received substantial help for dance activities from the Sports Council.

11 The central European influence In the mid-1930s, as these domestic influences developed, a European influence arrived which has exerted ever since an enormous impact on dancing in the schools and colleges of Britain. The atmosphere of the period has been recaptured very well by Diana Jordan in her book *Childhood and Movement*.[81] 'The 1933 Syllabus was but a few years old and only beginning to take its place in Teacher Training Colleges. Each specialist Physical Training College was developing its own system based on the work of Swedish and Danish pioneers, while Austrian gymnastics were also being explored in at least one College. In dance — Scandinavian folk dance had proved to be a popular addition to English folk dance, and on the expressive side Greek dance and various kinds of eurythmics were being widely introduced into schools.

'To a few in those days, all these forms of dance excluded sufficient opportunity for children to express or communicate their own ideas in their own way and in addition, the formal exercises of gymnastics, or in the primary school 'drill', far from helping children to dance, seemed merely to induce habits of movement which had to be broken down in the dance lesson in order to free the natural rhythmic and expressive abilities within the children.'

Among those in the mid-1930s who were questioning 'these forms of dance' was Joan Goodrich. Trained at Bedford College of Physical Education, she had just been appointed to the staff of the college but had also studied with Mary Wigman in Leipzig. She brought to the curriculum a form of dance called 'Central European Dancing'. The caution with which it was received can be seen in an extract from an article written in 1935:— 'English gymnasts tend to sweep it aside as an art allowing for infinite self-expression and individualistic movements but incompatible with English ideas of dance and movement . . . The so-called body training is built up on tension and relaxation and the intermediate degrees between the two extremes . . . (and) the widened vocabulary acquired gives increased resources at our command.'[82]

Leslie Burrows, a Margaret Morris pupil who later also studied with Mary Wigman and was an exceptionally gifted teacher and dancer, called this dance 'Modern Dance' and claimed for it '. . . freedom, bodily and expressive freedom.'[83]

12 Spread of modern dance In 1930 Leslie Burrows had established with Louise Soelberg in Chelsea, a Dance Centre whose objects were: 'to provide classes and to provide a centre to which visiting artists could go to speak, to show their work and to meet others in this country who are interested in dance.'[84] Joan Goodrich and Diana Jordan, author of the first English textbook on modern dance in education in 1938, were founder members of this centre which was forced to close in 1940 owing to the war. But members moved to different parts of the country and continued to teach 'Modern Dance'. The next important step, therefore, was a conference organised by the Physical Education Association in April 1941 — 'more in the nature of a feeler as to the educational possibitities of Modern Dance in schools and colleges than a conference proper on this form of dance.'[85] There had been a demand for such a conference and amongst the lecturers invited to speak were Rudolf Laban, Lisa Ullmann, Louise Soelberg, Joan Goodrich, Diana Jordan and Douglas Kennedy. But 'the real inspiration of the conference' said a report afterwards, 'lay undoubtedly, in the contribution of Rudolf Laban and Lisa Ullmann.'[86] Laban's name had come forward on previous occasions, for example, as the teacher of Mary Wigman, and in 1930 through a private course organised on 'the theories of Rudolf von Laban.'[87] It was Mary Wigman, too, who said that 'the extraordinary thing Laban gave back to the dance is movement, movement again . . . to move and to be moved.'[88] Now with Laban himself in Britain as a refugee from Nazi Germany, his ideas spread rapidly. He, with Lisa Ullman, became in great demand.

13 Influence of Laban Laban, as Hungarian by birth, had as a young man, studied the discipline of classical ballet but his interest was focused on human beings and the human body. He observed man in all his activities and realised that all human movement has a common basis. This is classified into '16 movement themes' which can be studied in greater detail in his book *Modern Educational Dance*.[89] There began a whole series of vacation courses in which Laban's ideas and principles were studied and practised. The first was at Newtown in Wales where Laban and Lisa Ullmann were given a home after their enforced departure, as aliens, from Dartington Hall. Then through the war years, Moreton Hall in Shropshire offered summer accommodation and Sheffield City Training College became the venue for Christmas vacation courses. From 1946 to 1961 these courses moved between Dartington, Bishop Otter College, Chichester, Ashridge, Chelsea College of Physical Education and Worcester College of Education. Teachers and college lecturers from all over the country attended regularly and in turn went back to teach their own students. Day courses were held in different regions and a number of education authorities encouraged, through their physical education advisers, the inclusion of this work in the curriculum of their schools. Here it was given particular impetus over the years by very strong support from His Majesty's Inspectorate, especially Ruth Foster,

Staff Inspector at the time. More advanced study was made possible by the opening in 1943 of the Art of Movement Studio in Manchester with Lisa Ullmann as Principal. Within two years the Ministry of Education recognised the Studio's Supplementary Course for Serving Teachers and a year later recognised also the Special Course. In 1953 the Studio moved to Addlestone in Surrey where it could operate on a larger scale to give initial and post-graduate education in the art of movement. A two year teacher training course was started, at first in co-operation with Trent Park College, and later with Whitelands College. It is continued today in the Laban Centre for Movement and Dance on the campus of Goldsmith's College, London, where students are able to take both the Certificate of Education or the Bachelor of Education qualification. Thus was initiated the major centre of influence upon dance in the maintained sector of British education during the post-war years. It had been made possible, however, by the earlier introduction of dance into official syllabi of physical education training in England, Wales and Scotland from 1909 onwards.

14 Problems of definition and content Almost parallel with Laban's appearance in Britain emerged another teacher and school to exert influence over the generation of teachers and dancers who began their careers between the late 1930s and early 1950s. Like Laban, Sigurd Leeder was a refugee from Nazi Germany, arriving in Britain in 1934 with Kurt Jooss and his dance company. In the early 1920s Leeder had been a student of Laban at the school in Hamburg and 'he found in Laban's teaching and experiments a compulsion strong enough to direct him permanently towards dancing for the rest of his career.'[90] From that time he worked closely with Jooss until 1947 when he established his own school in London. The way this happened belongs more to the history of private vocational training outlined in Appendix C. The problem which Leeder, Laban and others — especially Laban — posed for the maintained sector, however, was to analyse and describe accurately just what it was that had been introduced to British Schools. 'Modern Dance' and 'Modern Educational Dance' appeared on the timetables of some schools and colleges, but so also did 'Movement Education' and 'the Art of Movement'. In some cases 'movement' became synonymous with dance; in others it was a basic training for all forms of activity. In many primary schools it was seen as a force to liberate expressive powers. This indicates a degree of confused thinking and argument, which is still with us, about what the content of the work should be. A forum to discuss such problems was established to some extent in 1945 through the formation of the Laban Art of Movement Guild and its biannual Magazine. Much the most important centres of discussion and experiment, however, were provided by the Women's Physical Education Colleges. To these were added the Art of Movement Studio and men's colleges like St. John's, York, and St. Luke's, Exeter, which had included dance in their curricula from the early 1960s.

15 Support for dance teachers During all this period of development the problem was and remains to develop teachers with sufficient confidence, knowledge and understanding to teach the subject and particularly to carry it beyond the first year or two at secondary level. Insecurity of dance knowledge and lack of adequate support to overcome that insecurity have been major obstacles to the development of dance in schools over the last two decades. Experience during the same period shows that this situation need not arise when an adequate initial in-depth teacher training course is given and relevant local education authority in-service courses are available. Outstanding in this respect during the 1960s were the West Riding of Yorkshire and Lancashire authorities. Additional support for dance teachers came from a Modern Educational Dance Section (later called Dance Section) formed in January 1960 by the Association of Teachers in Colleges and Departments of Education (now NATFHE) to provide an opportunity for exchanging ideas and practical work as a basis for further development. This has proved valuable not only to teachers but to the work of our Study.

16 Introduction of degree courses Three further developments bring the story of dance in British education to the present day — the introduction of the Bachelor of Education (BEd) degree; the introduction of new degree courses separate from teacher preparation; and growing contact with the dancing profession. The BEd courses introduced in the late 1960s placed on lecturers extra responsibility to incorporate not only practical work but a theoretical basis for dance studies. Much of today's advance in the understanding of dance can be credited to the demands made by universities or the Council for National Academic Awards (CNAA) in their validation of BEd courses. Through the same channels there is continuing discussion about the kind of dance which should be taught in schools and colleges, originally based almost entirely on Laban principles. Without doubt past years of work in dance, based on these principles, have provided a root from which there can be an abundance of growth. It needs to be nourished, however, by an openness of mind, so that the subject can continue to expand and grow, incorporating other influences particularly from the art of dance itself as it develops and keeps pace with the changing needs of society. The introduction of further new degree courses during the last four years, incorporating dance as a major option quite separate from teacher preparation, validated either by universities or by the CNAA, has created another stimulus for rethinking the content of courses at this level. These new courses are transforming the situation of dance in education. They place the theories of Laban, classical ballet and contemporary dance within the context of dance as a whole, thus confirming the point made in chapter 1 that dance as a general subject is an intellectual discipline in its own right as well as an artistic discipline. Hence there is good reason to conclude that a broadly based dance education which includes the theory, structure and history of dance as well as its execution, and above all a degree course in dance, can be just as much a preparation for, say, a civil service or business career as a degree in history or science.[91]

17 Contacts with the dance profession Equally important in changing the perspectives for dance education has been a growing contact with the dance profession. This began in a planned way in the early 1960s with the tours of the Royal Ballet's Ballet for All company.* It developed in the early 1970s through 'residencies' in educational institutions, an idea imported from the United States by the Contemporary Dance Trust. The residencies were carried out by groups of professional dancers or entire professional companies in different parts of Britain, teaching as well as performing. The event which really established the practice was a six week series early in 1976, mostly in Yorkshire and Lancashire, carried out by London Contemporary Dance Theatre in association with the Arts Council of Great Britain, local education authorities, regional arts associations and the colleges concerned. During their residencies the company, founded on the technique and dance-style of the great American dancer, Martha Graham, led workshops with students and school boys and girls, gave lecture demonstrations, allowed audiences to watch company classes, rehearsed and answered questions from interested spectators, and gave performances in schools, colleges and local theatres. The enthusiasm created was very great, its educational significance underlined by a weekend conference[92] at I M Marsh College of Physical Education, Liverpool, about half way through the residency, attended by a large number of dance educationalists of various persuasions, all of whom acknowledged the value of this development. Since then the residency tours of London Contemporary Dance Theatre have become annual events and the idea is spreading. Cycles Dance Company in the West Midlands, EMMA Dance Company in the East Midlands, Janet Smith in Yorkshire and Devon, as well as Moveable Workshop in Scotland, Moving Being in Wales and others now regularly make residency arrangements. Ballet Rambert joined the new movement when a section of the company moved into Dunfermline College, Edinburgh, in October 1978, taking a programme aimed particularly at the dance options in undergraduate courses but with sufficient breadth to offer opportunities also to dance staff and the general body of students.

---

* The older Educational Dance Drama Theatre, based on the principles of Laban, was largely composed of dance teachers or actors in its early days, rather than professional dancers. No hard line between teaching and performing was drawn by this Company until 1974 with the formation of the Movement Teaching Unit. Up to this time the policy was one of teaching by performance, related to creative dance syllabus, mainly in primary schools. See Chapter 2.

Outline history of dance training in the non-maintained sector

1 Beginning of professional training in Europe By the time of the Renaissance the styles of peasant and court dancing had long diverged, reflecting the development of class society. Nevertheless dancing at the Elizabethan and Stuart courts continued to use much the same steps and techniques, refined from peasant dances, whether for social dancing or for ballets and court entertainment. There were few professional dancers as such. The separation of dance into social dancing for everyone on the one hand and dance on stage by specialists on the other hand began only in the mid-17th century. Encouraged by Louis XIV, professional dancers in France introduced the beginning of professional training while continuing still to be much concerned with teaching manners and dance to children of the nobility.

2 Early professional training in England In England much the same development took place around the beginning of the 18th century. Significant teachers include Isaacs, John Essex, John Weaver, E Pemberton and Kellom Tomlinson whose written works still deserve study. The first signs of an English professional theatre school of dance occur in 1809 under J H d'Egville at the King's Theatre, London. The Canadian dance scholar, John Chapman, (to whom we are indebted also for details of an apprenticeship agreement of young dancers in 1815) has produced records of English dancers such as Gayton, Cranfield and Twamley held in high regard by critics who also praised d'Egville's teaching methods. A better known school organised by Benjamin Lumley forty years later,[93] also at the King's Theatre, was able to build on this experience, significantly supporting some of the most important creative work of Jules Perrot, best known today as co-choreographer of *Giselle.*

3 The nineteenth century We have shown already in Appendix B how the history of dance during the latter half of the 19th century reflects Victorian moral backlash — a gradual exclusion of dancing as a respected activity, first from the mainstream of general education, then after the 1850s, from theatrical culture itself. "The ballet was not recognised as a branch of the English theatre" wrote Ninette de Valois of the period before 1914. "Dancers were accepted as individuals on their individual merits and they had to search for their own teachers; how they arrived at their eventual state of execution was no one's concern."[94] Yet the classical school of the late nineteenth century made great technical demands on its dancers, particularly in relation to *terre à terre* and *petite batterie* steps, so there were certainly some good professional dance teachers in Britain during this period. The tradition of London as a great centre of romantic ballet in the 1840s was never completely extinguished. An audience had been formed, academic teaching had been encouraged, and dancers had been trained. These helped to make possible the spectacular ballets for which the Alhambra and Empire theatres in London became famous in the 1880s and 1890s.

4 Influence of foreign teachers The principal adornment of these productions was usually an Italian ballerina trained in the school of Milan, from which graduates were to be found across the world. One can trace in London, for example, a line of Italian teachers from the late 19th century into the 1920s. The late and greatest of them was Enrico Cecchetti who taught the Diaghilev Company from its formation in 1909. Cecchetti opened a London studio in 1918. Here he taught until 1923, exerting a formative influence over today's British ballet because so many of its future leaders studied with him during those five years. In the same way the School of Paris has been hardly less influential in Britain. Leon Espinosa, trained at the Paris Opera, opened a school in London in 1872. His son, Edouard, founded his British Normal School of Dancing in 1896, the first school in England to hold examinations and issue certificates. Edouard's son is the present head of the British Organisation.

5 Beginning of The Imperial Society of Teachers of Dancing, 1904 For every British teacher trained in these traditions and able to sustain high standards of classical ballet teaching there were many more whose knowledge was so slight that they were a danger to their pupils. Already, therefore, in 1904 a meeting of dance teachers had established what is today the Imperial Society of Teachers of Dancing to develop and safeguard their professional status and teaching standards. By the early 1920s this Society comprised some 258 members who were general practitioners with a knowledge of the social dances of the day, academic ballet, national and character dancing.

6 Beginning of the Royal Academy of Dancing, 1920 Nevertheless there was felt to be a need for a more specialist body, "an association of experts to guide teachers and young dancers in the correct technique of the ballet and to preserve the great traditions of our art."[95] Thus, inspired by Philip Richardson and Édouard Espinosa, there came into being on December 31, 1920, the Association of Operatic Dancing, known today as the Royal Academy of Dancing. The original committee represented the four main schools and methods of classical training then recognised in Europe — Italian, French, Danish and Russian — and it introduced its first elementary syllabus at the same inaugural meeting. Its first president was Adeline Genée, the Danish ballerina whose dancing and personality had transformed the quality of ballet at the Empire Theatre in the first decade of the century. The Association held its first elementary professional examination for teachers and dancers on May 9, 1921 and by 1923 had also inaugurated intermediate professional examinations. It was given the patronage of Queen Mary in 1928, and was granted a Royal Charter in 1935 to become the Royal Academy of Dancing.

7 Beginning of the Cecchetti Society, 1922 Meanwhile, the method of the great teacher, Cecchetti, was being codified by the dance historian and bookseller, Cyril Beaumont, assisted by the Diaghilev dancer Stanislaus Idzikowski and by Cecchetti himself. This work was published in 1922 as *A Manual of the Theory and Practice of Classical Theatrical Dancing (Cecchetti Method)*, probably the most influential manual of classical dance technique to have been written this century.[96] Around the Manual, animated by Beaumont, gathered many of those who had studied under Cecchetti to form the Cecchetti Society. Launched the same year as the Manual, also to perpetuate Cecchetti's system of teaching, the Society was thus in many ways a more specialist body even than the Royal Academy of Dancing with which, logically, it should have developed close links. Instead, the new Society became incorporated as a branch of the Imperial Society of Teachers of Dancing when that Society was re-organised into specialist branches for different styles of dancing in 1924.

8 Beginning of the British Ballet Organisation, 1930 Yet another teaching and examining body for classical ballet was established when Édouard Espinosa resigned from the Association of Operatic Dancing in 1930 and set up his own British Ballet Organisation, essentially expounding his own French style of the late nineteenth century. Thus was established the third of the teaching and examining bodies for classical ballet which have operated in the United Kingdom and Commonwealth from then until today. The first was the Association of Operatic Dancing; the second the Cecchetti Society, operating within the Imperial Society; the third was the British Ballet Organisation. All three have done much to raise the standard of teaching and dancing throughout Britain by their examinations, tests, scholarships and teaching.

9 Links with the Empire and Commonwealth All three also soon established their examinations, followed by branches, in the then British Dominions. These Imperial and Commonwealth links have proved immensely significant not only to the three organisations directly concerned, but to British ballet as a whole. The Royal Academy of Dancing, Imperial Society/Cecchetti and British Ballet Organisation have given much to the Commonwealth through their examinations and teaching standards. Commonwealth branches have given in return a greater financial security to their parent organisations and often, at least until the 1960s, the best of their young talent to teach or dance in Britain.*

---

* With the formation of classical companies in Canada, Australia, New Zealand and other countries, the growth of teaching opportunities at home and the introduction of regulations affecting immigration and employment, the Commonwealth element among professional dancers and dance teachers in Britain is now much reduced. In the early days, nevertheless, they made an important contribution to the establishment of classical ballet in the United Kingdom.

200

10 Beginning of other teaching and examining bodies for classical ballet Other teaching and examining bodies for classical ballet in Britain have been established since the Second World War, notably the classical ballet element of the International Dance Teachers Association (established after a merger of smaller associations in 1967,) and the Imperial Ballet branch of the Imperial Society, developing the traditions of the original group of members who taught 'operatic dancing' in 1904. Besides these national organisations there are other examining bodies, more regionally based. Thus was initiated today's plethora of teaching and examining bodies in classical ballet.

11 Other dance forms in the private sector Classical ballet, of course, is not the only element of the private sector. We have described already in Appendix B the considerable contribution of pioneers such as Ruby Ginner, Madge Atkinson and Margaret Morris. All three teachers remained prominent members of the private sector with an influence sustained today by their successors. The work of Margaret Morris is continued through Margaret Morris Movement. The work of Ruby Ginner and Madge Atkinson continues respectively through the Greek Dance Association Branch of the Imperial Society of Teachers of Dancing and the Imperial Society itself. Alongside these have grown up, between the wars and since, the Ballroom, Latin American, Victorian and Sequence, Historical, National, and Scottish Country Dance branches of the Imperial Society. Add the work of teachers in the International Dance Teachers Association and other organisations and there emerges a very broad range of dance offered in the private sector with an equally broad range of standards.

12 Growth in the number of private studios This spectrum of teaching and examining bodies partly stimulated, and partly was stimulated by, the growth in the network of private dance studios throughout Britain between the wars. These studios, mostly run by individual teachers, all began to offer a diverse range of tests and examinations introduced by the particular association or examining body to which they belonged. The examinations were unrelated to each other, or to anything in the maintained sector, although children might be given time off from school to study and take the examinations. The legacy of this growth remains today in the range of private studios and examinations described in Part III of our report.

13 Beginning of independent dance schools The period between the wars saw also the beginning of the idea of independent schools combining general education with a special training in classical ballet. The pioneer was the Bush School which had begun in Nottingham in 1914. In 1930 the founder's daughter, Noreen Bush with her husband, Victor Leopold, began to develop the concept of a general education combined with special dance training. In 1939 they formed a partnership which created the present Bush Davies Schools. These independent schools receive more attention in chapters 14 and 16, but are mentioned here partly for their historical significance and partly because examining bodies, such as the Royal Academy of Dancing and the Imperial Society of Teachers of Dancing, greatly influenced the syllabi and curricula of the schools through their examinations. Hence the examining bodies began to exert an educational influence outside the boundaries of their original aims to raise the standard of teaching.

14 Beginning of the Sadler's Wells/Royal Ballet Schools Since dancing was not recognised as a branch of the English theatre at the beginning of the twentieth century, no professional dance schools existed to offer a professional training. Such training was offered only in private studios. The first steps towards the establishment of professional schools linked with dance companies came in 1920 and 1926 with the founding by Marie Rambert and Ninette de Valois respectively of the Rambert School of Ballet and the Academy of Choreographic Art, now the Royal Ballet School. The Academy of Choreographic Art in Roland Gardens, Kensington, was de Valois' private school which she closed when she opened a company school for the Vic-Wells Ballet at the Sadlers Wells Theatre on January 12, 1931. In September 1947, this school moved to its present premises at Baron's Court, West London, and was expanded at the same time to offer a full academic education under Arnold Haskell as Director. Eight years later the school's junior section moved to White Lodge, Richmond Park, leaving an expanding upper school at Baron's Court. The distinction between lower and upper schools remains significant as we have seen in chapters 16 and 18.

15 Beginning of The Rambert School The Rambert School of Ballet was established in a studio in Bedford Gardens, London, as the Russian School of Dancing (Cecchetti method). Later it moved to larger premises in Ladbroke Road, Notting Hill, subsequently developed as the Mercury Theatre. In 1979 it moved again to the premises of the London School of Contemporary Dance. Until 1966 the school maintained a special link with its company, The Ballet Rambert. This link was ended when the company abandoned its traditional classical repertory to become the modern dance company it is today, the school becoming a separate, private school of classical ballet. The company is now developing in the Rambert Academy at the West London Institute of Higher Education, its own new educational and vocational training links in line with its new direction, described in chapters 9 and 16.

16 Influence of foreign classical teachers Although the Rambert and Vic-Wells Schools played a significant role as foci of professional training during the 1920s and 1930s, the presence in London of important teachers from abroad, especially from Russia, was hardly less significant in training the first generation of British professional dancers and teachers. It was, in short, a question of transferring to British physiques and temperaments two centuries of ballet tradition from other countries. The Royal Ballet's late Ballet for All company well summarised this transfer in one of its productions. "In London during the twenties, history assembled that tradition − from Italy through Enrico Cecchetti, great teacher of Diaghilev's Ballets Russes; from France through Édouard Espinosa; and Denmark through Adeline Genée, joining Philip Richardson to found what is today the Royal Academy of Dancing; from Russia through dancers and teachers like Legat and Astafieva in flight from the Russian Revolution. All these brought gifts to the classrooms of the young British ballet."[97]

17 Influence of Jooss Leeder in the modern field At the same time as a professional training for classical ballet began to be established in the 1930s the first signs began to appear in Britain of alternative 'modern' methods and styles of dance theatre. The influence of Isadora Duncan was long since acknowledged, of course, as a challenge to classical ballet but nothing emerged on the British stage from this challenge the way it had in Central Europe and the United States of America. Even jazz dancing, the other American import, lacked good teachers in London and so occupied a rather tentative place in British musical theatre. The first alternative to classical ballet arrived from Germany in 1934 with Kurt Jooss and his dance company. With them, as we showed in Appendix B, came the dancer and teacher Sigurd Leeder. Whilst Jooss created the ballets (Leeder choreographed only one in the early years in Britain − *Sailor's Fancy*), Leeder's training of the dancers showed exceptional ability and artistry. Consequently, when the Jooss Company became established in Cambridge after 1940, the Jooss Leeder School of Central European dance, deriving from early studies with Rudolf Laban, began to attract British teachers and dancers. Through this, and the children's classes begun at the same time, Leeder began to exert a direct influence upon British professional dancers and dance teachers in the 1940s and 1950s. He opened his own school in London in 1947 when Jooss returned to Germany and in 1958 joined the dance department of the University of Santiago, Chile. He returned to Europe in 1965.

18 Other foreign dance influences Leeder's considerable influence in his modern dance field − matching that of classical teachers from abroad like Seraphine Astafieva, Nicholas Legat and Vera Volkova − illustrates the continuing debt owed by British dance to teachers from abroad. The debt is not confined to classical ballet and modern dance but embraces jazz, tap and various other styles of stage dance, particularly introduced by teachers from the United States. The real development of these alternatives to classical ballet in the theatre, however, came after the Second World War.

19 Beginning of private teacher training One other initiative, important for the future, was taken just before the outbreak of war. In 1939 the Royal Academy of Dancing introduced a course of weekly lectures for dance teachers on the principles of education, anatomy, physiology and hygiene to extend over four years. The war interrupted the plan but the general need was clear. If the standard of dance teaching was to be raised in the private sector the private sector would need to match the provision for dance teacher training which had been developed in the maintained sector. Examinations were not enough. The needs of the private sector, in any case, were quite different from the maintained sector. Not only was the actual dancing different, but the approach to dancing and the whole philosophy which guided this approach. In 1944, therefore, the London College of Dance and Drama was established by Grace Cone with Anita Heyworth to train girls in the principles and techniques required for dance teachers in the private sector. This was followed two years later by the Royal Academy of Dancing which opened its Teachers' Training Course in 1946, building on its initiative before the war. These and other professional teacher training institutions in the private sector are examined in detail in chapter 18.

20 Summary By the outbreak of the Second World War, then, today's pattern of the private sector was largely established. A generation of skilled and dedicated private teachers had been developed, mostly through the work of the major examining bodies. The majority of these teachers taught classical ballet in private studios distributed throughout the country. Most of their students were children aged anything from four years upwards attending once a week.[98] Usually the lessons had no particualar vocational purpose but talented children might move in due course to receive vocational training at one of the private studios or schools run by a former professional dancer. A growing majority of the better private teachers belonged to, and entered children for the examinations of one of the major national examining bodies formed between the wars. A group of influential independent dance schools had been established and the first professional schools launched, linked with the Vic-Wells and Rambert ballet companies. In all this achievement teachers from abroad had played a vital role and Commonwealth dancers were beginning to do the same as members of Britain's professional ballet companies. Most significant of all, perhaps, an increasing number of candidates had begun to flow from private studios and the independent schools into the Vic-Wells and Rambert Schools, or into their companies, or into new dance companies which arose to meet wartime interest in dance. The foundations had been laid for an indigenous dance profession in Britain.

Appendix D

Dance and the Child: International

We reproduce below relevant articles from the Constitution of this new international organisation established to promote dance with and for children.

Dance and the Child: International
(DACI)
Constitution   Draft 1 Aug. 1979
Article I

Dance and the Child: International (DACI) is a non-profit making association founded in 1978 and subsequently entering the Conseil International de la Danse (CIDD), UNESCO, as an autonomous, fully constituted branch of CIDD with the aim of promoting the growth and development of dance for children on an international basis.

Article II

Aims and Purposes

The aim of Dance and the Child International is to promote everything that can benefit dance and the child, irrespective of race, colour, sex, religion, national or social origin; and that this aim shall be carried out in a spirit of peace and universal brotherhood.

Its objectives are to: —
- recognise the right of every child, including those with special needs to dance;
- promote more opportunities for children throughout the world to experience dance as creators, performers and spectators;
- reveal and respect the views and dance interests of the child;
- preserve a cultural heritage of all forms of dance for children;
- promote the inclusion of dance in general education and stimulate the exchange of ideas on dance programmes in schools and in communities;
- encourage research in movement and in dance which will benefit the child in all aspects of development;
- establish an information centre for books, films, videos and any other forms of documentation related to children's dance;
- establish a directory of teachers and other resource people experienced in various aspects of dance for children;
- organise a conference at least once every four years.

Appendix E

Statistics of private dance teachers in the non-maintained sector

The following statistics were compiled from information appearing on the record cards for examinations in 1975 by the four major examining bodies in the private sector in Britain — The Royal Academy of Dancing, The Imperial Society of Teachers of Dancing, The International Dance Teachers' Association, The British Ballet Organisation. BBO records did not present information to allow for a division under the heading 'what they teach' and therefore is added separately: advice from the organisers indicated that the total could be split evenly between those teaching ballet only and those teaching ballet plus another dance form. This information is incorporated in the final total but not analysed under Educational Authority areas.

This is the first comprehensive survey of a major section of dance teaching in private studios in Britain and we are grateful to the organisations concerned for their permission to undertake this research. In order to verify the accuracy of this survey a sample independent examination of the Greater Manchester Area was undertaken with the same result, indicating that the statistics presented are likely to be reasonably accurate. The division into geographic areas in England and Wales is guided by the Local Education Authorities' area boundaries. The geographic divisions in Scotland are guided by the regions determined by the Local Government (Scotland) Act 1973.

Analysis of dance teachers submitting candidates
for examination by the Royal Academy of Dancing, Imperial Society of Teachers
of Dancing, International Dance Teachers Association and British Ballet Organisation

Where they are	Ballet only	Other dance forms only	Ballet plus other forms	Number of teachers
Northern				
Northumberland	6	—	1	7
Cumbria	9	1	2	15
Durham	14	2	2	20
Cleveland	12	—	2	19
North Yorkshire	16	1	10	31
Humberside	19	—	10	48
Tyne and Wear	12	1	16	31
Lancashire	25	12	30	130
West Yorkshire	39	6	44	112
Merseyside	27	4	19	90
Greater Manchester	48	3	21	89
South Yorkshire	19	5	36	99
North Western	25	3	8	48
North Midland				
Derbyshire	10	1	7	21
Nottinghamshire	23	5	17	66
Lincolnshire	4	—	12	17
Leicestershire	17	—	17	43
Northamptonshire	13	2	11	27
Midland				
Shropshire	6	4	3	15
Staffordshire	13	1	7	38
Hereford and Worcester	24	1	7	37
Warwickshire	15	—	8	25
West Midlands	54	4	53	129
Eastern				
Norfolk	11	—	9	23
Cambridgeshire	11	—	4	16
Suffolk	13	1	10	27
Bedfordshire	13	1	10	24
Hertfordshire	48	6	25	79
Essex	37	16	43	99
Metropolitan and South Midland				
Oxfordshire	16	2	2	23
Buckinghamshire	27	1	15	43
South Western				
Gloucestershire	14	2	10	42
Avon	34	5	14	59
Wiltshire	10	—	10	28
Somerset	21	1	5	31
Dorset	34	2	14	52
Devon	24	3	7	55
Cornwall	12	—	2	16
Greater London				
ILEA	48	6	33	92
Greater London	159	21	86	274

Where they are	What they teach			
	Ballet only	Other dance forms only	Ballet plus other forms	Number of teachers
Southern				
Berkshire	35	4	21	60
Surrey	75	7	29	112
Kent	44	6	52	104
Hampshire	65	13	40	119
West Sussex	37	2	15	55
East Sussex	22	3	23	64
Isle of Wight	5	—	1	6
Channel Islands				
Guernsey	1	1	4	6
Jersey	6	—	—	6
Isle of Man	2	—	—	2
Scotland				
Highland	2	—	—	2
Grampian	6	—	1	14
Tayside	2	—	—	3
Strathclyde	54	3	5	87
Central	4	—	—	4
Lothian	15	—	1	23
Borders	1	—	—	1
Wales				
Anglesey	2	—	—	2
Gwynedd	3	—	—	5
Clwyd	5	1	3	15
Dyfed	3	—	—	4
West Glamorgan	7	1	2	10
Mid Glamorgan	2	—	1	3
South Glamorgan	19	—	2	27
Gwent	6	—	1	14
Totals	1643*	402	843*	2888*

*British Ballet Organisation figures included

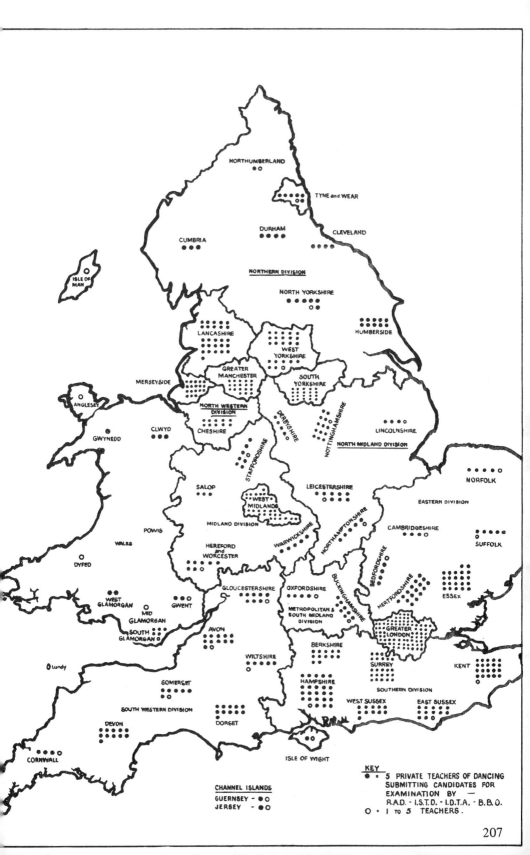

207

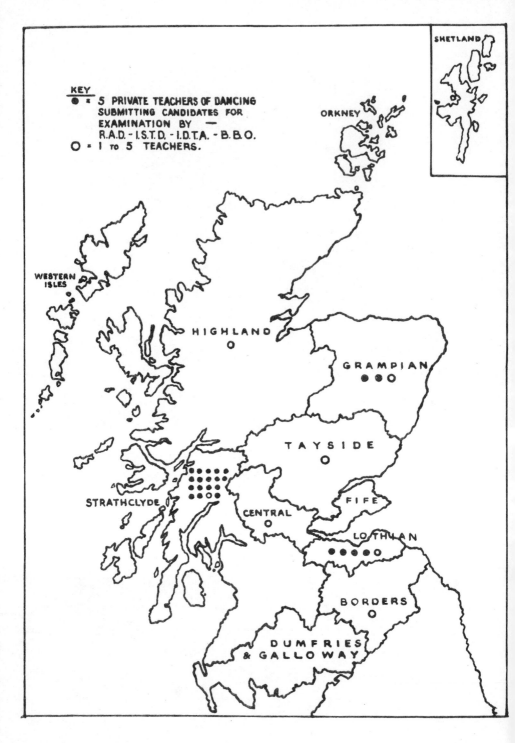

KEY

● = 5 PRIVATE TEACHERS OF DANCING
SUBMITTING CANDIDATES FOR
EXAMINATION BY —
R.A.D. - I.S.T.D. - I.D.T.A. - B.B.O.
O = 1 TO 5 TEACHERS.

SHETLAND

ORKNEY

WESTERN ISLES

HIGHLAND

GRAMPIAN

TAYSIDE

FIFE

STRATHCLYDE

CENTRAL

LOTHIAN

BORDERS

DUMFRIES & GALLOWAY

National Dance Councils

1. Council for Dance Education and Training
Address: 5 Tavistock Place, London WC1H 9SS Tel. 388 5770/387 9681 (messages)
Chairman: Michael Wood
Director: James Ranger
Secretary: Joan Maxwell-Hudson
Extracts from Constitution of the Council for Dance Education and Training

1 The Council (hereinafter called "the Council") shall be known as the "Council for Dance Education and Training".

2 The object of the Council is to advance the education of children, young people and students in the art of dance.

3 In furtherance of the above purpose but not further or otherwise the Council may: —
(i)   a) publish and provide information and advice on all matters connected with training and education for dance by all practicable means;
      b) encourage the general and technical training in the dance;
      c) provide and encourage publicity for the improvement of training and education for dance;
      d) draw-up and publicise an accredited list of those training establishments that meet criteria specified by the Council from time to time and to alter and vary the list of accredited establishments as and when the Council may so decide;
      e) advise and cooperate with departments of Government, local authorities and other interested bodies on all matters connected with education for dance and training for dance and for the teaching of dance;
      f) promote research and assess the changing needs and problems of dance education and in particular by encouraging the writing and production of text books and other literary works and materials in other media on dance as a subject for educational study;
      g) do all other lawful things as shall raise and maintain the standards of education for dance and training for dance and for the teaching of dance at all levels throughout the United Kingdom;
(ii) receive and accept subscriptions, donations, endowments and gifts of money, stocks, funds, shares, securities and any other assets whatsoever provided such assets are applied solely in furtherance of the object for which the Council is established;
(iii) receive and act as a channel for grants for distribution to schools institutions and individuals to be applied towards education for dance and the teaching of dance;
(iv) borrow or raise money with or without security for any of the purposes of the Council: provided that no money shall be raised by mortgage of any real or leasehold property of the Council situate in the United Kingdom without such consent or approval as may be by law required therefor;
(v) make and carry out any arrangement for joint working or cooperation with any other charitable society or body whether incorporated or not carrying on any work for the time being carried on by the Council;
(vi) invest moneys of the Council in or upon any investment authorised by Part I or II of the First Schedule to the Trustee Investments Act 1961, as amended or extended from time to time;
(vii) employ and pay any person or persons to supervise organise carry on the work of and to advise the Council and as employers of staff to make all reasonable and necessary provision for the payment of pensions and superannuation to or on behalf of employees and their widows and other dependents;
(viii) do all such other acts and things as are or may be deemed necessary to the attainment of any of the purposes of the Council or the exercise of any of its said powers.

4   a) The Council shall consist of a Chairman and not more than 24 members (of which not more than 6 members shall be individual members).

b) The first members of the Council shall be (i) the persons named in the first column of the First Schedule hereto each of whom shall hold office in their personal capacity until such time as the organisation specified alongside their name in the second column of the First Schedule hereto shall notify the Secretary in writing that it is willing to appoint a representative as a member of the Committee and shall notify the Secretary of the name of its representative and (ii) the persons named in the Second Schedule hereto (herein called "the individual members").

c) Each of the organisations set out in the second column of the First Schedule hereto and as may be nominated under subclause (d) hereof (hereinafter called "the participating organisations") shall be entitled to appoint one member to the Council who shall serve as such member until he shall resign or be dismissed by the organisation who appointed him.

d) The Council shall have power to nominate any other organisation connected with dance training or any duly constituted body representing organisations connected with dance training as being entitled to appoint and dismiss a member to the Council on such terms as the Council shall in its absolute discretion think fit provided that the total number of Council members appointed by the participating organisations shall not exceed eighteen.

e) The nearest whole number to one-third of the individual members of the Council shall retire at each annual meeting of the Council. The remaining members of the Council may at that annual general meeting or at any later meeting fill the vacancy caused by such retirement and in doing so may re-elect the individual member who has retired if he is willing to be re-elected.

f) Participating organisations may appoint deputies to replace representative members who are unable to attend any particular meeting of the Council.

g) The Council may invite any person or a representative of any organisation with an interest in professional training and education for dance but not being entitled to appoint a member to the Council to attend its meetings as an observer but without power to vote.

2. Scottish Council for Dance
Address: 261 West Princes Street, Glasgow G4 9EE
Tel: 041 331 2931
Chairman: Robin Anderson
Secretary: Vacant
Extracts from Constitution of the Scottish Council for Dance

1 The Council (hereinafter called "The Council") shall be known as "The Scottish Council for Dance"

2 The Council is established, maintained and managed for the purpose of public education by the promotion of all forms of dance and in particular:—
    1) to extend and improve the opportunity for participation in dance of all kinds.
    2) to publish and provide information on all matters connected with dance.
    3) to encourage and improve the general and technical training in dance.
    4) to further the public appreciation of all forms of dance, and
    5) to advise and co-operate with departments of Government, local authorities and other interested bodies in all matters connected with dance.

3 Membership of the Council shall be open to all individuals and established organisations interested in furthering its purposes. The first members of the Council shall be of the authorities, institutions, organisations and societies specified in the first schedule to this constitution and the individuals specified in the second schedule of this constitution. Other members may be admitted by the Council at their annual meeting or at any other general meeting or by postal vote in appropriate cases under procedure to be determined by the Executive Committee of the Council after application in writing to the Secretary

of the Council. Members shall pay such annual subscription as the Executive Committee may, from time to time determine and any member whose subscription is six months or more in arrears shall cease to be a member.

4 Subject to such directions as are given by the Council at any General Meeting, the general management and day to day affairs of the Council shall be conducted by an Executive Committee numbering fourteen persons elected as aftermentioned. The Executive Committee may co-opt a maximum of two additional persons to serve as members of the Executive Committee for a period not exceeding two years. The Executive Committee shall meet for the dispatch of business as and when it may determine but the Secretary of the Council shall send a notice of every meeting of the Executive Committee by post to each member thereof with an agenda at least seven clear days beforehand. All decisions reached by the Executive Committee shall be determined by a simple majority of its members present and voting and six members shall comprise a quorum.

The Executive Committee shall appoint from its own members a Chairman and a Vice Chairman. The Executive Committee shall also appoint a Secretary who is a member of Council or an accredited representative of a member of Council and Treasurer who need not be a member or an accredited representative of a member of the Council, who shall hold office until the Executive Committee otherwise determines, subject to the approval of the Council in General Meeting, that the Executive Committee may prescribe rules or regulations for the general conduct of the business of the Council and its Executive Committee.

5 The elected members of the Executive Committee shall be appointed in manner following, that is to say:—

Two members shall be elected by the accredited representatives of the members of the Council referred to in each of the six groups of members specified in the first schedule of this Constitution and a further two members by the members of Council specified in the second schedule of this Constitution. The elected members of the Executive Committee shall serve for a maximum period of three years but shall be eligible for re-election. The first members of the Executive Committee shall be elected at the first Annual Meeting of the Council. At each subsequent Annual Meeting, one third of the members of the Executive Committee shall retire by rotation. Those members who are to retire at the second and third Annual Meetings shall, unless otherwise agreed, be determined by lot. The Executive Committee may co-opt a member to fill a casual vacancy in its membership but such co-opted member shall only hold office until the next ensuing annual Meeting when the co-option may be confirmed or otherwise.

6 An Annual Meeting of the Council shall be held at such time, not being less than eleven nor more than thirteen months after the holding of the preceding Annual Meeting, and place as the Executive Committee shall determine. An extra-ordinary meeting of the Council may be called at any time by direction of the Executive Committee and shall be called within six weeks of the receipt by the Secretary of the Council of a written requisition requiring such a meeting to be held, signed by or on behalf of at least ten members of the Council.

First Schedule Corporate Members	Second Schedule Individual Members

Group A — Recreational Dance

Group B — Movement

Group C — Performing Groups

Group D — Formal Education

Group E — Higher and Further Education

3 Dance Council for Wales
Address: Welsh Arts Council, Museum Place, Cardiff CF1 3NX
Tel. 0222 394 711
Chairman: Sheila Griffiths
Hon Secretary: Felix Graham-Jones

The Welsh Dance Association, in the process of re-evaluating its purpose and objectives, has submitted for inclusion in this report the following draft Constitution which is awaiting final examination by its legal advisers and approval by the Membership at their Annual General Meeting in the Autumn of 1980.

Draft constitution

1 *Name* The name of the Council (hereinafter called 'the Council') shall be 'Dance Council for Wales — Cyngor Dawns Cymru'.

2 *Object* The Council is established to further the cultural appreciation of dance.
For the foregoing principal purpose the Council is empowered to do, perform and carry out any or all of the following acts: —

a. to encourage the development of regional dance associations within the Principality and to act as a co-ordinating body of its several member organisations and its individual membership;

b. either by direct action or through its members: —
i. to encourage and extend opportunities for participation in dance of many styles and forms;
ii. to encourage and improve general and technical training in dance;
iii. to promote research and study into all forms of dance activity;
iv. to establish a regular communication channel between its members;
v. to act as an information referral system for the general public;
vi. to help in the development of resources for the study, appreciation and practice of dance.

c. to advise and co-operate as appropriate with departments of government, local authorities, and other interested bodies in all matters connected with dance;

d. to do all such other acts and things as are, or may be deemed necessary to the attainment of any of the purposes of the Council or the exercise of any of its said powers.

3 *Membership* Membership of the Council shall be open to duly constituted organisations and to individuals who accept and support the objects of the Council and who pay the membership fee.

4 *Subscriptions* The annual membership fee shall be determined and may only be altered by the Annual General Meeting.

Schedule One
Category 1   Private Teachers of Dance/Representatives of Private Dance Schools.
Category 2   Representatives of Dance Teaching Organisations.
Category 3   Working Dancers and Choreographers/Representatives of Professional Dance Companies.
Category 4   Dance in State Education at Primary and Secondary level.
Category 5   Dance in State Education at Tertiary level.
Category 6   Recreational Dance and Movement Organisations and Community Dance Schemes.
Category 7   Promoting Organisations and the Media.
Category 8   Regional Dance Associations. (Elected from a different region each year on a rotational basis.)

Schedule Two
The individual membership of the Council electing one representative to the Executive Committee to take responsibility for each of the following (eight) counties: — Clwyd, Gwynedd, Powys, Dyfed, Gwent, West Glamorgan, Mid Glamorgan, South Glamorgan.

Appendix G

A Mobile Dance Stage

For many years — and in many parts of the world — the problem of suitable floors for dancing has troubled teachers, students and administrators. The ideal most often cited is that they should be wooden, sprung, unpolished, not less than 27m square, having a ceiling height which allows all kinds of lifts and steps of elevation, be acoustically secure and well ventilated. The reality is often wooden blocks on concrete, polished or semi-polished, of erratic size, all-purpose, noisy with low ceilings and airless.

These conditions cannot be changed overnight but the Leicestershire Education Authority in discussion with East Midlands Arts Association and the Calouste Gulbenkian Foundation concluded the situation was sufficiently urgent to commission Anthony Hill Designs of Shepshed, Leicestershire, to investigate the possibility of a portable stage for drama and dance performances, capable of providing the elements essential for dancing.

After some years of experiment the stage which has emerged is made of aluminium and is easily erected and dismantled with the minimum of labour. It is light to carry and to transport but is also stable and capable of being used in sections to accommodate a range of requirements from small studio productions to large dance presentations. It is constructed from a simple kit of parts and is modular in essence being built from strong light-weight aluminium sections, (see illustrations inside front and back covers).

A standard 10m x 10m stage weighs 2.2 tons, it can be stored within a space measuring 5m x 1.2m x 1.7m and fits into a Box or 'Luton' type van. Two men can build it in under three hours or take it apart in under two hours. Two heights of stage are available and split-level layouts are possible. The surface is flat, safe and slightly sprung and a vinyl covering is desirable. A range of auxiliary items is available, including ramps, stage steps, extra cast supports and superstructures for curtains, lighting and presentations requiring a proscenium arch. The cost in April 1980 was about £10,000.

213

The Dancers' Resettlement Fund

Background to the Scheme
The Opera and Ballet Inquiry which was set up by the Arts Council in 1966 and reported in 1969, studied the conditions of employment and security for dancers. Although concern was expressed about the problems encountered by ex-dancers in to-day's competitive world, it was not until the meetings to discuss pension arrangements for the profession took place that any positive steps to improve the position could be taken. Up to that time there had been no proper channel through which ways of alleviating these difficulties could be explored.

While the Welfare State was steadily increasing the provisions and protection for the majority of citizens, the measures taken seemed to offer little or no answer to the special needs of dancers. In some ways, they made matters worse by enabling others to compete more easily for the available opportunities. With the growing emphasis on adult education, more people took the chance to study for examinations they had missed earlier in life. There were evening classes, day and sandwich release courses and the Open University. The dancer's life usually entailed a working day from morning to late at night, an irregular programme, and a great deal of travelling. This made it virtually impossible for them to take advantage of such provisions for further education. When their employment as a dancer ceased, they discovered that few authorities would give them a grant for GCE studies and these were frequently a prerequisite for entry to vocational courses.

The Royal Ballet Benevolent Fund was dealing with an increasing number of applicants whose need was for re-training and vocational guidance rather than relief of poverty as such. Apart from the difficulty of entering a new career, a dancer had to cope with the strain of adapting to a new way of life and of earning a living in whatever way was possible. Into the bargain, they may have had to fight against a fairly widespread belief that dancers could do nothing else but dance.

In 1971, meetings between dance company administrators, representatives of the Arts Council of Great Britain and British Actors' Equity Association were called to consider the problem, following discussion at the committee for CODA (Co-ordination of Dance Activities). They noted a recurrent question from dancers in their talks about pension schemes. 'Why can't we have a lump sum or a pension when we leave the profession? That is when we really need it'.

A sub-committee was appointed to explore schemes to ease the two periods of insecurity in the lives of many dancers; at the end of their dancing career and at normal pension age. Few dancers could hope that these periods would be simultaneous; it was envisaged that most dancers would be coming to the end of their career in their mid-thirties. By linking membership of a pension scheme and a resettlement fund, both periods could be covered. The financial help would be of great benefit, but it was also envisaged that a resettlement officer could offer encouragement, information and guidance during the transition from one career to another.

Constitution
The Scheme was established under a Trust Deed on April 1st 1973, for the furtherance and the assistance of dancers so that they may usefully undertake some occupation other than or additional to that of dancer. Trustees are nominated by each of the dance companies participating in the Scheme, the Arts Council of Great Britain and the British Actors' Equity Association. The Fund is financed mainly by the dance companies, each of which pays five per cent of the salaries of the members of the Dancers Pension Scheme. There are, however, provisions for donations to the Fund from other sources. Members or ex-members of the Dancers Pension Scheme are eligible for benefit from the Resettlement Fund.

Awards from the Fund
All awards are strictly discretionary. They may include fees, maintenance and allowances for dependents. In some cases, grants or loans may be given towards the capital ex-

214

penditure needed to start a business. The Fund aims to assist those who are thought to be disadvantaged because they have had a serious dancing career. For example, a dancer who had completed some eight years in the profession would be considered to be almost certainly at a disadvantage compared with those in other kinds of employment who had been able to continue their further education or take vocational training other than dancing at school-leaving age. The Fund also assists those dancers who have suffered illness, accident or redundancy and have been unable to complete as many years of service as they would normally have done. The Resettlement Officer arranges for applications to be made to the Fund. All relevant information and details of proposed courses are assembled and a report given to the Trustees. Contact between the applicants to the Fund and the Resettlement Officer continues during re-training and, when it is necessary, an award can be reviewed.

Dancers' Resettlement Office, 9 Fitzroy Square, London, W1P 6AE. Telephone: 01 387 2666

Appendix I

Note on a Swedish Committee of Inquiry into Dance Education 1976

The Swedish Committee noted the "widespread interest in an expansion of dancing instruction under municipal auspices which the Committee find gratifying. Dancing instruction within, say, the framework of the Municipal Music School would open up opportunities for those who want such instruction but who shy away from the substantial costs which often accompany private instruction. Further, an expanded system of municipally provided dancing education would serve to spread educational opportunities across the country instead of being concentrated in a few large cities as at present." The Committee sees the main function of municipal dance education as provision "for all children and young people who want to devote themselves to dancing as a hobby and leisure pursuit." Within this general provision might go special provision for those with special aptitude because "a system of municipal dancing instruction would constitute a valuable preparation ... for pupils who intend to head for the pre-vocational dance curriculum in a primary school".* The goal of "pre-vocational dancing education in the primary school should be to give the pupil a good physical foundation and sufficient dancing knowledge to pursue vocational training in the field of dance, to stimulate the pupil towards self-activity and personal creativity, to foster his or her musicality and sense of rhythm". Three such pre-vocational dancing courses should be established at primary schools in Malmö, Gottenburg and Stockholm in liaison with the relevant theatres in each city. This it is hoped will make Sweden self-sufficient in native dancers, ending the present situation where every third professional dancer in Sweden is a foreign national. Pre-vocational education in the three selected primary schools would start at about the age of 10 without actually laying down any fixed age because "physical qualifications and motivation will vary from one individual to another". The education would be founded on classical ballet techniques with provision also for improvisation, acrobatics, folk dance and character dance, modern dance, jazz and music including options in the two highest grades for specialisation in particular dance techniques. The total number of hours per week in 40 minute classes varies from 13 at the age of 10 to 18 at the age of 16. Of these hours slightly more than half will fall within the school curriculum, sometimes in the form of double classes. The rest will fall outside the curriculum with safeguards for the student's leisure time. After pre-vocational education in a primary school a successful

---

* Primary education in Sweden covers a wider range than in Britain. Just before the Committee began work public education in Sweden was re-organised to provide 9 years compulsory schooling from the age of 7—16 in the Grandskolan, ie primary school; further education from 16 to 18/19 in the Gymnasia; the universities.

215

pupil could move on at the age of 16 to a two-year vocational course within a secondary school in Stockholm, the content and scope of which is suggested by the Committee. From here the student would either enter a company or move into tertiary education where training as a dance teacher would be one option.

Appendix J

The Case for Dance in Universities

Summary of a paper arising from a conference on 'Universities and the Arts' convened by the Arts Council of Great Britain at the University of East Anglia, 14th – 16th September 1979.

1 Background. Dance has been an academic subject in the United States of America since 1927. Today 230 tertiary institutions offer dance degrees, many of them as major subject areas. Many institutions also offer post-graduate studies in dance. In the United Kingdom 8 universities. offer dance as an option within an honours course, and/or for post-graduate study. They are: Birmingham; Bristol; Hull; Kent; Leeds; Goldsmiths' College in London University; Manchester; and the Queen's University, Belfast – not counting those universities which validate BEd degrees including dance. There are also a growing number of degree courses outside the universities, validated by the CNAA, in which dance is a major subject area. Largely thanks to the support of the Arts Council of Great Britain, the art of dance now attracts audiences of all age groups throughout the United Kingdom in theatres, studios and on television. Of particular significance is the growing student interest in dance, giving reason to face the future with some confidence. It is an expanding field at a time of cutback.

2 What is meant by dance? For a minority dance implies performance and the possibility of a performing career, as in drama. Principally, though, dance should be interpreted in its broadest meaning and application – dance in community arts, dance criticism, dance administration, dance therapy, dance history, dance in various forms of education, dance changed by and helping to change our technological society. Most especially a degree in dance and the study of dance at tertiary level should be considered as valid a preparation for life in careers unconnected with dance as is, say, a study of literature, history or of the social sciences.

3 Why is dance necessary and unique as a subject? Dance is a necessary subject of study in a university because it is part of the history of: –
a) human movement; b) human culture; c) human communication.
Deriving from this and because universities are concerned with the architecture of the mind and all kinds of knowing, dance in a university context contributes essentially to: –
a) the nature of knowing, especially affective, non-verbal, sensory thinking, and the knowing which comes from the study of values; b) the nature and practice of communication; c) the proper balance of university life in the sense that a university ought to undertake and offer to faculty, students and the community a background range of study and experience.
Dance is unique because in each of these areas it presents a unique aspect of human experience, understanding and relationship to the environment, unique because the knowing, the communication, and the dance activity are through the human body and the process of knowing oneself. Therefore dance is part of any adequate system of education. Universities are much the poorer without it, and the individuals they produce will be less than complete.

4 How is all this valid academically? If dance is the unique and necessary subject described above it is a valid subject for study on its own at university. Indeed, the growth of dance throughout the world since the Second World War will only be really fruitful when

216

it has roots in the education curriculum at all levels, including the university curriculum. It is recognised, of course, that university degree studies are concerned primarily with the conceptual frameworks of a subject and that students are led to an understanding of the methods of working within a distinctive area of knowledge. In dance these conceptual frameworks are still in an early stage of development in relation to the tertiary sector, so the reluctance of some validating bodies to initiate courses in dance is understandable. Nevertheless, from the experience of dance in a wide range of institutions at tertiary level, five areas can be identified where it can be studied and assessed:—

a) choreography — its theory, craft and creativity; b) performance; c) notation and recording; d) appreciation; e) dance in relation to other disciplines, such as history, sociology, anthropology, medicine and so on.

In each of these areas study would need to be linked with music and production and each, of course, can be the subject of research and post-graduate studies.

5   What are the special needs?

a) Library resources. It is often thought dance has no literature. This is not true. It has a long history recorded in words, pictures and notation much of it only now coming to light. Additionally, the literature of dance includes film and video records.

b) Finance. Experience suggests that a mixed economy package may be needed, putting together what is relevant locally at a particular university. In assembling the package student interest, and therefore student numbers, provide the vital stimulus and ingredient.

c) Spaces. Special spaces in the form of dance studios and a theatre are as essential to dance as laboratories are to a scientist. There is plenty of information available on the nature of the spaces needed. In the present situation the provision of spaces has to be a balance between ideal provision and the practical. The key surely lies in the genuine sympathy and collaboration of a university community in sharing existing spaces and in recognising the particular needs of dance study — at the very least a special floor available most of the time and the use of production facilities some of the time linked with music.

d) Staff. Necessary staff are of two kinds, academic and practical, who need not always be separate people. For practical studies it is essential to sustain close links with the dance profession partly through the use of artists in residence but also in terms of permanent positions of responsibility.

6   Accordingly, we recommend that:—

a) existing dance courses in UK universities should be safeguarded and developed as much as possible;

b) universities include dance, dancers and especially choreographers within the established practice of appointing artists in residence;

c) extra-mural departments should recognise public interest in dance and reflect it in their work according to local need, drawing for help as necessary upon the dance profession;

d) Conference express its support for the University of Surrey in its dance plans;

e) the Arts Council develop by all means its dialogue with the universities so that both sides make the best use of each others resources, particularly through developing existing dance courses;

f) the dance profession do all it can to support and use university theatres and performance spaces and thus develop its relations with the university community;

g) the Arts Council and the dance community do all they can to encourage the use of university research capacity to advance dance.

List of organisations and individuals who submitted written or oral evidence or gave information to the Inquiry, or were consulted or visited by members of the Committee.

In addition to those listed below, and at Appendix A, the Chairman and Committee wish to thank the Rt Hon Shirley Williams (former Secretary of State for Education and Science), the Rt Hon Norman St John Stevas (Chancellor of the Duchy of Lancaster), Sir James Hamilton, Walter Ulrich and D E Lloyd Jones of the Department of Education and Science, the Scottish Education Department and a number of organisations and individuals who asked not to be named, for information and guidance during the preparation of this Report.

Organisations:

Academy of Ballet, Edinburgh
Advisory Council for Adult and Continuing Education (ACACE)
Province of Alberta, Canada, Ministry of Education
Another Dance Group
Anthorne School, Potters Bar
Arts Council of Great Britain
Arts Educational Schools, Tring & Golden Lane, London SE1
Associated Examining Board (AEB)
Association of Ballet Clubs
Australian Association for Dance Education
Australian Ballet
Avon Region, RAD
Ballet for All, Royal Ballet
Ballet Rambert
Bingley College of Further Education, Yorkshire (now part of Ilkley College)
Bisham Abbey National Sports Centre
Borders Regional Council
Bretton Hall College of Further Education, Yorkshire
British Actors' Equity Association
British Association of Teachers of Dancing (BATD)
British Ballet Oganisation (BBO)
British Columbia, Canada, Department of Education
Bromley Arts Council
The Brooking School of Ballet and General Education
Bush Davies Schools, East Grinstead
Canada Council
Cecchetti Society
Central Council of Physical Recreation (CCPR)
Chelsea College of Physical Education (now Brighton Polytechnic)
City of Bristol Treasurer's Department
City of Leicester Treasurer's Department
City of Manchester Treasurer's Department

Conference of Lecturers in Physical Education, Scotland
Consultative Committee on the Curriculum, Edinburgh
Council for Dance Education and Training (CDET)
Council for National Academic Awards (CNAA)
Crewe and Alsager College of Higher Education
Dance in Canada Association
Dance and the Child: International (DACI)
Dance for Everyone
Dancers' Resettlement Fund
Dance Theatre of Harlem
Dartington College of Arts
Dartington Hall School
Doncaster College of Higher Education
Dumfries & Galloway Regional Council
Dunfermline College of Physical Education
East Anglian Dance Theatre
East Anglian Region, RAD
Eastern Arts Association
East Midlands Arts
Edinburgh Schools Dance Association
Educational Institute of Scotland, Advisory Committee on Physical Education
Elliot-Clarke School, Liverpool
Elmhurst Ballet School, Camberley
Eltham Adult Education Institute
EMMA Dance Company
English Folk Dance and Song Society (EFDSS)
Essex Region, RAD
Extemporary Dance Company
Fairlop Secondary Girls School, Hainault
Fife Education Authority
Finchley Manor Hill School, London N.12.
Foxfield Junior School, London SE18
French Embassy, London
Friern School, Dulwich, London

Germany, Embassy of the Federal Republic, London
Grampian Regional Council: Banff & Buchan, South Grampian
Great Cornard School, Sudbury, Suffolk
Greater London Arts Association (GLAA)
Greensward School, Hockley, Essex
Grove Vale Primary School, London SE22
Guildford School of Acting and Drama Dance Education
Guildhall School of Dancing, Norwich
Guildhall School of Music and Drama
Hallfield Junior School, London
Hammond School, Chester
Helix (Cambridge Contemporary Dance Group)
High School of Art, Manchester
Hillingdon Arts Association
Holy Family Convent School, Enfield
Hull, University of
Imperial Society of Teachers of Dancing (ISTD)
Inner London Dance Teachers' Association (ILDTA)
Inner London Education Authority (ILEA)
Institute of Choreology
Intake High School, Leeds
International Dance Teachers' Association (IDTA)
International Federation of Actors
Irish Ballet Company
Islington Dance Factory
Islington, London Borough of, Directorate of Recreational Services
Italia Conti Stage School, London SW9
Marianne Jepson School of Dancing, Oldham
Jordanhill College of Education, Glasgow
Juilliard School of Music, New York, Dance Department
Laban Centre for Movement and Dance
Language of Dance Centre
Leeds, University of, Department of Physical Education
Legat School, Mark Cross, East Sussex
Leicester Polytechnic
Leicester, University of
Lincolnshire and Humberside Arts Association
London College of Dance and Drama (LCDD)
London Contemporary Dance Theatre (LCDT)
London Festival Ballet
London Region, RAD
London School of Contemporary Dance (LSCD)

London Youth Dance Theatre
Loughborough University of Technology
Ludus Dance Group
Madeley College of Education, Cheshire
Stella Mann School of Dancing, London NW3
Margaret Morris Movement
I M Marsh College of Physical Education, Liverpool Polytechnic
Merseyside Arts Association
Middlesex Polytechnic
Midland Region, RAD
Misbourne School, Buckinghamshire
Modern Dance Society, University of Edinburgh
Moving Visions Dance Theatre
National Association of Teachers in Further and Higher Education (NATFHE)
New Brunswick, Department of Education, Canada
New College, Durham
National Endowment for the Arts, New York
New London Ballet
Nonnington College of Physical Education, Kent
Northern Arts
Northern Ballet Theatre
North West Arts
North West Region, Liverpool Section, RAD
North West Region, Manchester Section, RAD
Northwest Territories, Canada, Department of Education
Province of Nova Scotia, Canada, Minister of Education
Province of Ontario, Canada, Ministry of Culture and Recreation
Paris Opera Ballet School
Pattison Dancing Academy and College, Coventry
Physical Education Association (PEA)
Province of Quebec, Canada, Ministry of Education
Rambert Academy, Isleworth
Rambert School of Ballet, London WC1
Rolle College, Exmouth
Royal Academy of Dancing
Royal Ballet School (Lower and Upper)
Royal Netherlands Embassy, London
Royal Scottish Country Dance Association
Province of Saskatchewan, Canada, Department of Education
College of St Hild and St Bede, Durham
St Joseph's College, Bradford

De La Salle College of Higher Education, Manchester
Schools Council
School of American Ballet
Scottish Arts Council
Scottish Association of Advisers in Physical Education
The Scottish Ballet
Scottish Central Committee on Physical Education
Scottish Council for Dance
Scottish Official Board of Highland Dancing
Scottish Region, RAD
Scottish Sports Council
Scottish Universities Physical Education Association
Scottish Women's Keep Fit Association
Sheffield, University of
Society of Russian Style Ballet Schools
South East Region, RAD
Southern Arts Association
Southern Region, RAD
South Wales Region, RAD
South West Arts
South West Region, RAD
Barbara Speake Stage School
Standing Conference of London Arts Councils
Starcross School, Islington, London N1
State College of Victoria, Hawthorn, Australia
State College of Victoria, Rusden, Australia

Strathclyde Regional Council: Argyll & Bute, Ayr, Renfrew
Sunderland Polytechnic
Sunshine Fund for Blind Babies
Sydenham School, London SE26
Tayside Regional Council: Perth & Kinross
Theatre School of Dance and Drama, Edinburgh
Theatre Workshop, Edinburgh
Tower Hamlets Arts Committee
Tower Hamlets School, London E1
Trinity and All Saints' Colleges, Leeds
Wales, Polytechnic of
Weekend Arts Colleges, Inter Action, London
Weguelin School of Russian Ballet, Tunbridge Wells
Welsh Arts Council
Welsh Dance Association/Dance Council for Wales
Welsh Dance Theatre
West Byfleet County Secondary School
Western Australia Arts Council
West London Institute of Higher Education
City of Westminster Arts Council
West Midlands Arts
Yorkshire Arts Association
York University, Toronto, Canada, Dance Department
Youthaid
Yukon Territory, Canada, Government Executive Committee

Individuals:

Mollie P Abbott
Janet Adshead
Elizabeth Aggiss
A Aitkenhead
Eileen Alexander
Hubert Allen
J A van Alphen
Robin Anderson
Werdon Anglin
Professor J F Arnott
John Auty
Gideon Avrahami
Eva Barnes
Michael Barnes
Jean Battersby
Dr Alan Beattie
Karen Bell-Kanner
C A Beresford
Doreen Bird
S Bishop
Professor John Blacking
Jean A Bowden

K C Breckon
Vivien Bridson
Jonathan Brill
Louise Browne
L W K Brown
P Brown
Dr Vi Bruce
D J Buchanan
Dawn Buckle
Roderick Bunce
Esme Burtles
Noreen Bush
Jane Butchart
Jo Butterworth
Joyce Butler
Dr Eileen Byrne
Annette Cairncross
Bob Carlisle
Sarah Carter
M M Cassie
T H Caulcott
John Chapman

John Clegg
G E Cloughley
John de la Cour
Peter Cox
S Creevy
R Crook
Bridget Crowley
Gordon Curl
Anne Day
John Day
Michael Dawson
W G Dear
Pamela Dellar
John Dilworth
Peter Doman
G Donald
Nicholas Dromgoole
Bill Dufton
Alexander Dunbar
C Duncan
Lucien Duthoit
J A Dyble

220

Fergus Early
Junius Eddy
Angela Ellis
Warwick Ellis
Konrad Elsden
William J Eltham
Bridget Espinosa
Ann Evans
Elizabeth Every
Felicity Excell
Rita Fenton
Barbara Fewster
G C Finlayson
T F Fitzgerald
E W Foulser
K Fraser
Joan Freeman
Ruth French
Wendy Frost
David Gayle
Barbara Geoghegan
P N G Gilbert
P Giles
Irene Grandison-Clark
Felicity Gray
Vera Gray
Sheila Griffiths
Professor V S Griffiths
Dorothy H Guise
Pat Halley
Michael Hammet
Iris Hanson
Mary Hanson
Emily Hargreaves
Sheila Hargreaves
Mark Harris
Muriel Hasland
David Henshaw
A G Hetherington
Colin Hicks
John Hipkin
Dr Richard Hoggart
Janice Holliday
Roger Howlett
Nina Hubbard
Margaret Hurd
Michael Huxley
M A Inniss
S C Ireland
Christine Iweins
Marie Jack
John James
Robert James
Margaret Jamieson
Rt Hon Hugh Jenkins
Marianne Jepson
Karol Johnstone
Peter Jones
Dr John Kane

H M Kastrati
Mary Kelly
Vera Kelly
I Kerr
Bill King
Audrey Knight-Ellis
Dorothy Kuya
Tim Lamford
Margaret Lawford
Brian Lee
Colin D Lee
Sheila K Lee
A Legat-Pinnes
Victor Leopold
Paul Leopold-Kimm
Keith Lester
Dr Warren Lett
Gina Levete
Veronica Lewis
E Liddell
K M Lockhead
Beryl Loveridge
Mary Lowden
Jean-Claude Luc
J MacDonald
Dr Alwynne Mackie
Margaret S Mackie
Stella Mann
Beryl Manthorp
Margaret Markham
Harold Marks
Timothy Mason
Alan Mather
Allan Matten
Joy Matthews
Sidney Matthews
Helen McBuff
Marie McCluskey
Shirley McKechnie
Joan McLaren
Archie McMillan
Michael Merwitzer
Donald Meyer
Monique Michaud
Gillian Middleton
P A Mitchinson
M Monkhouse
M J Morgan
Professor Derra de Moroda
Susan Morris
G Mortimer
Reverend John and Mrs Mortimer
Sir Claus Moser
William Mowat-Thomson
D E Mumford
Simon Mumford
Donald Naismith
Stephen Newman
Jenny Nicholson

Teresa Noble
D J Nuttall
Betty Osgathorp
Roger Pahl
L Paine
Barbara Pass
Betty Pattison
Peter Pearson
Kedzie Penfield
Joyce Percy
A C Perkins
Colin Pickles
Maurice Plaskow
Peter Plouviez
Maureen Pope
James Porter
Geoff Powell
Dame Peggy van Praagh
Alan Pratten
W K Pringle
Alwyn Probert
J Queen
John Ranelagh
James Ranger
Charles Reinhart
Jeanne Renaud
J H Rensen
Ann Ridler
June-Elizabeth Roberts
I M Robertson
Claire Robilant
Colin Roth
David Rowlands
Margaret Russell
Mary Schaefer
Brian Scott-Hughes
F Seatree
Betty Sellar
Anne Sheward
Zena Skinner
P T Sloman
Sissie Smith
H Lotte Smock
Barbara Speake
A Stainer
Wolfgang Stange
Jean Stanley
Dorothy Stevens
D Stewart
Joline Stiddard
A K Stock
Professor Grant Strate
Elizabeth Sweeting
Annette Thomson
Elma Thomson
D B Thrower
Reverend Dr G Tolley
John Tomlinson
Ian Trethowan

Joan Tucker
I Tulloch
Muriel Tweedy
Dame Ninette de Valois
Lyndon Wainwright
Margaret Walker
Chris Wallock
Mary-Jane Watson

K L Webster
Catherine Weguelin
Alison White
Paul White
Sister Wilfrid
Jean Williams
June Williams
Peter Williams

Sophia Williams
Faith Wilson
G B L Wilson
Peter Wilson
Brenda Woods
Patricia Woodall
Anthony Wraight
Janet Wright

Glossary

Advisory Council for Adult and Continuing Education. Established 1977 under the chairmanship of Richard Hoggart to advise the Government and has produced a succession of papers, pamphlets and reports on aspects of the subject.

A-level Advanced level examination for the General Certificate of Education in England and Wales usually taken after two years in the sixth form. See GCE.

AEB Associated Examining Board. One of the eight examining bodies in England and Wales and the only one not connected with a university.

British Actors' Equity. The Trade Union for actors, dancers, singers and most other performing artists.

BBO British Ballet Organisation, a teachers' organisation concerned with teaching and standards of classical ballet. Has an important representation in Australia as well as UK.

CDET Council for Dance Education and Training. See Appendix F.

CDS Conference of Dance Schools, a constituent organisation of the CDET above. There is a Conference of Drama Schools (also CDS) on the pattern of which the Conference of Dance Schools was founded.

CEE Certificate of Extended Education. An experimental examination still waiting to be officially recognised taken at 17+ following a one year sixth form course as a follow-up to the CSE examinations (qv).

CIDD Conseil International de la Danse. UNESCO sponsored body of which DACI (qv) is now a member. The body through which the British dance world could most appropriately develop its international contacts.

CNAA Council for National Academic Awards. Established by Royal Charter in 1964, it is the validation body for degree courses in non-university institutions in UK.

Consultative Committee on the Curriculum. Scottish equivalent of the Schools Council (qv)

CSE Certificate of Secondary Education, an examination open to boys and girls in any school in England and Wales who have completed five years of secondary schooling. Usually taken at around the age of 16, it is awarded in 5 grades and is controlled largely by serving teachers sitting on 14 regional boards.

DACI Dance and the Child: International. International organisation established following a conference at Edmonton, Canada in July 1978. For its purpose and other details see Appendix D.

DES Department of Education and Science, the responsible ministry for much of education in England and Wales, under a Secretary of State having Cabinet rank. Its powers and relationships are complex although ultimately it makes the decisions in the educational field through its control of finance, control of minimum standards of educational provision and content of the training, supply and distribution of teachers. Functions in connection with schools, further education and teachers relate primarily to England. Functions in relation to the universities are exercised through the UGC (qv). In Wales responsibility for nursery, primary and secondary education, and for non-university institutions of further, higher and adult education is exercised by the Secretary of State for Wales. The DES does not itself run any schools, colleges, or engage any teachers, or prescribe textbooks or curricula.

DHSS Department of Health and Social Security. Responsible for the administration of the National Health Service in England and for the personal social services run by local authorities in England for children, the elderly, the infirm, the handicapped and other persons in need. Responsible also for the social security services in England, Scotland and Wales. Responsibility for the administration of the Health Services in Wales resides with the Welsh Office (qv) and in Scotland with the Scottish Office (qv) through the Scottish Home and Health Department and the National Health Service, Scotland.

17

EFDSS English Folk Dance and Song Society, founded by Cecil Sharp in 1911 to study, record and encourage folk dancing and folk music.

GCE General Certificate of Education. Examination for secondary school pupils and others in England and Wales upon which depend many openings to higher, further and vocational education and many job opportunities. Conducted by eight examining bodies and set at two levels: O (Ordinary) and A (Advanced). For Scotland see SCE.

GLC Greater London Council. The Local Authority responsible for the government of the Greater London area comprising 610 sq miles and nearly 7 million people. The Council and the 32 London Borough Councils were constituted under the London Government Act, 1963.

HMI Her Majesty's Inspectorate. Her Majesty's Inspectors inspect schools and other educational establishments in England, apart from universities, reporting to the Secretary of State for Education and Science on the efficiency of the educational system. They also offer independent professional advice, based on their observation and judgement, to the Secretary of State, the DES (qv), LEAs (qv) and teachers. There are separate Inspectorates for Scotland and Wales fulfilling similar responsibilities. (The Dance Study received invaluable and continual help from all three Inspectorates.)

IBA Independent Broadcasting Authority. Responsible for providing television and local radio services additional to those provided by the BBC. Its authority covers all the UK and is exercised through the appointment of programme companies; ownership and operation of transmitters; supervision of programmes; and control of advertising.

ILEA Inner London Education Authority, the local education authority for an area corresponding with the area of the twelve inner London boroughs and the City of London. It is the largest authority of its kind in UK and one of the largest in the world.

ISTD Imperial Society of Teachers of Dancing. The oldest society of dance teachers in the Commonwealth, founded in 1904. Conducts its own examinations and issues diplomas in ballroom and most other types of dancing.

LEA Local Education Authority. The education service is a national service locally administered through local education authorities responsible for providing state primary, secondary and further (but not university) education to meet the needs of their areas.

LCDT and **LSCD** London Contemporary Dance Theatre and London School of Contemporary Dance. The professional dance company and vocational dance school jointly administered by the Contemporary Dance Trust from headquarters at The Place, London. The School opened in 1966 and the Company gave its first performance in 1967.

MSC Manpower Services Commission. The body established by Government to initiate and administer schemes covering training, re-training, re-settlement and other services to assist those unemployed, redundant and seeking work.

NALGO National and Local Government Officers Association, the largest trade union covering workers in local government having a membership of approaching ¾ million.

NATFHE National Association of Teachers in Further and Higher Education, the principal trade union for teachers in further and higher education other than universities who are served by the Association of University Teachers.

PE Adviser Physical Education Adviser, the subject specialist appointed by a local education authority to advise it on the efficiency and teaching of physical education, the supervision of this subject, teacher training, teacher recruitment, student grants and almost all other activities to do with physical education in a local authority area, usually including dance. London and a number of other authorities maintain an inspectorate, members of which cover particular areas of education, including physical education and dance.

RAA Regional Arts Association. England and Wales are divided into groupings of local authorities comprising associations to develop and encourage the arts in their regions. The Arts Council of Great Britain now devolves a substantial part of its funds and functions to RAAs.

RAD Royal Academy of Dancing, an examining body and association of teachers founded in 1920 aiming to improve the standard of classical ballet teaching and dancing in UK and the Commonwealth. It is not concerned with ballroom dancing or modern dance, except as part of the training of classical dancers, and now conducts examinations in many countries outside, as well as within, the Commonwealth.

SCD Scottish Council for Dance. See Appendix F.

Schools Council. The Schools Council for the Curriculum and Examinations was established in 1964 as an independent advisory body co-ordinating the work of examining boards, or advising them. It represents all educational interests with teachers forming a majority of its members and is particularly concerned with promoting and encouraging curriculum study and development.

SCE Scottish Certificate of Education, conducted by the SCE Examination Board, roughly corresponds to GCE (qv) in England and Wales. Conducted at two grades, Ordinary O-grade and Higher H-grade. The Board also grants a Certificate of Sixth Year Studies.

SED Scottish Education Department, responsible to the Secretary of State for Scotland for the general supervision of the national system of education in Scotland, except for universities. This national system has developed independently from that of England and has a number of distinctive features which, of course, influenced the conduct of the Dance Study in respect of Scotland.

Scottish Office. The Department of State responsible for the Affairs, Government and Public Offices of the Kingdom of Scotland as distinct from the Kingdom of England.

SHAPE Name of the organisation established in 1976 by Gina Levete to enable individual artists, or groups of artists of every kind, to apply their art in settings which can help handicapped, sick or otherwise incapacitated people.

STUC Scottish Trades Union Congress. National centre for the trade union movement in Scotland. Formed in 1897.

TSA Training Services Agency. Part of the MSC (qv) responsible for training services.

TUC Trades Union Congress, founded in 1868 as a voluntary association of trade unions. It has met annually since 1871 and is now the main policy-making body of the trade union movement responsible also for conducting relations on behalf of the movement with Government, Government departments and many other bodies.

UGC University Grants Committee, the body exercising the responsibility of the Secretary of State for Education and Science in respect of universities throughout Britain. There are 44 universities in UK. Of these, 33 are in England, 8 in Scotland, 2 in Northern Ireland and one (a federal institution) in Wales. There is also the Open University directly grant-aided by the DES which does not come within the UGC system. Although all universities have freedom in academic matters, the Government, through the UGC, determines the total size of the university student population, strongly influences its distribution between arts, science, medicine etc, and determines the role of the university sector in the whole higher education system.

UNESCO United Nations Educational, Scientific and Cultural Organisation. An agency of the United Nations working for 'the advancement of mutual knowledge and understanding of peoples . . . to give fresh impulse to popular education and to the spread of culture . . . to maintain, increase and diffuse knowledge.' See also CIDD.

WDA Welsh Dance Association. See Appendix F. The Association is in the process of becoming the Dance Council for Wales with functions similar to those of the Scottish Council for Dance.

Welsh Office. The Department of State responsible for the Affairs, Government and Public Offices of the Principality of Wales.

Notes and Bibliography

1 *Going on the Stage* Calouste Gulbenkian Foundation London 1975
2 *Training Musicians* Calouste Gulbenkian Foundation London 1978
3 *Making Musicians* Calouste Gulbenkian Foundation London 1965
4 *A Report on Opera and Ballet in the United Kingdom 1966–69* Arts Council of Great Britain London 1969
5 *The Education of the Adolescent* Board of Education HMSO 1926
6 *15–18* Ministry of Education HMSO 1959
7 *The Open Classroom Reader* Charles Silberman (Ed) Random House Inc., New York 1973. Quoted in *Coming to our Senses* (cf 25)
8 *Art in Secondary Schools* Curriculum Paper 9 Scottish Education Department HMSO Edinburgh 1971. 'Society at present is sorely in need of many of the qualities which art is capable of giving to the educational experience'. See also *Physical Education in Secondary Schools* Curriculum Paper 12 HMSO Edinburgh 1972. "We believe," says the report, "that all young people should have the opportunity to dance."
9 *The Arts and the People* Transport House The Labour Party
10 *The Arts: The Way Forward* Conservative Central Office 1978
11 *The TUC Working Party Report on the Arts* A Consultative Document Trades Union Congress 1976
12 *The Arts Britain Ignores* Calouste Gulbenkian Foundation, Arts Council of Great Britain and Community Relations Commission 1976
13 *Support for the Arts in England and Wales* Lord Redcliffe-Maud Calouste Gulbenkian Foundation 1976
14 *Arts and the Adolescent* Schools Council Working Paper 54 Evans/Methuen Educational 1975
15 *Arts and the Curriculum* A study commissioned by the Calouste Gulbenkian Foundation under the chairmanship of Peter Brinson and organised by Nicholas Usherwood. Expected to report 1980.
16 *The Creative Arts in the Secondary School* Inner London Education Authority 1974
17 *Hansard* House of Commons Report, London. Debate on Specialist Musical Education, 1st August, 1978.
18 *Aspects of Secondary Education in England* A survey by Her Majesty's Inspectorate HMSO 1979 (especially advice and pronouncements on a core curriculum)
19 Annual Report of the Royal Opera House, Covent Garden 1977/78
20 *Memories and Commentaries* Igor Stravinsky and Robert Craft London 1960, New York 1959
21 *The Art of Making Dances* Doris Humphrey New York 1959 Reissued by Horizon Press, New York 1978
22 Draft Constitution of Dance and the Child: International, Article II August 1979.
23 International Labour Organisation Report prepared for a joint meeting of ILO and UNESCO August 1977.
24 *Education of Professional Dancers* Summary of a report from the Swedish Committee of Inquiry into Dancing Education. Stockholm, June 1976. The Summary is available through Swedish Embassies. The full report can be obtained from the Ministry of Education and Cultural Affairs, Stockholm.
25 *Coming to our Senses* David Rockefeller Jr (Chairman) The significance of the arts in American education, a panel report, American Council for the Arts in Education McGraw-Hill 1977
26 *Perspectives on the Arts and General Education* Junius Eddy An Information Paper for the Rockefeller Foundation January 1974

27   Statistics supplied by the Department of Education and Science and Scottish Education Department. We are indebted for other statistics in this report to published government documents, especially *Trends in Education* (HMSO), *Education in Britain* (HMSO 1977), *The Educational System in England and Wales* (DES 1977) and *Scottish Education*, a Scottish Information Office Fact Sheet, 1977. All England and Wales data referred to have been published in the *Statistics in Education*, Vol. I (HMSO 1977).

28   *Education* Page 49, 20th January 1976 and *The Government's Expenditure Plans* 1978—9 and 1981—82, HMSO 1978 (Cmnd 7049). The estimates are expenditure forecast figures and represent a slightly increased provision in view of declining pupil numbers. The figures do not take into account unemployment following recent Government cuts.

29   *11—13* HMSO 1978

30   *Physical Education in Secondary Schools* Educational Building Note 15 Scottish Education Department HMSO Edinburgh 1979 See also description of portable aluminium stage at Appendix G

31   *Primary Education in England* A survey of HM Inspectors of schools HMSO 1978 Neither this survey nor our own included dance in Scotland

32   *Movement: Physical Education in Primary Years* HMSO 1972/74

33   *Report of the Committee of Enquiry into the Education of Handicapped Children and Young People* HMSO 1979

34   *Education* Page 251, 22nd September 1978

35   *In Search of Promise* National Children's Bureau A long term national study of able children and their families E M Hitchfield — Longman 1973

36   The National Association for Gifted Children publishes a bulletin and regular information from its headquarters at 1 South Audley Street, London W1.

37   *Gifted Young Musicians and Dancers* Report of a working group set up to consider their general and specialised education. Scottish Education Department HMSO 1976

38   *Find the Gifted Child* Devon Education Department, County Hall, Exeter. 1977

39   *Needing a Push: How the Arts Neglect the Disabled* Greater London Arts Association 1979. The report illustrates how buildings used for the arts by one London borough are often impossible or hazardous for handicapped people and argues for physical conditions which take into account handicapped needs.

40   *Education* page 478, 2nd November 1979. Dr Rhodes Boyson, Parliamentary Under Secretary of State, speaking at the annual meeting of the Standing Conference of Principals and Directors of Colleges and Institutions in Higher Education.

41   *Expression in Movement and the Arts* David Best Lepus Books London 1974. An examination of the relationship between philosophy and movement.

42   *Education: A Framework for Expansion* Government White Paper December 1972 *Teacher Education and Training* Department of Education and Science HMSO 1927.

43   Report of the National Council for Diplomas in Art and Design, published February 1964. (Council now amalgamated with the CNAA, 344—354 Gray's Inn Road, London WC1)

44   Such as *Trends in Education* (HMSO 1977) on in-service training and *Curriculum 11—16* (HMSO 1978) working papers by HM Inspectorate and *Local Authority Arrangements for the School Curriculum* November 1979.

45   *Education in Schools* A consultative document HMSO 1977 (Cmnd 6869) The idea of some institutions becoming recognised as national or regional centres of development and resources in particular fields and subject areas.

46   Final Report of the Adult Education Committee Ministry of Reconstruction 1919

47   *Adult Education and the Arts, a Case for Closer Integration* Roy Shaw *Adult Education* January 1978

48   *Adult Education: A Plan for Development* HMSO London 1973

49   *Adult Education — The Challenge of Change* HMSO Edinburgh 1975

50   For example, *After Expansion: A Time for Diversity* Richard Hoggart Advisory Council for Adult and Continuing Education Leicester 1978

51   See *Report of a Community Education Seminar* 1978 Goldsmiths' College, University of London and the British Association of Settlements and Social Action Centres organised 12th November 1977.

52   For example, the response (November 1978) of the Advisory Council for Adult and Continuing Education to the White Paper on Broadcasting (Cmnd 7294) and *Broadcasting and Youth* the report of a study commissioned by the BBC, Calouste Gulbenkian Foundation, IBA and MSC. Calouste Gulbenkian Foundation 1979

53   For example, *Education and Training for 16—18 Year Olds* HMSO 1979 *A View of the Curriculum* HMI Series Matters for Discussion HMSO 1980 (cf. 54)

54   *Education and Training for the 16 to 19 Age Group* National Union of Teachers 1980

55   *Inside the Colleges of Further Education* Adrian Bristow HMSO 1977

56   The National Union of Students has provided a useful discussion paper proposing *A Strategy for Recurrent and Part-Time Education*, to which we are indebted. NUS January 1978

57   Since this report was written a fuller treatment of dance in adult education has been presented by Peter Brinson as a chapter in *Adult Education and the Arts* to be published by the Department of Adult Education, University of Nottingham in 1980.

58   We have in mind publications like directories of relevant organisations in particular areas. The East Midlands Region of the Sports Council, for example, has published a directory of members on behalf of the Association for Movement and Dance in the East Midlands, formed in 1977.

59   *Education* page 547, 23rd June 1978. John Crawford, Chief Education Officer, Birmingham.

60   Report of the National Conference on Youth, 1977 National Youth Bureau, 17—23 Albion Street, Leicester. See also *Youth Arts Manifesto* (October 1978) a working document following a two-day conference on 'The Arts and the Youth Service', prepared by the Director of Cockpit Arts Workshop, Gateforth Street, London NW8 8EH. It includes a series of interesting recommendations many of which parallel ours in this study, and others which we endorse.

61   The Education Supplement of the Greater London Arts Association, Spring 1978, offers interesting ideas to develop the provision of arts for young people outside school hours.

62   *Report of the Committee on the Future of Broadcasting* Chairman: Lord Annan HMSO London 1977 (Cmnd 6753)

63   Formal Statement and Recommendations on Broadcasting and Adult and Continuing Education Advisory Council for Adult and Continuing Education 1978

64   *Report on Education* No. 93 Department of Education and Science August 1978. Assessing the performance of pupils

65   *Education* page 241, 8th April 1977. Report of the GCE and CSE Boards to a Select Committee of the House of Commons on the attainment of the school-leaver.

66   *Dance as an Examination Subject* Joan White Paper submitted in part fulfilment of the requirements for the degree of MA, Department of Physical Education, University of Leeds, March 1977. It is to be published during 1980 by the Margaret Morris Movement.

67   A unique account of infant classes is given by Beryl Manthorp in *Towards Ballet* Dance Books London 1980

68   *Dance* page 1, July 1979. Journal of the Imperial Society of Teachers of Dancing

69   *Dance* page 24, May 1979. Journal of the Imperial Society of Teachers of Dancing

70   *The Governor* Sir Thomas Elyot (1531) Dent London 1937 Introduction to the Everyman edition

71   See *Essay towards an History of Dancing* John Weaver, 1712; *Anatomical and Mechanical Lectures upon Dancing* John Weaver, 1723 and *The Art of Dancing* Kellom Tomlinson, 1735. *The Spectator* eg No 66 (Steele) 15th May 1711, Vol I. *An Essay for the Improvement of Dancing* E Pemberton London 1711.

72   *The Contribution of Modern Dance to Education* June Layson Unpublished MEd thesis, University of Manchester 1970 Reference to this thesis has been of the greatest help in this study. We are also indebted to Margaret Dunn for many historical details.

73   *A History of Anstey College of Physical Education, 1897–1972* Colin Crunden Anstey College 1974

74   See *Syllabus of Physical Training 1909, Syllabus of Physical Training 1919, Syllabus of Physical Training 1933* and *Syllabus of Physical Training 1937* Board of Education, HMSO

75   *The Revived Greek Dance, its Art and Teaching* Ruby Ginner Methuen London 4th Edition 1947

76   *The Technique of the Revived Greek Dance* Ruby Ginner The Imperial Society of Teachers of Dancing London 1963

77   *The Dance based on Natural Movement* Madge Atkinson The Dancing Times December 1925

78   We are grateful to Anita Heyworth for permission to use material in this section from a letter to a student at Bingley College of Education.

79   *Creation and Dance in Life* Margaret Morris Peter Owen London 1969 Republished 1978

80   Apart from the acknowledgement already made we have drawn information for paragraph 10 in Appendix B from *Margaret Morris Dancing* (Kegan Paul, Trench and Trubner, London 1926); from an unpublished MA thesis *A Pamphlet with Honour* by Joan White, submitted to Leeds University 1977; and from the International Association of Margaret Morris Movement and the Central Council of Physical Recreation who gave us a report and other material about the Movement.

81   *Childhood and Movement* Diana Jordan Basil Blackwell London 1966

82   *Ling Leaflet* March 1935 Joan Goodrich

83   *Ling Leaflet* July 1936 Leslie Burrows

84   *Ling Leaflet* August 1939 Diana Jordan

85   *Ling Leaflet* May 1941 Notice

86   *Ling Leaflet* May 1941 Report

87   *Ling Leaflet* December 1930 Advertisement

88   *The New Era* Vol 40 No 5 May 1959 Mary Wigman

89   *Modern Educational Dance* Rudolf Laban MacDonald Evans, London 1948 1st Edition

90   *The New Ballet* A V Coton Dennis Dobson London 1945. This book together with *Modern Dance* by Jane Winearls A and C Black London 1958 2nd Edition 1968, and a valuable contribution from Margaret Dunn, have provided source material for this section.

91   See also Lord Vaizey's introduction to *Training Musicians* Calouste Gulbenkian Foundation 1977 which argues the same point for music in the same terms.

92   *Technique Considered* Report of the Conference February 1976 published by the Association of Principals of Women's Colleges of Physical Education.

93   An account of this school, and Lumley's attempts to establish it on a permanent basis, is given in *The Romantic Ballet in England* Ivor Guest Phoenix 1954

94   *Come Dance with Me* Ninette de Valois Hamish Hamilton London 1957

95   *The First Fifty Years* Phyllis Bedells in *Dance Gazette* No 1 1971 The Royal Academy of Dancing

96   *A Manual of the Theory and Practice of Classical Theatrical Dancing (Cecchetti Method)* Beaumont and Idzikowski Beaumont London 1922

97   *Birth of the Royal Ballet* a production by the Royal Ballet's Ballet for All company, first produced at Spa Pavilion, Felixstowe 13th October 1972

98   See *Autobiography* Fonteyn W H Allen London 1975 and *How I Became a Ballet Dancer* van Praagh Nelson London 1954 Margot Fonteyn and Peggy van Praagh both record starting lessons about the age of four.

In addition to acknowledgements above we have drawn also on the following documents and publications.

Art and Artists in the Federal Republic of Germany Inter Nationes Bonn 1976

Central Council of Physical Recreation Annual Reports

Community Action in the Cultural Sector Bulletin of the European Communities Supplement Commission of the European Communities June 1977

DES Reports on Education

Digest of Statistics No. 14 London School of Economics 1979

The General Teaching Council for Scotland Handbook Edinburgh 1977

Impulse Termly magazine of the Inner London Dance Teachers' Association

Information Bulletins of the Arts Council of Great Britain Published bi-monthly

Life is not an Academic Subject Youthaid Education Statement 1979

Momentum Journal on Dance published from Dunfermline College of Physical Education, Edinburgh

Music in Scottish Schools Curriculum Paper 16 HMSO Edinburgh 1978

Physical Education in Secondary Schools Curriculum Paper 12 HMSO Edinburgh 1972

Report of the Task Force on the Education, Training and Development of Professional Artists and Arts Educators National Endowment for the Arts New York 1978

Secondary School Examinations: A Single System HMSO 1978 Cmnd 7368

Social Trends Annual Reports from the Government Statistical Service since 1975

Summary Report 1970—77 Selected summaries of Boekmanstichting research in the field of art and culture in Holland Boekmanstichting 1977

The Training of Teachers for Further Education Advisory Committee on the Supply and Training of Teachers 1975

Whitaker's Almanack 1978—80

Youth in Society Bi-monthly journal, published by the National Youth Bureau

Index

Numbering refers to paragraphs or, where indicated, chapters.

Sports Council, 52, 182, 188, 263
Staff, school, 118, 119, 204; universities 144
Standing Conference of Young Peoples' Theatre (SCYPT), 223
Statistics and facts, 5, 64, 66, 70, 80, 81, 82, 107, 110, **135**, 243, 350, 351, **354**
Statutory bodies, 186
Students, see Pupils
Summerson Committee, 147
Support, financial and moral, 22, 31, 53, 64, 106, 118, 119, 126, 133, 184, 224, 229,
236, 278, 286, 293-296, 309
Sweden, **65**; Swedish Committee of Inquiry into Dance Education, 65; Swedish Council
for Cultural Affairs, 65; unemployment in, 179; visits to, 57
Switzerland, 57

Teachers, 38, 55, **74**, 87, 88, 95, **Ch. 10**, 184, 307, 308, 312, **334**, 342, 344, 345, 347,
356; graduates, 121, 148, 324; head t. 47, 75, 89, 118, 119, 263; licencing
system, 246, **247-248**, 254, 256, 309, 319, 353; male t. 89, 118; peripatetic t.
91, 112, **123**; private studio t. 319, 320, 324, 326, 328; promotion of, 120, 121;
qualifications, 74, 118, 121, 144, 150, 258, 319; quality of t. 95, 115, 118,
120, 123, 126, 127, 133, 168, 255, 256, 274, 319; status of t. 119, 121, 122,
249, 253, 324, 330, 343; visiting t. 101, 123, 124, 254, 307, 308, 317, Scotland,
90
Teacher training institutions, 89, 90, Ch. 10, 150
Teacher training institutions, dance, 34, 55, 131, Ch. 10, 297, 299, 312, 318; Holland,
64; private, 211, Ch. 18, **323-328**
Teacher training and re-training, 34, 95, 120, Ch. 10, 152, 255, Ch. 18; apprentice
system, 249, **256**, 318, **319**; in-service courses/training, **40**, 87, 91, 101, 112,
127, 144, **167**, 189; Professional Dancers' Teaching Courses, RAD, **322**; re-
training professional dancers, 306, 312, 313, 314, 316, 318, **321**; Canada, 62;
Teachers' Training Course, RBS, 323, 328, 330, 350
Teaching aids, 30
Teaching dance, 159
Theatre, commercial, 352; subsidised, 349
Third World, 56, 57
Timetables, 92, 98, 116, 156, 288
Trade Unions, 24, 46, 53; Trades Union Congress (TUC), 8, 53; Scottish Trades Union
Congress (STUC), 53
Training Opportunities Scheme (TOPS), 322
Training Services Agency, 174, 179
Treaty of Rome, 60

Unemployment, 77, 179
UNESCO, 8, 59
United States of America (USA), 20, 56, 57, **66**, 67, 136, 142; National Research Centre
of the Arts, 66; National Endowment for the Arts, 66; universities, 136
Universities, 42, 58, 62, 67, **138-140**, 141, 147, 163, 183, 203, 298, 301, 302, 311,
320; Alberta, Canada, 58; Birmingham, 138; Bristol, 138; British Columbia,
Canada, 62; Edinburgh, 139; Simon Fraser, Canada, 62; Glasgow, 138, 139;
Hull, 138, 139; Leeds, 138, 139, 140, 141, 147, 163; Liverpool, 19; London, 17,
138, 141, 298; Manchester, 138; Montreal, Canada, 62; New England, Australia,
58; Open University, 134, 135; Oxford and Cambridge, 17, 139; Strathclyde,
165; Surrey, 311; USA, 67, 136; Waterloo, Ontario, Canada, 62; York, Toronto,
Canada, 58, 62; postgraduate study, 138, **163**; undergraduate study, 138
Universities and the Arts Conference, 140
University of Cambridge Local Examination Syndicate, 195, 198
University of London School Examinations Department, 198

Visits and displays, 26, 85, 110, 112, 125, 189, 209
Voluntary organisations, 46, 53, 79, 186, 340

Wales, Dance Council for, 1, **4**, 60, 191, 219, 232, 248, 252, 253, 273
Weekend Arts Colleges, 186, **187**
Welsh Arts Council, 4, 25, 31, 50